Life in the Presence of God

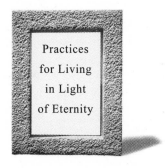

Practices
for Living
in Light
of Eternity

KENNETH BOA

IVP Books

An imprint of InterVarsity Press
Downers Grove, Illinois

InterVarsity Press
P.O. Box 1400, Downers Grove, IL 60515-1426
ivpress.com
email@ivpress.com

InterVarsity Press® is the book-publishing division of InterVarsity Christian Fellowship/USA®, a movement of students and faculty active on campus at hundreds of universities, colleges, and schools of nursing in the United States of America, and a member movement of the International Fellowship of Evangelical Students. For information about local and regional activities, visit intervarsity.org.

All Scripture quotations, unless otherwise indicated, are taken from The Holy Bible, New International Version®, NIV®. Copyright © 1973, 1978, 1984, 2011 by Biblica, Inc.™ Used by permission of Zondervan. All rights reserved worldwide. www.zondervan.com. The "NIV" and "New International Version" are trademarks registered in the United States Patent and Trademark Office by Biblica, Inc.™

While many stories in this book are true, some names and identifying information may have been changed to protect the privacy of individuals.

Published in association with the literary agency of Wolgemuth & Associates.

Figure 7.1: Adapted from Roger N. Shepard, Mind Sights: Original Visual Illusions, Ambiguities, and Other Anomalies (New York: Palgrave Macmillan, 1990).

Figure 7.2: Twisted cord illusion by Guy Walker, Logo Arts, www.cr31.co.uk/logoarts/pict/gall11/twist.html.

Cover design: Chris Tobias
Interior design: Daniel van Loon
Image: © David-W/photocase.com

ISBN 978-0-8308-4516-3 (print)
ISBN 978-0-8308-8898-6 (digital)

Printed in the United States of America ∞
InterVarsity Press is committed to ecological stewardship and to the conservation of natural resources in all our operations. This book was printed using sustainably sourced paper.

Library of Congress Cataloging-in-Publication Data
Names: Boa, Kenneth, author.
Title: Life in the presence of God : practices for living in light of
    eternity / Kenneth Boa.
Description: Downers Grove : InterVarsity Press, 2017. | Includes
    bibliographical references.
Identifiers: LCCN 2017042138 (print) | LCCN 2017041209 (ebook) | ISBN
    9780830888986 (eBook) | ISBN 9780830845163 (pbk. : alk. paper)
Subjects: LCSH: Spirituality--Christianity. | Spiritual life--Christianity.
Classification: LCC BV4501.3 (print) | LCC BV4501.3 .B594 2017 (ebook) | DDC
    248.4/6--dc23
LC record available at https://lccn.loc.gov/2017042138

| P | 21 | 20 | 19 | 18 | 17 | 16 | 15 | 14 | 13 | 12 | 11 | 10 | 9 | 8 | 7 | 6 | 5 | 4 | 3 | 2 |
| Y | 36 | 35 | 34 | 33 | 32 | 31 | 30 | 29 | 28 | 27 | 26 | 25 | 24 | 23 | 22 | 21 | 20 | 19 | 18 | 17 |

Dedication

In *Conformed to His Image*, I wrote that private prayer consists of mental prayer (meditation and contemplation), colloquy (conversational prayer with God), and the prayer of recollection (practicing the presence of God). This recollection of God can be habitual or actual (see also p. 102 of this book). *Habitual recollection* is analogous to a man's or a woman's love for a spouse or children, and does not require an ongoing consciousness. Just as we can form a habitual identity as being a husband, wife, or parent, so we can ask for the grace to form a habitual state of mind as a follower of Jesus Christ. *Actual recollection* involves the developing habit of turning to God at regular times throughout the course of the day. This is more along the lines of what Brother Lawrence, Frank Laubach, and Thomas Kelly pursued in their quest for a more conscious awareness of God in the routines of everyday life.

As I reflected on this dedication for *Life in the Presence of God*, it became obvious to me that my clearest experience of life in the presence of another person has been with my beloved wife, Karen. Our five decades together has been such a rich and profoundly rewarding mutual journey. In a fallen but soul-forming world, this all-encompassing journey necessarily entails places of difficulty and misunderstanding. But the mutuality of covenant love and commitment has weathered these places and enriched our lives together in ways we could have never anticipated.

Our love story is Beatrix Potter's *The Tale of Pigling Bland*, and it ends with the poignant image of "over the hills and far away"—

an evocative metaphor of our true home: "They ran, and they ran, and they ran down the hill, and across a short cut on level green turf at the bottom, between pebble beds and rushes. They came to the river, they came to the bridge—they crossed it hand in hand—then over the hills and far away she danced with Pigling Bland!"

In Your presence is fullness of joy.

PSALM 16:11 NASB

Contents

Introduction

Stop, take a deep breath, and read just long enough to see if this is worth considering. What I'm asking you to do will take no more than a second, but it will also take the rest of your life. It won't require you to sign up for a Bible study or commit any block of time to a group of people. You don't have to buy a study guide (unless you want to) or find a babysitter on a Tuesday night. It'll be easy, but at first it may take a lot of discipline—until it becomes habit. Then, in many ways, it will be effortless, as natural as breathing. And it will be the most important, most fruitful, most enjoyable thing you do.

I'm talking about learning to live in God's presence. It's something I've been learning to do more of lately, so I've written this book as much for myself as for you. And my goal is simple: to learn with you how to practice the presence of God better in every facet of our lives. By *practice*, I mean discerning and developing habits of awareness of God's presence—if not all day, every day, at least much more often than most of us typically do.

The Bible calls this "abiding," "remaining" in Christ, "walking with God," or "keeping in step with the Spirit." Whatever you want to call it, God's Word is clear that it's important. Without abiding in him, Jesus said, we will accomplish nothing of lasting value (John 15:5); we won't live like God wants us to live. We also won't get what we want out of life.

Outside of this book is a great, big world all around you. It clamors for every bit of your attention, and usually, because it's loud and incessant, it wins. Christians are often taught that our main line of defense against this clamorous, invasive world is a daily quiet time. If we're disciplined enough to practice this, we usually "complete" it before leaving our homes in the morning. Then we head out into the rest of our day, having compartmentalized our God life, leaving our Bible and our relationship with Jesus on our desk or bedside table.

Sure, it's good to give the first—or the last—moments of our day to God. But what about the rest of the day? It's so easy for our hearts and heads to end up somewhere else. Is that how God really wants us to live? Is that what he really had in mind when he said he'd give us abundant life (John 10:10)?

I'm proposing that we take our life with God—and our awareness of his presence—with us everywhere, not just into our quiet times but into our noisy times too, incorporating practices into our lives that help us keep that awareness right in front of us, throughout the day, every day.

Anyone can do this. This book is for followers of Christ of every age and maturity level. It's for those who consider themselves mature Christians but who, for whatever reason, have never learned how to abide in Christ. It's for new believers who are just learning what it means to walk with Jesus. And it's for those who want to rekindle an intimacy they once enjoyed with God that has since faded. It's even for people who already feel close to God, because, really, none of us is ever finished drawing near to him—not in this life. As with a relationship with a good friend, there are always new ways of spending time with him, of drawing closer to him, no matter how mature we are.

I hope I can convince you that becoming more conscious of God's moment-by-moment presence is something you need and can have. It's not something just for "super-Christians" (a category of people that doesn't exist). It's not for the superspiritual or the ultramature. It's actually an innate capacity that every true follower of Christ has and can cultivate. From the time a person first believes, God puts his Holy Spirit in every believer, and that Spirit is now available to us every second of every day (Romans 8:11; 1 Corinthians 3:16; Ephesians 1:13-14). Most of us live largely unaware of this divine presence, to our own detriment and impoverishment. More than that, we do so at risk of being disobedient to the commands of Jesus (John 15:4-8).

In many ways, this book is a sequel to my last book, *Rewriting Your Broken Story*.[1] That book focused on the power of an eternal perspective. This book talks about how to develop that kind of perspective from a practical standpoint. While that book aimed to convince you of the value of an eternal perspective, I hope this book will teach you how to have that kind of perspective, so you can realize the eternal longing God has placed in your heart and in every human heart (Ecclesiastes 3:11).

We were made for more than this world, and only when we live with that understanding can we fulfill the true purpose for which God made us. In one sense, only God himself can give you this perspective, but we can do certain things to make ourselves more open to his working in us and to hearing what he wants to teach us. Those things are what this book is about.

Lord of All Pots and Pans and Things

For many people, one writer comes to mind when they hear the phrase "practicing the presence of God": Brother Lawrence. Maybe you've heard of this well-known French man from the seventeenth century. A poor dishwasher and cook in a monastery kitchen, Brother Lawrence experienced so much peace and joy in God's presence that people were drawn to him. He mentored many during his lifetime. He kept a record of his experiences, and after his death his thoughts were compiled into a book: *The Practice of the Presence of God*. This humble man had come to the point of "keeping [his] mind in His holy presence, and recalling it as often as [he] found it wandered from Him."[2] He developed "an habitual, silent, and secret conversation of the soul with God" as he went about his business—which he considered as sacred in as outside of the cathedral.[3] Since his assigned work area was the monastery's kitchen, he's best known for this prayer:

> Lord of all pots and pans and things . . .
> Make me a saint by getting meals
> And washing up the plates![4]

Brother Lawrence's deep but simple teaching echoes an earlier tradition of the Benedictine monks of the fifth and sixth centuries: *ora et labora* ("pray and work"). The idea is to work while praying and pray while working. In other words, everything matters to God, and every moment can be devoted to him; there's no need to separate the sacred and the secular. In fact, we *can't* separate them. Life simply isn't bifurcated this way. The spiritual and the physical worlds overlap and are integrated. We live in both, and we have to stop thinking of them as two separate parts of our lives.

Brother Lawrence isn't the only one who's written on this theme. Thomas R. Kelly and Frank Laubach are two more recent examples that you'll meet in this book. Reading writers like these, and studying their lives, can be extremely inspiring and helpful. I've studied many myself and drawn great inspiration and encouragement from them. But there's something I've never really gotten from any of them, at least not in any detail. I've never found any satisfactory answer for this question: *How did they do it?* *How* did they maintain such a centered life, with Christ so *daily* at the center of everything they did? *How* did they offer their lives as a continual sacrifice of praise, seeming to radiate the presence of Christ—in mundane things as well as in the midst of huge trials, suffering, even persecution? Was there some secret to their success at being what Hannah Whitall Smith described as souls with "happy hearts" able to "walk in triumphant indifference through a sea of external trouble"?[5]

My desire through this book is to resurrect the spirit of Brother Lawrence, along with the spirit of other writers and practitioners of God's presence over two millennia of church history, and to explore what it means to follow their example in our own context. My goal isn't to leave you in awe of their lives but to discover their secrets with you. I want to take what may have been ineffable experiences to them and put words to them, and then learn how to put it into practice ourselves.

I hope I can show you how you can be more aware of his presence, no matter what your life is like. And as you become more aware, I hope you'll also learn to respond to his voice and his leadings. I pray that this book will be a catalyst for you—to grow in intimacy with him yourself and lead others to do the same.

No Magic Formula

The fact is, it's one thing to aspire to walk closely with God, but it's another to actually do it. None of the saints of the past came to enjoy the abiding presence of God in their lives by default, accident, or magic. There's no pill they took to suddenly develop the sense that Jesus was with them or to learn how to communicate with him regularly. You and I can just as easily discover what they understood. We can live in the presence of God every day too. And my goal in this book is to provide you with some intensely practical ways to cultivate that kind of life—some concrete steps, a suite of practices, to help you develop a closer life with Jesus.

I must emphasize one thing, though: *There's no formula* for walking with God! If you're looking for a five-step plan, you can set this book aside right now. (No such plan exists!) There are many ways to draw near to God—lots of practices and methods. They all have one thing in common: every single one goes through the person and work of Jesus Christ. Jesus calls himself the gate, the door, *the* way (John 10:7, 9; 14:6), and he makes very clear that a relationship with him is our only point of entry into this kind of life with God.

Some methods I give you may be helpful for you but not for others, and vice versa. And some may work for a season of your life but grow stale over time. The goal isn't to find *the way* to practice God's presence but to have a number of possible ways, and to keep in mind that they are only means to an end. The ultimate goal is communion with a very real and present God, something—*Someone*—we can enjoy in part on earth and will one day enjoy perfectly (1 Corinthians 13:12).

One of the greatest practitioners of the way of life I hope to show you was Watchman Nee. Nee was a brilliant young man and a church planter during Mao Zedong's communist takeover of China. Being often sick and knowing he would either die from illness or in a communist "reeducation" camp, Nee felt the Lord calling him to write, so he did, getting as much on paper as he could before his arrest in 1952. Though he planned and organized his writings well, he knew that without the Holy Spirit, no one would really comprehend what living and abiding in Christ means. These words, which he wrote about his own books, speak somewhat prophetically to the way we've learned to scan and skim books in our quest for rapid answers:

> God, I have discovered, does not do things [our] way, and much less does he let us do them. We human beings are not to produce "perfect" books. The danger of such perfection is that a man can understand without the help of the Holy Spirit. But if God gives us books they will ever be broken fragments, not always clear or consistent or logical, lacking conclusions, and yet coming to us in life and ministering life to us. We cannot dissect divine facts and outline and systematize them. It is only the immature Christian who demands always to have intellectually satisfying conclusions. The Word of God itself has this fundamental character, that it speaks always and essentially to our spirit and to our life.[6]

I hope you'll read this book slowly enough to engage the power of the Holy Spirit. I pray that you find practices in it that speak to your spirit and bring you life.

In the first part of this book, we'll explore what the Bible has to say about living in God's presence—some of which might surprise you, even if you're already familiar with Scripture. We'll also take a look at some people whose lives were changed by the experience of God's presence.

Then, in part two, we'll discover some answers to the *how* and *why* of this practice by looking in some unusual places (like the worlds of neuroscience and sport), and through some real-life stories.

For additional practices, exercises, and resources, see the companion "A Guide to Practicing God's Presence" available online at ivpress.com and kenboa.org.

As you read, I pray that you draw inspiration as well as conclusions, and that these pages spur you to find new life in the presence of Christ.

PART 1

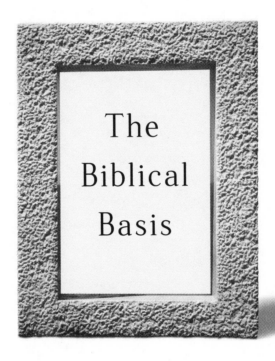

The
Biblical
Basis

The Secret

Abide in me, and I in you.

JOHN 15:4 ESV

Anne was ninety-seven years old and recovering from hip surgery. She had lived a beautiful life, but she was tired and ready to go home. She stared blankly at the ceiling. "Why Lord?" she pleaded. "Why am I still here? Isn't it about that time?" She'd been in conversation with the Lord for decades, learning to hear his voice, and his response came quickly and clearly to her: "Anne, I still have something for you. Get out there and look around."

Minutes later, Anne grabbed her walker and slowly made her way out of her room into the central gathering room of the senior living center where she was staying. She scanned the faces: mostly women, a few men. Almost all were nodding off to sleep while a sitcom played on the muted television they were circled around.

"This is ridiculous," Anne muttered, still in the conversation that had led her here. "At least they could turn on the volume!" But then Anne noticed one lady, off to the side, who had gone into a coughing fit. Her hacking pierced the room, where the only other noises were some snoring and an occasional labored breath.

"All right, Lord, I get it," Anne silently prayed. "There's still more for me to do. Use me, even here." Anne eased over to the coughing lady, touched her back gently, and began to sing an old tune. Soon, two voices were joined in song, belting out lyrics written when these ladies were in their twenties. When they finished every verse, the lady who had been coughing fell silent. A contented smile spread across her aged face. Anne told her about how much God loved her, then edged away.

Anne went to each person in the room in similar manner, placing her arm around them tenderly, sometimes just asking about their life stories, but always telling them about the One who loved them most, her Savior.

This is a true story. And Anne is a picture of what most of us would probably want to be like if we reach such a ripe old age. She's a picture of the biblical "good life" described in Psalm 92:

> The righteous will flourish like a palm tree,
> > they will grow like a cedar of Lebanon;
> planted in the house of the LORD,
> > they will flourish in the courts of our God.
> *They will still bear fruit in old age,*
> > they will stay fresh and green,
> proclaiming, "The LORD is upright;
> > he is my Rock, and there is no wickedness in him."
> > > (Psalm 92:12-15, emphasis added)

I find Anne's story remarkable, not only because she's fulfilling the calling to continue to bear fruit as long as she draws breath, but because of the natural way she entertains an ongoing dialogue with the invisible God. Did you notice that? There's no doubt she's suffering from aches and pains, and is perhaps discouraged by her shrinking sphere of influence in life. But she's still deeply connected to God, aware of his presence wherever she finds herself. She is never alone. Do you want a relationship like that? Would you like to talk to God honestly all day long, no matter where you are or what you're going through? Did you know you *can*? That this is how a Christian life is *supposed* to be lived— always in his presence? Did you know that he *wants* that for you?

Look at how Anne struggled at first. Every bone in her body probably cried out against the effort. Her soul longed for home. But she looked up to God first, then outward, rather than succumbing to the temptation to give in to exhaustion or feelings of uselessness, which would be totally understandable at her age.

Anne has spent a lifetime learning, *practicing* God's presence. She works to overcome distractions, to slow down enough to listen to him, to conquer the desire in herself to disobey when God calls her to do something. And this practice has led her to a peace that marks her, an ability to keep reaching out to people, and an assurance about her future. Jesus is drawing people to himself through Anne, loving people *through* her. She is a visible manifestation of God's presence in others' lives, just as God's presence is manifest in her own.

Most of us aren't ninety-seven. We have busy lives and too little margin of free time. Maybe we want more of God in our lives in theory, but we don't see how it can happen; nor do we stop and take time to think about it much. Is there a way to have more of God *now*, instead of waiting until we're retired or so over-scheduled or exhausted that we're *forced* to take a break? Do we even *want* more of him?

What Do You Want?

"Delight yourself in the LORD, and he will give you the desires of your heart" (Psalm 37:4 ESV). We all have to back up and start here. Ask yourself, *What do I want?* I mean, what do you *really* long for? Whatever your answer is, that's what will shape you. The destination you choose will define your journey. Your intention defines your outcomes. The finish line you envision determines the course of your race. You get the picture. You've got to know what you want!

So, do you want more of God in your life? Do you want him to be involved in what you do every day? Or does the thought of that frighten you? Your answer depends on where you are in your relationship with God, what you think about him, and your level of commitment. We're all in different places. But if the thought of God's closeness makes you afraid—worried, maybe, that he'll ask you to give up something you're not ready to give up, or that he'll see you for who you really are—that's okay. Lots of people feel this way. And most of us, if we're honest, are hiding some sins or fears in the recesses of our hearts. This can make the idea of total exposure to a perfect and holy God a little scary.

But these fears are unfounded if we're believers. They're based on a view of God that doesn't take into account the magnitude of his goodness and love for us. Maybe we don't exactly see him as an angry tyrant or an easily disappointed parent who's ready to slap us for every wrong move. But most of us aren't fully convinced he loves us *that much*. Thankfully, he is not all of the things we think he is!

God sent Jesus to bring us freedom, to live a full life, to experience joy, to live in his family. He's a loving Father who wants us to curl up beside him, lean on him, rest in him, and realize he already knows all the things we're hiding or holding back from him anyway. We are his pride and joy, and he wants to help us, to change us in good ways, to give us power to go out and live extraordinary, full, and satisfying lives.

Psalm 16:11 says, "In your presence there is fullness of joy . . . pleasures forevermore" (ESV). Do you believe this is true, and not just for later, after you die? Do you believe it's possible to experience joy in being with God *now*, or have you not even thought to hope this could be true?

C. S. Lewis is well-known among Christian readers. In his book *Surprised by Joy* he detailed how, beginning at a young age, he noticed a longing in his life for something more than this world had to offer, "an unsatisfied desire which is itself more desirable than any other satisfaction."[1] He explained how memorable these moments were, so much that he even found himself longing for the longing to return so he could try to put a name to it. He didn't come to faith in Christ for a long time afterward. He was a smart loner, isolated by choice, and a devout atheist. But his biographer, Devin Brown, noted that people who knew him after his conversion said his whole life took on a tone of joy, the kind most of us reserve for Christmas and birthdays.[2] In Christ, Lewis found real *life*, filled with a kind of joy that was different than he ever could have expected but which also had the familiar sense of those experiences so long before. Lewis explained how he came to understand the difference between what we often pursue and what we really want:

> Our Lord finds our desires not too strong, but too weak. We are half-hearted creatures, fooling about with drink and sex and ambition when infinite joy is offered us, like an ignorant child who wants to go on making mud pies in a slum because he cannot imagine what is meant by the offer of a holiday at the sea. We are far too easily pleased.[3]

In *The Joyful Christian* he explains, "Aim at Heaven and you will get Earth 'thrown in': aim at Earth and you will get neither."[4]

See, we're called to far more than what the world tells us to pursue. *The ambitions of this world aren't big enough for eternity;* they're not strong enough to sustain us for the long run. The poet George Herbert wrote:

> If souls be made of earthly mould,
> > Let them love gold;
> > If born on high,
> Let them unto their kindred fly:
> > For they can never be at rest,
> > Till they regain their ancient nest.
> Then silly soul take heed; for earthly joy
> Is but a bubble, and makes thee a boy.[5]

Here's the point: the pleasures this world offers are just toys that make us fools and sell us short. We're meant for more. Even our best imaginations of the good life are inadequate. Only God really knows what we're meant for and what we're made to do. Our identity and purpose are revealed in the Bible and understood in relationship with him. But most of us are so busy with our mud pies that we don't see how much is promised to us in that Book. The whole Bible, and especially the teachings of Jesus, talk about the *real* purpose of life. And it's only by engaging with God's Word that we can begin to understand how to grow and thrive and prosper.

Jesus asked a couple of his followers this fundamental question: "What do you seek?" (John 1:38). He wanted to know, "What are you really after? Is it me or is it something you hope to get from me?" So let's go back to the question I asked a moment ago: *What do you want?* What do you see as "the good life," the ultimate, satisfying life? Whether you believe it or not, the truest satisfaction comes from finding out where Jesus is going, following him, and then staying with him there (John 1:39).

Steady the Pendulum!

In one of his most famous lines, St. Augustine of Hippo wrote, "Thou hast formed us for Thyself, and our hearts are restless till they find rest in Thee."[6] When your allegiance to God is split with your allegiance to your boyfriend or spouse, your boss or board of directors, or anyone or anything else, you'll find yourself in constant inner turmoil. Restless. Like a pendulum, swinging between two extremes—worshiping God sometimes, with certain people, and devoted to the priorities and activities the world tells us are important at other times. You'll focus on God in one moment and push him to the back of your mind most of the rest of the time.

The Bible talks a lot about an undivided heart, how one true allegiance makes you one whole person (see Psalm 86:11). You're going to have to steady the pendulum and stop swinging if you want to find your center. It's my goal to help you, because what you'll find when you stop swinging is that you've gained more than you've given up.

The book of 2 Chronicles tells the story of the new king Solomon, of whom God asked: *What do you really want?* Realizing he didn't have what it took to do the job God just gave him, Solomon asked God for wisdom. When he answered, it was like on a game show when all the bells go "ding, ding, ding, ding" and the lights flash. Solomon chose the right answer, and God was so pleased with him that he not only granted Solomon's request, but he gave him everything he didn't ask for too. In essence, God said,

> Since this is your heart's desire, and you didn't ask for wealth, possessions, or honor (or for me to kill your enemies) or for long life, but instead you asked me for wisdom and knowledge

to lead my people, you will get what you asked for. And I will give you everything you didn't ask for too: wealth, possessions, honor, more than any king has ever had or will ever have again! (2 Chronicles 1:11-12, my paraphrase)

Under Solomon, the nation of Israel began to fulfill the promise God made to Abraham years before: a nation of people who served a good God in the land he'd given them. For a time, their king was so wise and their lives so good that news of Israel spread throughout the world.

I think we miss that we're being made a similar offer. We may not be the king of Israel, but if we're Christians, we're supposed to be leading lives that attract others to Jesus. It's like God is asking us, all the time, to choose what we *really* want: do we most want the life he offers, or do we want something else more? Today, there's still only one answer that will make the bells ding and the lights flash.

God, in his Word, calls us to make a choice and steady the pendulum, to unite our life and world. No more dividing things between what is sacred and what is secular. God doesn't divide the two, and when we try to, the result is a divided, restless, unhappy life. Jesus said we can't serve the world and God too; we cannot serve two masters (Matthew 6:24). And he didn't say it without reason. Attempting to serve two masters makes us miserable and unproductive, which is why God and the Bible don't allow it.

But *how* do we pledge our allegiance to God while we're still living in this world? *How* do we keep from dividing our hearts when we have a foot in two different worlds at once? And how can we commit to the invisible world when we still have responsibilities and plans here on earth?

There are people who have mastered this, or are in the middle of mastering it, and we can learn from them.

The Secret

Some people just seem good at being Christians. They're "happy Christians," people who seem to really *know* God personally, can talk to him like a close friend, and *enjoy* their relationship with God. Their lives and character seem infused with a supernatural quality. They're more peaceful, steadier, kinder. They appear to get more accomplished with less work and worry. Have you known anyone like this?

We're drawn to these kinds of people. They're real, live people— not just the Christian "greats" like C. S. Lewis, Thomas Merton, A. W. Tozer, Billy Graham, Dwight Moody, Martin Luther King Jr., and Corrie ten Boom (the list could go on) that we read about in books—but people we've watched and been touched by firsthand: that older couple at church who invite you to their home and explain Scripture to you in ways you've never heard before; the friend who drops everything on a busy day just to come over and pray with you; the youth pastor whose front door was always open, so you could hang out with his family when you were going through a rough time with your own. There's a sense of something very real and holy about all of these people.

But they're just *people*, like you and me. There's nothing particularly unique about them except one thing; they've learned a simple secret: the Christian life means *life in Christ*. The motions of these people's lives may be similar to ours, but because they take Jesus seriously when he says to abide in him (John 15), there's an entirely different and much sweeter quality to their lives. These people reflect what the *extraordinary* life of Jesus looks like in *ordinary* life. They're fulfilling the Great Commandments: loving

God with all their hearts, souls, minds, and strength; and allowing that love to overflow into the people around them. They're living out these commands imperfectly but faithfully, here and now, one day at a time—not *someday*. And you and I can too.

The key is this: instead of just mentally believing in the gospel of Christ, we need to start living this *in-Christ* life now. We need to become *practitioners*, not following biblical laws to check a box but doing practical things to get close to God—like we do with anyone we want to be close to.

None of this happens by human effort alone. All of it requires the help of the Holy Spirit, who lives in every believer. As we offer our lives to God, through practices that draw us to him, it may feel less natural at first. Growing close to someone takes time. A relationship doesn't deepen and mature overnight, and there are those awkward moments in the beginning. But if we keep practicing and don't give up, we'll find that time spent cultivating our life in God is worth more than anything else we've ever done.

First Things

If we want to take this secret and run with it, there are two things we have to do. The first is trust, and the second is train. After this chapter, we'll focus a lot on training. So here we have to talk about trust.

Without trust, our training is in vain. Faith in Christ is always the starting line in the race of pursuing God. He's the initiator. He pursues us before we ever begin to pursue him. But when we respond to him, surrendering our lives to him (like a lump of clay surrenders to the artisan at the potter's wheel), then he uses our practice to change us. He does the work of bringing us into his good life, but he needs a willing participant. And in the Bible the first thing people do to participate with God is trust him.

This trust is nonnegotiable. The chance to live with God is a privilege reserved for his children, not something we deserve or can conjure up or control. So we start with trust. Without it, it's impossible to please God or draw near to him (Hebrews 11:6). Any effort we make to enter God's presence without faith in his Son will fail. But for those who put their trust in him, this promise is true: "You who once were far away have been brought near by the blood of Christ," and through him, "we . . . have access to the Father by one Spirit" (Ephesians 2:13, 18).

In the Gospels, Jesus tells us to "believe" in him. The Greek word he uses was *pisteuō*. It implies a transfer of trust and a mutual, personal reception. It means taking our trust off of ourselves (or someone else) and handing it over to Jesus. So to believe in Christ is to embrace him. This idea is radically different from the rest of the religions of the world. In Christianity, we don't trust in our own work to attain, achieve, or merit favor in the next life (or this one either). It's exactly the opposite: God working salvation on our behalf, even when we were still sinners (Romans 5:8). As soon as we transfer trust to Christ, God embarks on his mission to conform us to the image of Christ, making us able to experience life with him, now and forever. And he does this in the same way he saved us: by grace through faith (Ephesians 2:8).

So this secret of practicing God's presence starts *and* ends with trust, and even the best spiritual training program in the world will fail if we don't start there.

A Single-Minded Pursuit

Trusting God leads to single-mindedness over time. Jesus, especially in his parables, encouraged his followers to bet the farm on his character, to go for broke when it comes to seeking him. He can't be the first priority among many. He is *the* priority, or he's no priority at all. As C. S. Lewis said, "Christianity is a statement which, if false, is of *no* importance, and, if true, of infinite importance. The one thing it cannot be is moderately important."[7] Too many people see Jesus as moderately important. Especially in America, many who call themselves Christians attend church weekly (or less often) and view two hours on a Sunday morning as enough. Jesus, to them, is *a component* of their lives. But this mindset is a huge mistake. Jesus is the pearl of great price, the hidden treasure in a field. Real Christianity is throwing everything in for him, dying to self, and following him—every day. *That's* what trust means. It means not just *saying* we believe the bridge will hold, but proving our trust to be true by stepping out and walking across it.

Fellowship with God, not our own satisfaction, has to be the primary goal we pursue. If we pursue satisfaction as an end, we'll never obtain it—it will always elude us. But if we pursue God first, we'll find satisfaction is often a byproduct. This is risky; and it's not always easy, because it requires self-denial. But Jesus never invites anyone to give up something without offering something better. And he promises that if we lose our lives for his sake, we'll find them. But if we try to save our lives, we'll end up losing them—forever (Luke 9:24).

Loving and trusting God makes us worthy before him. Scottish theologian Henry Scougal said:

> The worth and excellency of a soul is to be measured by the object of its love. He who loveth mean and sordid things doth thereby become base and vile, but a noble and well-placed affection doth advance and improve the spirit into a conformity with the perfections which it loves. . . . The true way to improve and ennoble our souls is by fixing our love

on the divine perfections, that we may have them always before us, and derive an impression of them on ourselves.[8]

We can't put our trust in Christ one time and stop. We have to go on, continually, single-mindedly trusting and coming and following him the rest of our lives. This commitment is radical and total. It's an "absolute surrender," as the South African author Andrew Murray called it. It demands our all. But this total commitment is an accumulation of many small commitments to practice his presence, *to live in Christ*, every moment. And making the most of those small moments is what this book is about.

Amphibious

Frank Laubach was an American missionary in the Philippines who learned by practice the value of making the most of small moments. He and his wife had moved to the Philippines early in their marriage, with a dream of working among the Moro—a people known as "the worst troublemakers American soldiers had ever faced."[9] The Moro people were Muslims with a four-century track record of resisting foreign rule, and their long, armed conflict with the American military had ended just a year before. The Laubachs felt called to reach these people—no mission field was ever so untrodden or so in need. But the military forbade it. Young, inexperienced preacher-teachers had no business there. So the Laubachs settled for work in other parts of the Philippines, even as they held on to their dream to reach the Moros.

After fourteen years in the Philippines, Frank was finally allowed to enter Dansalan, where the Moro lived. But he found them totally resistant to his teaching. One day, completely discouraged, he climbed a hill behind the cottage where he was staying. He sat and tearfully poured his heart out to God: "I hate myself. My plans have all gone to pieces." Then he begged God to come and work through him. God showed him that he'd been acting like he was superior because he was a white, literate American. He immediately asked the Muslim religious leaders to teach him about what they believed, and his mission field opened up. Frank found ways to reach them that he'd never thought of before. The hill behind his home became Laubach's place of on-going conversation with God. Wanting even more, Laubach made a great experiment that year of first trying to think of God every fifteen minutes while he worked (or at least every half-hour), and eventually trying to think of God one second of every minute. It sounds impossible, but by the end of that year, it had become his habit, so much a habit that he continued it for the rest of his life. In his diary, which was later published as *Letters by a Modern Mystic*, Laubach explains how adjusting his thinking this way took some effort at first but became completely natural. And it empowered him, revolutionized his life and ministry, because he was, every single minute, with God.

Laubach said it was pretty clear that this was what Jesus was doing all day, every day. It's also clear, he said, that it's not what most of his followers have been doing. In his book *The Game with Minutes*, he said that people who practice these things experience the same world as the rest of us, yet they see "it has a new glorious color and a far deeper meaning."[10]

Laubach was right that this is how Jesus lived. Christ was in constant communion with the Father, and he intended for us to learn this from him. The Bible makes clear we were designed to live in two worlds at once: the one we were born into and the one into which we've been born again (John 3). That world most of us rarely visit is more real than the one clamoring for our attention (2 Corinthians 4:18). It's the world where he promised we'd be able to go in and out freely, and find good pasture (John 10:9). Jesus wasn't speaking nonsense. He was talking about the very thing Laubach was doing.

In a letter to his father, Laubach wondered if *everyone* could actually do this:

> Can a laboring man successfully attain this continuous surrender to God? Can a man working at a machine pray for people all day long, talk with God all day long, and at the same time do his task efficiently? Can a merchant do business, can an accountant keep books, ceaselessly surrendered to God? Can a mother wash dishes, care for the babies, continuously talking to God? . . . Can little children be taught to talk and listen to God inwardly all day long, and what is the effect upon them? Briefly, is this a thing which the entire human race might conceivably aspire to achieve?[11]

The answer is that everyone *can* become aware of God in this way. And if everyone *did*, the results would be evident and the life of Christ more visible in all of his followers. Why so few churches talk about this is a mystery to me. We seem to think we have to wait until we die to experience this invisible world. But Jesus clearly didn't think so. Otherwise, why would he say, "Here I am! I stand at the door and knock" (Revelation 3:20)? Jesus is no fool. He doesn't stand at a door that won't open until we die. He's standing at *your* door, waiting for you now. The gate between these two worlds is Jesus, and if you've trusted your life to him, the gate is open.

Great Christians know this kind of living. C. S. Lewis said that humans are sort of "amphibious beings." Frogs are amphibious because they can survive on land or in water. They're able to live in the water, but they can also hop on land. We're not amphibious from a biological standpoint, but we are from a spiritual one. Like frogs, we live in one world while belonging to another. We can be with the God of heaven while our feet are planted firmly on earth.

A lot of us live as if there's a God world and a separate material world; we develop a sort of sacred-secular dichotomy, keeping the two worlds separate in our mind and practice. But we weren't made to live like this! God hardwired us to grasp both worlds simultaneously. He "set eternity in the human heart" (Ecclesiastes 3:11). The visible and the invisible are both real, and they're not separate. They're integrated, and when our lives reflect this fact, we become more the people God intends for us to be.

We can train ourselves to embrace our amphibious nature. We can train our hearts and our minds to discern the eternal, invisible, transcendent things of God at the same time as we're engaged in the immediate and visible world. As we bring the extraordinary into our ordinary lives, God's splendor into our mundane routines, we thrive. And as in Laubach's life, it will bring us a vitality we will surely notice in ourselves—and others will notice it too.

This is the practice of living *in* Christ. It's how Christians have endured persecution and found joy in unlikely circumstances. It's the difference between a happy Christian and one who doesn't seem very much like Christ at all. It's not an impossible life. It's an imminently possible life, when Christ is in us. And it's the life we all long for, whether we recognize it or not.

Listen to God in His Word

Read John 15:5 a few times through, and then write it down. Keep it with you in your pocket or your wallet or a place where you'll see it all the time. Try to recall it throughout the day and say it as a prayer that you've personalized, something like this: "Without you, Lord, I can't do anything. Please let me abide in you."

Practice His Presence
Your Game with Minutes

Look back at this chapter to see what I said about the secret to life in the presence of God. Then look at how Frank Laubach brought himself more into the presence of God, at first every hour and then every minute. (Consider reading his *Letters by a Modern Mystic*, as it gives more detail than I have space for here.) Put your own spin on this. How often do you think you can bring the Lord to mind in a day? What sentence or sentences would you say to remember him? How would you check in with him? Set a realistic goal for yourself to try it out. If it's not too distracting for you, consider setting an alert or reminder on your smartphone at several points in the day. (Over time, your check-ins should become habit, part of your ongoing dialogue with God. But at first, external prompts, as from a phone, can be helpful for instilling a new practice.) Then record your experiences in a journal or on a pad of paper.

2

The Images

I am the vine; you are the branches. . . .
Apart from me you can do nothing.

JOHN 15:5

Jesus knew how human minds are wired. He knew that if his words painted a picture, it would be easier for people to remember the truths he taught. And he knew that just as we live in two worlds at once, our minds can comprehend two levels of meaning at the same time. That's one reason he used a lot of metaphors, allegories, and Old Testament images that would have been well-known to his original audience. Such tangible, everyday scenarios and references—to things like fishing or farming or other familiar activities—helped give his hearers a gut-level understanding of deep spiritual truths.

The apostle Paul seems to have had a similar knack for words. Like Jesus, he also used familiar images, mostly to describe what life in Christ is like. The Bible is full of imagery about how to live in God's presence. And we don't have to dig too far into these images to discover that God is gently using them to show us that training for—and entering into—this life isn't something only special, religious people strive for. Growing in God's presence is a process ordinary Christians go through.

Watchman Nee called this the "normal Christian life," which is summed up in Galatians 2:20: "I have been crucified with Christ and I no longer live, but Christ lives in me. The life I now live in the body, I live by faith in the Son of God, who loved me and gave himself for me."

We often gloss over these words in our Bibles because we don't take them seriously, and we also breeze past them because we think they're too high for us to understand. But Watchman Nee didn't think so. Paul wasn't talking about some higher level of Christianity; he was merely presenting "God's normal for a Christian, which can be summarized in these words: I live no longer, but Christ lives his life in me."[1]

Nee went on to say that God only has one answer for every human need. That answer is Jesus. Need salvation? Get Jesus. Need forgiveness? Get Jesus. Want a better, deeper, more meaningful life? Get Jesus. In fact, get Jesus, and get out of the way. Jesus wants to live his life through you. This isn't life for an *extraordinary* Christian (although, in a very real sense, *every* Christian life is extraordinary) but life for every follower of Christ.

We're going to look at some people who lived this way and who were used by God to do great things. But please don't get the idea that I want you to sit and admire them. *They* wouldn't want that. They'd want you to go out and allow him to live his life through you, so he can then reproduce it in others. God made each of us for this purpose.

It's a process of becoming who Jesus has already made us. The Bible calls this growth "sanctification," and it takes time and single-minded commitment. "Purity of heart is to will one thing,"

Søren Kierkegaard said, and the Bible is clear that we can't live a half-hearted, double-minded life (Psalm 119:113; James 1:8). At the same time, the apostle Paul experienced inward turmoil as he strived to bring his life into unity with Christ. We have this new nature in Christ (the "spirit") alongside our fallen human nature (the "flesh"), which will never completely go away while we're on earth. This is a function of our amphibious nature. Our sinful nature, officially, is dead and crucified with Christ, but it's still kicking around while we're in our earthly bodies. So, we practice walking in his presence day by day, becoming more and more led by the Spirit and indulging our flesh less, so that we can enjoy the freedom and joy he's made available (Romans 8:13).

Practicing God's presence isn't about perfectionism, and it's not about a product. It's about a process of drawing nearer to a person who loves us and wants us to come close to him, to look to him in every circumstance of life as the eternal source of all goodness and truth. This is extremely important not to miss. As a young boy, I was very involved in my family's church, taking part in all kinds of activities and even making a confession of faith as a teen. But in college, having totally overlooked the relational aspect of faith, I set my Bible on a shelf—literally—never intending to pick it up again. I was done, tired of all the activity and the religiosity. It wasn't until God made himself personally known to that twenty-one-year-old hippie (who I was at the time) that I realized how wrong I'd been about him.

Knowing God and living in his presence is the best thing that can happen to us; it's life giving, not draining. Intimacy with God (through Christ) grows like any relationship, over time, and naturally overflows into activity. As we explore these New Testament images for this relationship, we have to keep in mind that he's looking for love for, and devotion to, him as a person—not dedication to a program or even a system of beliefs. You'll see this idea emerge as you read through these images.

Abiding in the Vine

It was the week of Passover, and Jesus had been saying some really hard things to his closest followers, the disciples. One of them was going to betray him. Peter was going to deny him. And was their Messiah telling them he was going to die? Didn't the Scriptures say Messiah would remain forever? But he said he was going somewhere that they couldn't come, at least not yet. The Holy Spirit was coming to help and would *never* leave them, Jesus told them. But meanwhile, yes, he was going away. It was only to prepare a place for them, though. Later, he'd return to take them there, he promised. Then he said,

> I am the true vine, and my Father is the gardener. . . . Remain in me, as I also remain in you. No branch can bear fruit by itself; it must remain in the vine. Neither can you bear fruit unless you remain in me.
>
> I am the vine; you are the branches. If you remain in me and I in you, you will bear much fruit; apart from me you can do nothing. (John 15:1, 4-5)

There were plenty of things Jesus' disciples didn't understand during his last days. But he used the image of a vine this time, because he *knew* they would get it. To a Jew (Jesus and all of his followers were Jews), any mention of a vine was a reference to the nation of Israel. (Read Psalm 80 to see for yourself.) God had made a covenant with Abraham (in Genesis 12) that he would make Abraham's descendants into a great nation of people and use them to bless the whole world. God kept his end of the bargain, growing Abraham's family into the nation of Israel,

planting them in a beautiful land, providing them with everything they needed, and cultivating them by his law and with tangible reminders of his presence. The promises to Abraham were
almost realized.

But, because of selfishness, the people of Israel had failed in
their role as the vine and had split in two. The prophet Hosea said
that Israel had become a worthless vine, because it brought its
blessings only to itself; and the more its fruit increased, the more
altars it built to worship other gods (Hosea 10:1). Jeremiah said
the vine had grown "corrupt" and "wild" (Jeremiah 2:21), and
Ezekiel said the vine's branches wouldn't even make good
firewood (Ezekiel 15). Ouch!

This vine image was clear and meaningful to first-century Jews,
though not in a positive way. And Jesus had used it before. He
had told a parable (Mark 12) about the owner of a vineyard and
the evil tenants who lived there while the owner was away. Every
time the owner sent a servant to collect grapes, the tenants killed
him. Finally, the owner of the vineyard sent his own son, a son he
loved, saying, "They will respect my son" (v. 6). But the tenants
killed him too. "What then will the owner of the vineyard do?"
Jesus asked (v. 9). "He will . . . kill those tenants and give the
vineyard to others." Mark makes clear that the chief priests and
teachers of the law *knew* he was talking about them.

But now Jesus was saying he is the *true vine*. In contrast to the
unfaithful vine that Israel had become, which kept its blessings
for itself and dishonored God, Jesus was true—faithful, trust-
worthy, and strong enough to provide them with everything they
needed to bear fruit. God still had plans to bless the whole world
through a vine that spread its fruitful branches wide. He'd just be
using new root stock. Through Jesus, God *will* bless the whole

world, and already has, through those of us who are connected to him.

A branch that abides never leaves the vine. It's constantly drawing health and energy from the vine. When it stops doing this, it loses its vitality, fails to produce fruit, and eventually withers and dies. So Jesus is showing us that we either stay with him, drawing our life from him, depending 100 percent on him, and blessing the whole world, or we wither and die. There's really only one option here, but do we realize how amazing that option is? John 15:11 shows the heart of Jesus' offer: "I have told you this so that my joy may be in you and that your joy may be complete."

Along with the energy to produce fruit comes joy—the joy of a branch that produces a flower and then a fruit. It has a singular purpose and realizes it. Imagine knowing that you're doing exactly what you were created to do, and you're also being empowered to do it. This is exactly what Jesus wants for you; it's what he's offering.

Again, we've come upon the secret of Christians who seem so different. They *are different* because they're drawing on the life of Jesus. They're living every day in the presence of God. Not only are they *in him*, but he is *in them*, streaming his abundant life to and through them. If you're a Christian, this is the life you're meant to be living: constantly, consciously dependent on him, aware that your life is not your own. Jesus is living his life *in you* and *through you*, *as you*.

We are only branches. Abide. Stay. Be in Christ. But when we do, there's joy—he promised!

Setting Your Mind and Heart

Imagine this. Charles sits in his desk chair with a lamp beside him. It's the first of the month: bill-paying time. Like most people nowadays, Charles manages many of his bills online, but since he's older, he's also kept an old habit from the days when he wrote checks: next to him, on the desk, is a list in his own handwriting of every bill he needs to pay: mortgage, gardener, water, gas. Each time he clicks "submit," confirming his payment online, he adds a checkmark beside the corresponding item on the list. Under some items, he writes a sentence. There's a rhythm to his work, like he's been doing this every month for a long time.

After he writes a sentence under the last item, he stands up and stretches. He puts his hand on the list and closes his eyes, just for a second. Then he turns out the lamp and leaves the room. If this were a movie, we could zoom in and see his list. He's a simple man, so nothing fancy:

- Mortgage

  Thank you, Lord, that you're my shelter. You provide for me and meet my needs.

- Gardener

  Let him have health, a long life, and pleasure in his work.

- Water

  Jesus, you are living water. Help me drink from your well.

- Gas

- Cell phone

- Natalie's birthday

  2 Timothy 3:14-15 for my granddaughter, Lord.

What was Charles doing? Making the most of his time—living in two worlds, talking to God, even while he's paying bills. Someone suggested it to him eighteen years earlier, and he'd tried it. Through the years, he discovered that this "paying and praying" strategy gave him a deep sense of peace while doing something that used to be a serious source of stress for him. What he writes isn't necessarily profound. It's just a simple way of placing his trust in God while doing an ordinary, mundane task.

The apostle Paul would say Charles was setting his mind on things above (Colossians 3:2) and on what the Spirit desires (Romans 8:5).

Our minds easily stray. They get fixated on the wrong things, maybe not even bad things, just not the *best* things. This tendency plays out in people's lives differently. For some, the temptation is most intense while home paying bills or when the baby wakes up crying in the middle of the night. For others, it's on the computer, in the bedroom, in the grocery aisle, at a clothing store, or in the office or boardroom. Wherever it is, our minds are prone to wander—toward anxious, proud, or angry thoughts, and toward ignoring God and his moment-by-moment presence and faithfulness.

Though we aren't responsible for every thought that enters our heads, we *are* responsible for what we do with them. That's why Scripture calls us to "set our minds" on God's things. Paul said it was a choice between life and peace—or death:

> Those who live according to the flesh have their *minds set* on what the flesh desires; but those who live in accordance with the Spirit have their *minds set* on what the Spirit desires. The mind governed by the flesh is death, but the mind governed by the Spirit is life and peace. (Romans 8:5-6, emphasis added)

Paul's letters make up much of the New Testament, but even while he was writing them, he was struggling. Though he'd been made alive in Christ, he still sinned. The Lord had taught him that we can't eradicate sin just by trying harder. We can't live a godly life by our own strength. Our new identity is *in Christ*. And before he left the earth, he said the Holy Spirit would help us live this life. Now, in Romans 8, Paul was saying we stay away from sinful thoughts by learning to let the Spirit guide our thinking.

John 15 focuses on *Christ in us*, but Romans 8 focuses on *his Spirit in us*, and how that works out in our lives. Our part in this is the *mindset*. We can think about setting our minds the way we set a television channel. We can flip through a dozen channels (or hundreds, if you have cable), but we "set" the channel where we want to stay a while. Similarly, setting our minds has to do with where we let our minds stay. The Spirit can work with our consciences, helping us see where our minds *shouldn't* be, and where they should linger—on a Bible verse, how to honor God in the task at hand, or something that reminds us of him, like the sound of the wind or the beauty of the clouds or trees.

Paul wrote similar words in Colossians as he did in Romans, but notice what he added:

> Since, then, you have been raised with Christ, *set your hearts on things above*, where Christ is, seated at the right hand of God. *Set your minds on things above*, not on earthly things. For you died, and your life is now hidden with Christ in God. When Christ, who is your life, appears, then you also will appear with him in glory. (Colossians 3:1-4, emphasis added)

In these verses, Paul suggests we need not only an ongoing mindset, but an ongoing heart-set—a tuning of *both* our minds and our hearts to the things of God. Our approach to each day goes beyond our thinking and includes our desires and affections too. In fact, whatever we aspire to in our hearts is what ultimately shapes us. "You are what you love," as James K. A. Smith put it in his recent book.[2]

Philippians 4:6-8 shows us more of what setting our minds and hearts on the things of God looks like—how it's not just about eliminating wrong thoughts and desires, but replacing them with better ones:

> Do not be anxious about anything, but in every situation, by prayer and petition, with thanksgiving, present your requests to God. And the peace of God, which transcends all understanding, will guard your hearts and your minds in Christ Jesus.
>
> Finally, brothers and sisters, whatever is true, whatever is noble, whatever is right, whatever is pure, whatever is lovely, whatever is admirable—if anything is excellent or praiseworthy—think about such things. (Philippians 4:6-8)

The last part of that passage—"think about such things"—is translated "dwell on these things" in the New American Standard Bible. Dwelling is ongoing. It's about what we allow not just to pass through but to take up residence in our minds. Letting our minds *dwell* on something means we meditate on it, we chew on it—we stay there.

If we're honest with ourselves, the things most of us dwell on are the *opposite* of the things we see in Philippians 4:8. I've become very aware of this tendency in my own life in one particular area: driving. When a driver cuts me off on the highway, my first thought doesn't naturally incline toward something honorable or right. Same thing when I'm stuck in traffic: "I've got so much to do—I don't have time for this!" How quickly our contentment and focus on God can be disrupted by one small incident on the road!

One way we set our minds on things above is to stop *listening* to ourselves so much. Instead of feeding ourselves whining, grumbling, or worried thoughts, we need to *talk* to ourselves more—or rather, let God's Spirit speak truth to ourselves, inwardly. We may not even be thinking a lot of wrong or untrue thoughts, but many of our daily thoughts simply aren't *helpful* true thoughts—things that edify us and build up our souls.

I'm not just talking about overcoming negative self-talk with positive self-talk, like a self-help book might emphasize. I'm referring to the kind of self-talk that David did in Psalm 103, where he told his own soul to "praise the Lord" (v. 1), to "forget not all his benefits" (v. 2), and so on. He was gathering God's truth from Scripture to speak to his soul, so he would dwell on what was good and true and honorable, rather than despairing or worrying. And you and I can do the same thing.

God has given us an incredible capacity to set our minds and hearts on the spiritual realm, even while we live in this visible one. This doesn't mean we ignore things on earth, but we choose to play to an audience of one (God), cocking one ear to heaven as we go about our days. Setting our minds and hearts on heavenly things doesn't carry over from one day to the next; we have to *keep doing* it. Sometimes adjusting our thoughts and desires will be easier, a gentle shift; other times, we'll have to tackle wrong thoughts, taking them captive to destroy them (2 Corinthians 10:5). Either way, the Spirit is always present to guide and empower. This is never something we do alone, by willpower, but through his strength (Colossians 3:4).

Walking

Let's move from our minds and hearts (how we think and feel inwardly) to our actions (what we do outwardly). The next images are about living in the Spirit, applying Christ's life in us to our lives:

So I say, walk by the Spirit, and you will not gratify the desires of the flesh. (Galatians 5:16)

Since we live by the Spirit, let us keep in step with the Spirit. (Galatians 5:25)

As we live and move through our day, we aren't walking by our natural, fleshly default and inclinations, but by his Spirit. We're keeping in step with him, not lagging behind or jumping ahead. Wherever we go, God is with us—close at hand, our faithful companion, leading our way. We're living with wisdom: doing the right thing for the right reason at the right time by his power. We're constantly discerning and acting, based on the prompting and moving of the Spirit. We're talking to him, listening to him, seeking to value and prioritize what he values and prioritizes.

This sounds like a lot of work if we think about doing it *without* Jesus. But it's *not* a lot of work for Jesus, and if we're abiding in him, *it is Jesus* who is doing the work through us! The energy and ability to follow him, to walk with him, comes from him. We don't need to work really hard to muster it up. He does it.

Before we put our trust in Christ, we don't have the option of doing the works of the Spirit. Even our best efforts are tainted. But if we're walking with the Spirit, we're increasingly led *away* from sin. Sin no longer has the final say, because we're being progressively delivered from its power. (One day, we'll be completely delivered not only from sin's power but also from its presence.) And we have this new power within us to bear fruit— to produce good things that last (John 15:16; 1 John 2:17).

Running

In the book of Hebrews, the walking becomes running. It's almost like God is saying there will come a point when walking isn't going to cut it. Keeping our faith will be more a matter of not giving up than quietly experimenting with new ways to enjoy his presence. This is different from day-to-day walking. It'll take more effort and more commitment. There will be times when we're tempted to drop out. God wants us to stay the course, sticking close to him. Here are the words straight from the Scripture:

> Therefore, since we are surrounded by such a great cloud of witnesses, let us throw off everything that hinders and the sin that so easily entangles. And let us run with perseverance the race marked out for us, fixing our eyes on Jesus, the pioneer and perfecter of faith. (Hebrews 12:1-2)

If you have your Bible handy, it might help to back up a chapter before these verses. In Hebrews 11 the author talks about the Bible's "faith hall of famers." These were people—Noah, Abraham, Moses, and others—who put their faith into action. They walked with God, and their lives showed it. There are many other Christians who've followed in their footsteps. Though they may not be in the Bible, they have been through all kinds of struggles, and they did what good runners do: they kept their attention ahead, focused on the end goal.

The key to running a Christian life with endurance is keeping our eyes *fixed on Jesus*—our finish line—and not on our circumstances (the sidelines or the road below) or on the other runners. It's easy to look at people around us and compare, but comparison is the enemy of contentment. So, instead, we focus on Jesus, staying with him, and putting all our effort toward finishing well.

A woman (I'll call her Laura) recently trained for her first half-marathon. Laura is in her forties and only began running for exercise a few years ago. She started her half-marathon training far in advance, and with the help of a professional coach, steadily built up, half a mile at a time. Two short runs during the week, a longer run on the weekend, cross-training the other days, and one day of rest. She ran on hills and flat ground, in all conditions—snow, rain, heat, and humidity. By race day she was well prepared. The day was hot and humid—not ideal, but she knew the circumstances were beyond her control. As the gun fired to start the race, several friends ran by her side. She felt good the first six miles or so. About halfway through, the aching began. But she kept at it—spurred on by encouragement from her more experienced running buddies beside her.

Then something happened, around mile eleven. First, her buddies, eager for a better race time, shot ahead of her. Laura was left to finish the final 2.2 miles on her own. The first thing she noticed was how much harder it was to keep going alone. The second thing she noticed was how much her lungs hurt from the humidity. (For some reason, she hadn't noticed it until now.) Gasping for breath, she heard herself moan, silently to herself, *I'm done; I just can't* . . . With the choice to quit or keep going before her, and months of training behind her, words of a song suddenly popped into her mind. She began to sing, silently, "O Lord my God, when I in awesome wonder, consider all the worlds Thy hands have made . . . How great Thou art . . ."[3]

Laura's legs moved mechanically beneath her as she made her way through each stanza. Then she moved to a second praise song—and a third. As she crossed the finish line minutes later, her legs wobbled weakly, but her spirit soared. Almost without knowing it, she'd done what Paul told the Ephesians to do, in a literal sense, when he was telling them to make the most of their time on earth: "Sing and make music from your heart to the Lord" (Ephesians 5:19).

Laura's race was physical perseverance; the apostle Paul's was spiritual. Both ran in the same enduring spirit. By the time he wrote his letter to the Philippians, Paul had preached the gospel in nearly fifty cities. He'd been robbed, beaten, falsely accused, and imprisoned. He knew he would die soon, but he also knew his work wasn't finished. Like Laura, he pressed on:

> Not that I have already obtained all this, or have already arrived at my goal, but I press on to take hold of that for which Christ Jesus took hold of me. Brothers and sisters, I do not consider myself yet to have taken hold of it. But one thing I do: Forgetting what is behind and straining toward what is ahead, I press on toward the goal to win the prize for which God has called me heavenward in Christ Jesus. (Philippians 3:12-14)

Paul pushed toward his finish line: Christ Jesus. He didn't dwell on the past. Like other wise people, he realized even his mistakes could become the stuff of redemption. He kept his focus on living in the present, seeing his pains and struggles as the underside of a beautiful tapestry God was weaving with his life.

Offering Yourself Up

Paul gave another image of the dynamic of the spiritual life in Romans 12—a constant offering of our lives to him:

> Therefore, I urge you, brothers and sisters, in view of God's mercy, to offer your bodies as a living sacrifice, holy and pleasing to God—this is your true and proper worship. Do not conform to the pattern of this world, but be transformed by the renewing of your mind. Then you will be able to test and approve what God's will is—his good, pleasing and perfect will. (Romans 12:1-2)

If we're abiding like branches in a vine, we're submitting ourselves to be used. We're offering God our bodies and minds, inviting him to make us more like Jesus and more the people he created us to be. For a lot of us, that may be the hardest thing to take. We're giving up our independence, but in the exchange, we get the ability to discern God's will, which is "pleasing and perfect." God's will is our good. So when we let him work in us, this spiritual submission becomes an act of worship.

Flowing out of our submission is the idea of renewing our minds—another process that goes on and on for the duration of our lives. The reason we need this renewal is that God's truths have a way of slipping through our fingers. They're so countercultural that it's easy for them to be forgotten or thrown aside as we run back toward the noisy world. If you're like me, you go to a spiritual conference or event, and come back feeling renewed, committed to remembering and living by all that you heard. Yet, in a matter of days, you're back to your old habits. Retreats are great, but they aren't as important as our ordinary, daily lives. We don't live on mountaintops. We live the bulk of our lives on the flat plains—or even on the uphill or in the valley. The way we train ourselves spiritually should ready us for all of these terrains, and I hope this book helps you do just that.

■ ■ ■

There's so much rich imagery in the Bible that shows how we are able to live close to God, in his presence, relying on him for everything, in a process that lasts our entire lives. This imagery can be lost on us today if we don't take time to understand the context and think deeply about it.

The bottom line is that life with Christ and in Christ is how we *must* live as Christians. But not only that, it's how we should *want* to live. We run ourselves ragged and get exhausted when we don't live this way, and then we wonder why we feel like we're in the middle of the desert, parched! Remember, Jesus said, "Apart from me, you can do nothing." Who wants to accomplish nothing? Yet, if we don't abide in Jesus, our lives will be flat and full of failure.

We can't live the Christian life without him—it's impossible! But *with* him, all things are possible. So let's start exploring some ways to get more of him in our lives.

Practice His Presence
Images of Living in His Presence

Look through the thirteen images below that describe the on-going process of life in God's presence. These are just a few of the many images we could have chosen from Scripture; we looked at several in this chapter, and there are even more not listed here!

Choose one that you most resonate with. Then read the passage, write it on an index card, and keep it by your bed. Read through it every night for a week (or longer!). Don't just read it, though: meditate on the phrases that stand out to you the most, and ask God to help you live out or obey it. You might also try to read the card in the morning and another time midday as a reminder.

1. *Abide in Jesus*, and you will bear fruit; without him, you can do nothing. (John 15:4-5)

2. *Love God* with all your heart, soul, and mind, *and love your neighbor* as yourself. (Matthew 22:37-40)

3. *Set your mind* on what the Spirit desires, not what the flesh desires. (Romans 8:5-6)

4. *Walk by the Spirit*; keep in step with him. (Galatians 5:16, 25)

5. *Set your heart* on things above, making Christ first in your heart. (Colossians 3:1-2)

6. *Rejoice always.* (1 Thessalonians 5:16)

7. *Pray continually.* (1 Thessalonians 5:17)

8. *Give thanks* in all circumstances. (1 Thessalonians 5:18)

9. *Run with endurance*/perseverance the race marked out for you, fixing your eyes on Jesus. (Hebrews 12:1-2)

10. *Submit to God, offering yourself* as a living sacrifice to him, not conforming to this world's pattern but being transformed by the renewing of your mind. (Romans 12:1-2)

11. *Press on* toward the goal to win the prize of the upward call of God in Christ Jesus. (Philippians 3:12-14)

12. *Dwell on* the true, the noble, the right, the pure, the lovely, the admirable—anything that is excellent and praiseworthy. (Philippians 4:6-8)

13. *Remember* God's faithfulness and provision, how we do not live on bread alone but on the food of God's Word. (Deuteronomy 8:2-3)

Another Exercise to Try

God can use physical objects and visual images in powerful ways to remind us of spiritual realities. To help you remember to set your mind and heart on him, try one of these things this week:

- Find an object (like a small cross or a nail) that reminds you of God and what he's done for you; carry it in your pocket, and let it remind you, every time you touch it, to set your mind on things above.

- Write or type Philippians 4:8 and tape it to your workstation or dashboard. See if reading it and seeing it often helps you complain and whine less, and think of the "whatevers" more: *whatever is true, whatever is noble, whatever is right, whatever is pure, whatever is lovely, whatever is admirable.*

- Use a photograph of God's creation as the background on your phone or computer (for me, images of outer space can be a great way to reset my perspective—and it helps if I change the image daily or weekly).

3

The Exemplar

I pray . . . that they may be one as we are one—
I in them and you in me. . . .
Then the world will know that you sent me and
have loved them even as you have loved me.

JOHN 17:20, 22-23

One day, Jesus' good friends Mary and Martha
sent urgent word to him that their brother, Lazarus, was sick.
Jesus loved this family, John 11 says, but he was with his disciples
at the time, some distance away. Still, his response in John 11 is
somewhat puzzling: "Jesus loved Martha and her sister and
Lazarus. So when he heard that Lazarus was sick, he stayed
where he was two more days, and then he said to his disciples,
'Let us go back to Judea'" (John 11:5-7).

Wait! What? Lazarus is seriously ill, and his family has
somehow tracked down Jesus, sending a message for him to come
quickly. Why the delay? Why didn't Jesus rush to his friend's side
as fast as he could?

Eventually, Jesus arrived at Lazarus's home in Bethany. But before he even got there, he told his disciples, "Lazarus is dead, and for your sake I am glad I was not there, so that you may believe" (John 11:14-15).

Let's think about this: All along, Jesus knew what was wrong with Lazarus. He knew his family was worried. And he knew Lazarus would die before he arrived. Instead of running there in a hurry, Jesus stayed calm and waited until the timing was right—knowing his Father was going to make this one of the most teachable moments of his ministry.

But how could the timing be right if Lazarus was dead? Not only was he dead, but he'd been dead four days—the point when Jewish tradition said a person's soul was completely gone from their body, with no chance of return. In other words, all hope was gone, and to everyone around him, Jesus seemed to arrive too late. Martha said as much when she met him on the way in: "Lord, if you had been here, my brother would not have died" (John 11:21). The question was implied: *Why didn't you come sooner, Jesus?*

Jesus, unfazed, replied, "Your brother will rise again" (v. 23). Martha, putting on her brave face, said, "I know he will rise again in the resurrection" (v. 24). I wonder if Jesus smiled, knowing what she was about to see. Mary came running out of the house just then, collapsing in tears at Jesus' feet and repeating her sister's words: "Lord, if you had been here, my brother would not have died" (v. 32).

The sisters then took Jesus to the place where Lazarus was buried—and he cried (v. 35). He cried not because Lazarus was dead but because he really loved these people, and it's painful to see people you love hurting. Being in the flesh gave Jesus solidarity with the human condition; he wasn't immune to their pain. When they got to the tomb, Jesus ordered the stone removed from its entrance. Then he prayed:

"Father, I thank you that you have heard me. I knew that you always hear me, but I said this for the benefit of the people standing here, that they may believe that you sent me."

When he had said this, Jesus called out in a loud voice, "Lazarus come out!" The dead man came out. (John 11:41-44)[1]

Thank you that you heard me? What kind of a prayer was that? Obviously, Jesus had been in conversation with the Father about this already. Now God was using it to show those around Jesus that Jesus was his beloved Son, who was doing *his* will by *his* authority and power. This miracle and this prayer were gifts. Jesus was showing his followers something they could believe, because that's the first step to getting closer to God. Jesus and the Father had already made a plan. But this part was for the people, including us today, so they (and we) could believe, and many of them did (John 11:45).

Author Thomas R. Kelly notes that an inward orientation—a practice of inward worship, listening, and conversation—was "the secret . . . of the inner life of the Master of Galilee, [and] he expected this secret to be freshly discovered in everyone who would be his follower."[2] In John 11 we see Jesus inviting his followers to discover that secret. He was modeling the amphibious, two-level life we're all meant to have, seamlessly integrating an awareness of both heaven and earth. He was inviting Martha, Mary, and the others to life in his Father's presence.

When Jesus walked this earth, he laid aside some of the rights of divinity (John 1:14; Philippians 2:5-8) and faced the same limitations we face while in physical bodies. But this story makes very clear that even in his physical body he still had clear communication with the invisible God of heaven, while living and working with people. We can learn a lot from his example.

His Trust

We imitate Christ by identifying ourselves with him. That's why he wanted the people in Bethany that day to believe. Trusting in Jesus is a prerequisite to experiencing the presence of God. And when we repent of our sins and place our trust in him for salvation, we receive his Spirit. Without the Spirit, we can never live like Jesus, but with him we can.

Once we decide to follow him, coming in the humility of a child (Matthew 18:3-4), we experience a continual *becoming* in practice what he's already made us in position. Because of the blood Jesus shed on the cross for our sins, when we entrust our lives to him, we're immediately in good *standing* with God. We're righteous in his eyes and sanctified (set apart) for his purposes (1 Corinthians 6:11). But we aren't perfect yet. We're still in a sinful *state*, and the process of sanctification—being made into what we've already been declared to be—takes time. Immersing ourselves in God's presence on earth shapes us and prepares us for the immediate presence we'll experience after we die. All of this requires child-likeness, a humble attitude that instinctively trusts God's love for us, even when we're not sure why or how he's leading us.

One of Jesus' names is Immanuel, which means "God with us." For thirty-three years on earth, the people of Jesus' day experienced what it's like to have God present in a way that you and I can't experience. This is why Jesus told Thomas after the resurrection, "Because you have seen me, you have believed; blessed are those who have not seen and yet have believed" (John 20:29). It's interesting, though, that even when God was present among people, not everyone recognized him as God (actually, most didn't), and not everyone immediately believed in him. It's easy to think we're handicapped by not being able to physically see

Jesus, but the fact is that many stood near Jesus and had no idea they were in God's presence. Only by the Spirit can a person see Jesus for who he really is.

Even though Jesus was God in the flesh, time after time he sought the Father's presence, going out alone to be with him, seeking to know his will, to hear his voice, to be comforted by him. Jesus wasn't only fully God but also fully human. He too was amphibious for a time, raised by parents—trusting, learning, and growing like any child. Luke tells us, "Jesus grew in wisdom and stature, and in favor with God and man" (Luke 2:52). Even the Son of God went through the process (granted, without ever sinning). And now that we're in the process of growing in wisdom and faith, we can learn from his example.

His Identity

How do you start your prayers? If you scan all four Gospels, you'll find that Jesus addressed God as "Father," with only one exception—when he was hanging on the cross. Jesus never doubted his identity as the Son of the living God. He carried this understanding with him wherever he went. He knew who his Father was—almighty God and Creator of the universe. But he also knew him personally, as a loving Father who delighted in his Son. That pleasure was made clear when, after Jesus' baptism, a voice came from heaven: "This is my Son, whom I love; with him I am well pleased" (Matthew 3:17).

Do you understand the stamp of approval and the great pleasure God has toward *you* (assuming you've placed your trust in him)? We aren't children of God in the exact same way as Jesus is, but as new creations in him, we *are* his beloved children and no longer objects of wrath. We need to pray and see ourselves this way. Jesus taught us to approach God like he did: "This, then, is how you should pray: 'Our Father . . .'" (Matthew 6:9). He didn't mean we literally start every prayer with these exact words, but we come to God as his children, with an awareness of the intimate relationship and access we have to him through Christ. Paul echoed this in Romans, "The Spirit you received does not make you slaves, so that you live in fear again; rather, the Spirit you received brought about your adoption to sonship. And by him we cry, 'Abba, Father'" (Romans 8:15).

Abba is like *Daddy*. The Father's love is lavished on us as children he delights in (Ephesians 1:8). At the same time, we view our heavenly Father with reverence and awe, so we follow our address with this: "Our Father *in heaven, hallowed* [holy] *be your name*" (Matthew 6:9, emphasis added). How would it change our lives if we lived with this understanding: that we are sons and daughters of a Father who loves us deeply, who is at the same time perfect in power and holiness? A. W. Tozer, in his classic *The Pursuit of God*, spoke of our need to awaken to this reality:

> [Christians] have been taught to pray, "Our Father, which art in heaven." Now personality and fatherhood carry with them the idea of the possibility of personal acquaintance. This is admitted . . . in theory, but for millions of Christians, nevertheless, God is no more real than He is to the non-Christian. They go through life trying to love an ideal and be loyal to a mere principle. Over against all this cloudy vagueness stands the clear scriptural doctrine that God can be known in personal experience . . . with at least the same degree of immediacy as they know any other person or thing.[3]

Jesus played to an audience of one: the warm, loving Father who delighted in him. And he calls us to do the same, remembering that we're loved because we belong to him.

A father I know of used to tell his daughter, whenever she left the house, "Remember who you are." She was the daughter of a King, he would tell her, and she should live in this truth. He said it often enough that it became embedded in her thinking and shaped who she was. We all need this kind of regular reminder because it's too easy to allow the world to define us, almost without even realizing it. Do nothing and the world will shape you by default. It takes energy and effort to resist that downstream pull. God will enable you to resist, but you have to entrust yourself to *his* upstream pull. That's why it's so important to form habits that bring you into his presence—to remind you of your true identity and purpose.

His Agenda

Early in his ministry, when it was time to choose the disciples he'd poured the most of his teaching and time into, Jesus went up on a mountain and prayed all night (Luke 6:12). In the morning he went out and chose them. Either God had told him or he was about to show him which ones to choose.

As he stood on the Sea of Galilee teaching, he was surrounded by a crowd of people. Two boats off to the side caught his attention. One of them belonged to Simon Peter, who was on the shore washing his nets. It looks like Jesus kept talking as he went, and the crowds stayed. He made his way to Simon's boat and got in. Did Simon wonder, *What's that guy doing in my boat?* Here's Jesus, with people crowded all around him, and his gaze is fixed on Simon Peter, the first of the twelve disciples he'd choose. By the time he finished teaching, Simon was back at the boat. "Let's go out into deeper water," Jesus said. And then he worked exactly the right miracle to let this fisherman know who he was—nets that had come up empty earlier were now so heavy that they were tearing, with fish enough to sink two boats!

When they got to shore, Peter left behind the boats and the nets full of fish. The fish needed processing, and the nets need to be cleaned. This had seemed so important before, but now all Peter wanted was to be with Jesus. Jesus had spent the whole night in the presence of the Father, and now—though there were crowds swarming all around him—he knew exactly which person to choose.[4]

Jesus had perfect focus. Never distracted or derailed from his purpose, he did whatever the Father wanted him to do. He was always with God, following his direction and carrying the message of the kingdom. Of course, Jesus had the benefit of being one with the Father in a way that you and I aren't (John 14:11). But he still faced temptations to be derailed from his Father's plan. Take a look at Jesus' request in the Garden of Gethsemane shortly before his arrest (the entire account in Matthew 26 or Mark 14 is well worth taking a moment to read): "*Abba*, Father," he said, "everything is possible for you. Take this cup from me. Yet not what I will, but what you will" (Mark 14:36).

Here we have the supreme example of submission to the Father's will—Jesus' most agonizing moment, as he came to that awful realization not just of the unimaginable physical pain and cruel punishment he was about to experience, but of the coming separation from his Father's presence. This concept was inconceivable. He'd been with the Father since before matter, energy, space, and time were created. He always is and has been with the Father. It was unimaginable that he could live without him through the hardest moment of his life, yet he surrendered himself to his Father's will.

Jesus' whole being and presence in this world was about representing, demonstrating, and disclosing God's interests—pursuing God and treasuring him above everything else. Even at a young age, he seemed aware of it. He worried his parents sick one day because they couldn't find him when he hung back from them at the temple in Jerusalem. "'Why were you searching for me?' he asked. 'Didn't you know I had to be in my Father's house?'" (Luke 2:49).

Again, in Mark 1:12, Jesus willingly submitted to his Father's agenda: "At once the Spirit sent him out into the wilderness." It was *always* God, through the Spirit, who impelled him. Nothing he ever did or said was outside his Father's will, and all of it he did voluntarily, on the Father's initiative. Throughout the Gospel of John, the centrality of the Father's agenda in Christ's life is impossible to miss:

"My food," said Jesus, "is to do the will of him who sent me and to finish his work." (John 4:34)

Very truly I tell you, the Son can do nothing by himself; he can do only what he sees his Father doing, because whatever the Father does the Son also does. (John 5:19)

Jesus answered, "My teaching is not my own. It comes from the one who sent me." (John 7:16)

No one takes [my life] from me, but I lay it down of my own accord. I have authority to lay it down and authority to take it up again. This command I received from my Father. (John 10:18)

I did not speak on my own, but the Father who sent me commanded me to say all that I have spoken. I know that his command leads to eternal life. So whatever I say is just what the Father has told me to say. (John 12:49-50)

These words you hear are not my own; they belong to the Father who sent me. (John 14:24)

While he lived in human form, Jesus' vitality came from doing his Father's will, and the power to do it came from the Spirit. Everything Jesus did on earth, he did together with his Father and his Holy Spirit.

This kind of focused life wasn't meant just for Jesus. He prayed for us to enjoy the same kind of purpose and unity with his Father: "I in them and you in me" (John 17:23). Earlier he prayed, "As you sent me into the world, I have sent them into the world" (John 17:18). The apostle Paul echoed this theme when he called us "Christ's ambassadors" (2 Corinthians 5:20). In other words, Jesus was all about his Father's agenda, and he expects us to be too. We can and should draw our vitality from the Father, focusing our entire lives on making Christ's presence known to the watching world. We too are representatives of another kingdom, sent on mission. Do you see yourself that way? Do you have a strong sense of your own mission and heavenly citizenship, or does this feel theoretical or irrelevant to your daily life?

Practicing his presence means reminding ourselves often of not only our identity but also our purpose—our lifelong agenda. These reminders can come in a flash, in between or while we're doing other things. They don't need to take extra time out of our day. But they do require mindfulness and consciousness of God. These take time to develop, but they can become part of our default mode of thinking. And when we're constantly interacting with God, opening ourselves up to a real relationship with him and strengthening ourselves with his Word, this mindfulness becomes ingrained.

His Values

> The devil took him to a very high mountain and showed him all the kingdoms of the world and their splendor. "All this I will give you," he said, "if you will bow down and worship me."
>
> Jesus said to him, "Away from me, Satan! For it is written: 'Worship the Lord your God, and serve him only.'" (Matthew 4:8-10)

Because Jesus wanted to please God more than anything, because he understood who he was and why he was here on earth, and because he loved God's law, nothing could sway him. The best the world could offer him wasn't enough to tempt him to step out of the presence of the Father. Satan didn't stand a chance, because Jesus put the Father's values, not the world's values, first.

Jesus had no permanent home and few belongings. He lived a simple life. He wasn't an ascetic (like a lot of religious leaders in his day). He didn't refuse to drink or associate with people. He didn't hide out in the desert alone. He was surrounded by crowds every day, and yet he never once *over*indulged or became too close a "friend" with the world, because he knew it would damage his relationship with God (see James 4:4).

Listen to what he taught:

> Anyone who loves their father or mother more than me is not worthy of me; anyone who loves their son or daughter more than me is not worthy of me. Whoever does not take up their cross and follow me is not worthy of me. Whoever finds their life will lose it, and whoever loses their life for my sake will find it. (Matthew 10:37-39)

The Father was (and is) Jesus' highest priority, and Jesus expects to be ours. He demonstrated that all true values are God's values, and choosing any others takes us out of his will and his presence. In his best-known teaching, he taught those values. Here are a couple of them:

> Blessed are the pure in heart,
>> for they will see God.
> Blessed are the peacemakers,
>> for they will be called children of God. (Matthew 5:8-9)

So then, the truly good life—the "blessed" or happy life—is to see God and to be called his children. These are God's values: the things that bring his followers closer to him.

His Fearless Confession

Jesus lived with a mindset of making his Father known to the world. His allegiance was to another kingdom, another King, and he made that allegiance known. When Pilate questioned him, he responded: "My kingdom is not of this world. If it were, my servants would fight to prevent my arrest. . . . But now my kingdom is from another place" (John 18:36). When Pilate tried to then nail Jesus on the accusation that he was claiming to be a king, Jesus didn't hesitate: "You say that I am a king. In fact, the reason I was born and came into the world is to testify to the truth. Everyone on the side of truth listens to me" (John 18:37).

Jesus never minced words or fudged the truth, even in the face of dire consequences. Before he'd gotten to Pilate, he'd said almost the same words to the Jewish high priest: "'I have spoken openly to the world,' Jesus replied. 'I always taught in synagogues or at the temple, where all the Jews come together. I said nothing in secret. Why question me? Ask those who heard me. Surely they know what I said'" (John 18:20-21).

Life in God's presence means openly confessing our allegiance to God, especially when it's questioned directly. If we do, Jesus promised us, "Whoever acknowledges me before others, I will also acknowledge before my Father in heaven" (Matthew 10:32).

This confessional lifestyle of acknowledging Jesus in front of people means always being ready to give an answer for the hope we have (1 Peter 3:15). It's a mindset Jesus himself had about his Father. He was never ashamed of his identity and association with his Father, and neither should we be:

> For I am not ashamed of the gospel, because it is the power of God that brings salvation to everyone who believes: first to the Jew, then to the Gentile. (Romans 1:16)

> So do not be ashamed of the testimony about our Lord or of me [Paul] his prisoner. Rather, join with me in suffering for the gospel, by the power of God. (2 Timothy 1:8)

His "Quiet Time"

Jesus sought solitude. We don't have to be alone and away from the world to walk in his presence; he can be present in our noisy times too. But spending time in quiet is a necessary part of practicing God's presence. If we don't take it, we won't have the strength or vision to *carry* him into our noisy times.

Jesus was in incessant demand and easily could have been busy all day, seven days a week, if he'd chosen to be. But he didn't; he chose to make time for solitude—going away from everyone to be alone with the Father. Luke 5:16 says this was his habit. Even though he was, no doubt, sometimes up late at night, he often went off to be alone at the beginning of the day, seeking the Father's presence before going into the world:

Very early in the morning, while it was still dark, Jesus got up, left the house and went off to a solitary place, where he prayed. (Mark 1:35)

At daybreak, Jesus went out to a solitary place. The people were looking for him and when they came to where he was, they tried to keep him from leaving them. (Luke 4:42)

Jesus often escaped the crowds, only to be tracked down quickly (see Matthew 14:13; Mark 3:7)—and this long before Google and social media! He was almost always followed, his time and attention requested—sometimes for *good* reasons, other times for selfish ones. Jesus always knew to seek the best thing first: his Dad. He guarded this time, never allowing the world to drown it out. He didn't try to find time in his schedule for God—he *made* time with his Father a priority, the top priority.

This practice of silence and solitude empowered Jesus' life and ministry, and it's an example for us. Never have there been so many voices as there are now: do this, read that, hear this. Social media is killing people one click at a time—figuratively in most cases, though literally in some. Even non-Christians are waking up to the danger and emptiness of this lifestyle. We're addicted to the constant stream of input, which is so available that we have to go completely against the tide to stop the millions of voices around us. We have to silence our souls—and our technological devices—to listen for the voice of the Father. Sadly, silence has become frightening and foreign to us. But Jesus showed us we *have to* take time for solitude, to listen for the quiet voice of the Spirit of God. We won't hear it any other way.

His Prayer Life

Reading the Gospels, you get the sense Jesus' prayers were not only personal but almost *constant*. Jesus not only prayed first thing in the mornings but also as he went about his daily activities. That two-way communication with his Father didn't end with his morning "quiet time"; it continued all day long.

How about you—do you see prayer that way? Do you, like Jesus, talk to God as though he's always there (because he *is*)? This wasn't just something for Jesus—Paul said all Christians are to pray "continually" (1 Thessalonians 5:17). Personally, I do a lot of spontaneous, *silent* praying while talking to other people. These prayers aren't long or complicated, so they're possible to offer up while engaged in conversation. I call them "flash prayers" (some call them "arrow prayers," because you shoot them up like arrows shot with a bow).[5] Some Christians like to pray spontaneously for others *out loud*. They can be walking out of a building together and right there, in the parking lot, they start talking to God about some concern they've just discussed. Their eyes are wide open as they're walking together to their cars, but they're praying as they walk—as if God is a third person walking right beside them. And why not? God *is* right here with them, just as real as any person they can see.

Luke tells us that the day before Jesus chose Peter and the other apostles, "Jesus went out to a mountainside to pray, and spent the night praying to God. When morning came, he called his disciples to him and chose twelve of them, whom he also designated apostles" (Luke 6:12-13).

That night of prayer preceded one of the most important decisions he would ever make: picking the twelve men he would pour his time and teaching into. He made that decision together with his Father. Then, after that time of back-and-forth communication, God showed him the ones he would call. We too would do well to follow his example before any major decisions we make.

His Love

Jesus was always with people. He lived in relationships, with all of their pressures, demands, and joys, just like we do. He took time for the people others looked down on. He took time to lift up a blind man, a beggar, a prostitute, the diseased, and the demon-possessed. No person was too low on the social ladder for him to associate with. In fact, Jesus' disciples frequently got annoyed because he stopped so often to reduce his whole world to the needs of a single person. He was the opposite of self-important. He definitely wasn't concerned with his own business; this was his Father's business, and it included loving others and sacrificing whatever else he could be doing. He knew God would give him enough time to accomplish his purposes. So he stopped to take full advantage of a divinely invited opportunity—to look full in the face of a desperate man and heal him.

In the musical *Les Misérables*, the main characters sing together this moving line: "To love another person is to see the face of God." That was Jesus' motivation! Every time he looked in people's faces to heal or welcome or forgive them, he was seeing in them, and showing them, the face of God.

> "For I was hungry and you gave me something to eat, I was thirsty and you gave me something to drink, I was a stranger and you invited me in, I needed clothes and you clothed me, I was sick and you looked after me, I was in prison and you came to visit me."

Then the righteous will answer him, "Lord, when did we see you hungry and feed you, or thirsty and give you something to drink? When did we see you a stranger and invite you in, or needing clothes and clothe you? When did we see you sick or in prison and go to visit you?"

The King will reply, "Truly I tell you, whatever you did for one of the least of these brothers and sisters of mine, you did for me." (Matthew 25:35-40)

When we walk with God, even small exchanges with other people—things we might think are insignificant—are immeasurably significant to God because they're the overflow of Christ in us. No person is ever the same after coming to know Jesus, so investing in a single exchange has ripple effects beyond that individual. From the person who waits on your table to your spouse or child, every interaction is an opportunity to practice God's presence by showing his love.

Making time to love and serve the least, the last, and the lost was the heart of Jesus' work on earth, and it's seen best in his ultimate sacrifice. We're also called to die; to crucify our selfishness and place others' interests above our own, to be willing to be last instead of first. We're called to set aside our rights and become servants. We're called to follow the example of Jesus, who got on his hands and knees to wash feet and asked us to do the same.

Everyone in the Christian community wants to be *called* a servant, but no one wants to be *treated* like one. But if we're really walking with God, we won't be insulted when we're overlooked or taken for granted. We won't serve others to get praise. We'll do it because the one who provides us with unending life is leading us this way.

My friend Larry Crabb recently wrote a book about orienting our lives around sacrificial, Jesus-like love for others. He explained that Jesus was filled with and ruled by the Holy Spirit's passionate and undistorted love:

> Jesus endured no suffering as a helpless, unwilling victim. He was always willing and therefore not primarily a victim at all but rather a free agent choosing to suffer on behalf of people who were unworthy of His love. It is that kind of love, undistorted by self-centeredness, that brings the happiness we were created to enjoy even in the darkest night.[6]

His Sacrifice

Jesus was more than an example. He gave his life to rescue us from our sins. He didn't just *show* us what it looks like to practice God's presence; he gave us the power to do it. Without him, we wouldn't have free access to the Father and his Spirit *in* us. (Before Jesus, no one had this privilege.)

If we want to learn to experience God's presence, then reading, studying, and meditating on the life of Jesus is, hands down, the best place to start.

God brooks no rivals. Jesus made God's will and the desire to stay in his presence first in everything, living in a way no other person ever has or ever will. He took the gift of human life he'd been given and used it to draw as many as possible into the Father's family, to live in his presence. Then he laid it down in the sacrifice that would become our salvation.

Listen to God in His Word

Jesus' words are powerful. Choose one of the following sayings to focus on this week. Write it down (or type it out) and put it in a place where you'll see it often. Read it a few times during the day—whenever you see it. You might also want to get your Bible and take a look at the surrounding context of the verse you choose.

- Do not let your hearts be troubled. You believe in God; believe also in me. (John 14:1)

- I am the vine; you are the branches. If you remain in me and I in you, you will bear much fruit; apart from me you can do nothing. (John 15:5)

- Whoever wants to be my disciple must deny themselves and take up their cross daily and follow me. (Luke 9:23)

- It is written: "Man shall not live on bread alone, but on every word that comes from the mouth of God." (Matthew 4:4)

- Whoever finds their life will lose it, and whoever loses their life for my sake will find it. (Matthew 10:39)

- Come to me, all you who are weary and burdened, and I will give you rest. Take my yoke upon you and learn from me, for I am gentle and humble in heart, and you will find rest for your souls. (Matthew 11:28-29)

- If you love me, keep my commands. (John 14:15)

Practice His Presence
Meditate on the Life of Christ

Thomas à Kempis (1380–1471) was a follower of Christ who lived in a dark time; of all of the practices he engaged in, the one he said was of the highest importance (and most rewarding) was meditation on the life of Christ. This week, follow his example:

meditate on the life of Christ. You can do so in an easy way—using one of the four Gospels: Matthew, Mark, Luke, or John.

As you read, consider looking closer at the context of the verse you chose earlier. Or choose one of the characteristics of Jesus' life from this chapter—maybe one you struggle with or just want to learn more about—and look for it as you make your way through one whole Gospel: trust in the Father, living in awareness of his identity as God's Son, pursuing the Father's agenda, valuing what God values, confessing him before others, making time for silence and solitude, praying continually, and loving others sacrificially. Don't forget the most important step of studying the Bible: application. Brainstorm one way, even a small way, that you can apply Jesus' example to your own life this week!

Note: If meditation is new to you, here are a few hints. First, don't hurry! Take time to linger over a story or even just one sentence or phrase. It helps to *read* a passage several times—you'll notice things the second and third times that you missed the first. Then *reflect* on it (which words, phrases, and images stand out to you?), imagining it with all of your senses (this enables you to remember it better). *Respond* by praying the Scripture back to God: adoring him, confessing a sin, affirming a truth, thanking him, or asking his help to believe and obey. Finally, *rest* in silence for a few minutes, yielding yourself to God as you contemplate what you've read and learned. (You can use this *read, reflect, respond, and rest* method for any Scripture study, not just the Gospels!)

4

The Walk

Therefore as you have received Christ
Jesus the Lord, so walk in Him.

COLOSSIANS 2:6 NASB

The Bible is the tremendous, cosmic drama about God's relationship with humankind. Using the unique personalities of human authors, the Holy Spirit inspired its recording, giving us a patchwork of writings which connect together into one, grand narrative that climaxes with the person and work of Jesus Christ. The Bible gives us snapshots of many individual lives—people like you and me who lived in real time and space. These people encountered the presence of God in some way, inviting him in or rejecting his presence. Their stories are recorded for us so we too can understand the greatness of our Creator and the love he has toward us, a love so great that it led him to sacrifice his own Son for us.

In this chapter we'll zoom in on a few people in the Bible who seemed to experience God's presence deeply, walking closely with him. We'll start with the very first people God made, Adam and

Eve—the only humans, besides Jesus, ever to enjoy perfect, unbroken fellowship with their Maker.

Adam and Eve: From Oneness to Brokenness

In the beginning, Adam and Eve lived with God, enjoying his presence in what was likely the most beautiful place on earth. Their lives, and that garden, were gifts from their Creator. But the greatest gift was his presence. Adam and Eve knew God so well that they recognized the sound of God walking through the garden (Genesis 3:8). Since God is the source of every good thing (Psalm 16:11; Zephaniah 3:17; James 1:17), we can guess that that sound of divine "feet" was the best part of Adam and Eve's day. It was the sound of Daddy bringing home the best Christmas present ever—only infinitely better. Though they were naked, Adam and Eve were unashamed. They didn't even know what shame or any other negative thing was. They'd never known anything but openness and transparency with God.

All of that changes in the third chapter of the Bible. Here is the first time God has to look for Adam and Eve. They'd just eaten the fruit he'd told them never to taste, and for the first time they're hiding from God:

> Then the man and his wife heard the sound of the LORD God as he was walking in the garden in the cool of the day, and they hid from the LORD God among the trees of the garden. But the LORD God called to the man, "Where are you?"
>
> He answered, "I heard you in the garden, and I was afraid because I was naked; so I hid."
>
> And he said, "Who told you that you were naked? Have you eaten from the tree that I commanded you not to eat from?"
>
> The man said, "The woman you put here with me—she gave me some fruit from the tree, and I ate it." (Genesis 3:8-12)

There, the blame game began, continuing right on down to the present day. But look back at what God asked Adam and Eve: "Where are you?" Why would he ask that, since God knows everything? Was it a rhetorical question? In fact, God knew exactly where they were, but he wanted to initiate a conversation about what had just happened. In effect, he was asking, "Why are you separating yourself from me?"

Moments earlier, Adam and Eve had been naked and exposed, yet without shame or fear (Genesis 2:25); they had complete unity with God and each other. You might call their state "unconfirmed creaturely holiness." In other words, these moral agents—created by God to bear his image, to take care of his creation, to respond to his overtures—experienced no separation from their Creator, but neither had that unity been tested. The chapter division between Genesis 2 and 3 is telling. After the fateful acts of Genesis 3, the world's first people suddenly become terrified by the very thing that once brought them the most joy: God's presence. Because of their disobedience, they pushed back from him, making futile attempts to cover themselves so he wouldn't see them. All had been well with their souls, but now disharmony and an impulse to hide invaded their beings. That impulse is alive today. But as with Adam and Eve, no matter how much we think we can hide, God still sees and knows all things (Proverbs 5:21; Jeremiah 16:17; 1 Corinthians 4:5).

God couldn't let sin go unpunished, but his love and grace were also immediately evident from the moment people began to hide from him. He essentially told Adam and Eve, "Those fig leaves won't suffice." Their efforts to cover up were clumsy and useless; there's no fooling God! At that point God made the first sacrifice, killing an animal to provide the couple with clothing. That incident was later paralleled by Jesus' sacrifice for us—his own shedding of blood on our behalf so our sins could be completely covered, forever. By that sacrifice, Jesus bought us back from sin and made us able to enter his presence once again, without shame and without fear.

The first prophecy of Jesus' ultimate sacrifice comes in Genesis 3:15. The verse telling of God's judgment against Adam, Eve, and the earth also hints at the lengths God will go to in order to restore communion with his people. Ultimately, the seed of the woman, Jesus, will come to "crush" the head of the serpent, finally defeating both Satan and death (Luke 10:18; Revelation 20:10), and restore fellowship with his people. But first, Adam and Eve, and their offspring, would die—spiritually and physically.[1] This death spread into every relationship, resulting in brokenness, alienation, and separation from God, within themselves, with each other, and even with nature. The habit of hiding began. Since then, no effort to hide ourselves and conceal our sin has ever worked—and it never will; God will always find us out (Numbers 32:23)!

Jesus is God's plan to overcome this alienation with his people, caused by sin. Christ's sacrifice on the cross and his resurrection reversed the effects of the fall. That reversal is already completed in one sense (John 19:30), but it's also an ongoing process from a human standpoint (Hebrews 10:14). God will continue to restore his people and his creation until the day when our bodies are glorified and freed once and for all from this "bondage to decay" (Romans 8:21). When *that* happens, we'll know God face to face; we'll sit (and dance and revel and sing) in his presence the way we were meant to.

In the meantime, it's a great mystery why God even chooses to put up with us. He doesn't have to. If I were God for a day and could see the depth of wickedness in the human heart—not just one heart but multiplied by the 7.5 billion people on the planet today—I'd say, "Are you kidding? Who needs this grief? Thump, you are out of existence." You wouldn't even know I was God for a day because you would cease to be. I think most of us would do the same. But the God we deal with is mysterious and unsearchable, his mind unfathomable. He's a deeply personal God who, for reasons known only to him, takes pleasure in doing whatever it takes to make us his sons and daughters so we're able to become his children the way Adam and Eve were *supposed* to be. It's a love incomprehensible.

Enoch Walked with God

One of the most mysterious people of the Bible, Enoch, is keenly relevant here. This man's name is buried in a long list of other descendants of Adam in Genesis 5:

> When Jared had lived 162 years, he became the father of Enoch.... When Enoch had lived 65 years, he became the father of Methuselah. After he became the father of Methuselah, Enoch walked faithfully with God 300 years and had other sons and daughters. Altogether, Enoch lived a total of 365 years. Enoch walked faithfully with God; then he was no more, because God took him away. (Genesis 5:18, 21-24)

Besides another brief mention in Hebrews, that's all we're told about Enoch. Personally, I would have liked a bit more information. But God's Word is sufficient, never telling us less than we need to know. These verses give two key facts about Enoch. First, he was one of only two men in Scripture (the other was Elijah) who never died. We don't know exactly how or why that happened. The Bible simply says that God "took him away" and does not say that he died as it says of the other patriarchs. The other thing we learn about Enoch is that he "walked with God."

It's a simple statement also used of Noah in Genesis 6. It's remarkable when you consider the length of Enoch's life: 365 years! That's a long time to be walking with God. Enoch, evidently, "pressed on" (as Paul urged in Philippians 3:14) to the uttermost!

Enoch is proof that this kind of life—daily walking with God—is possible, not just in the short term but over a much longer lifetime than any of us will enjoy. If you're older and you're having difficulty persevering in your faith, just imagine how Enoch felt around age 260! We know Enoch's life was one of a steady faith that pleased God, because he shows up in one other place in the Bible, the great faith chapter of Hebrews: "By faith Enoch was taken from this life, so that he did not experience death: 'He could not be found, because God had taken him away.' For before he was taken, he was commended as one who pleased God" (Hebrews 11:5).

Like the others named in Hebrews 11—Abel, Noah, Abraham, Moses, and so on—Enoch led a life of faith worthy of emulation. He lived, as we are to live, in "the assurance of *things* hoped for, the conviction of things not seen" (Hebrews 11:1 NASB), and he walked with God, which is what I'm hoping all of us will learn to do better by the end of this book. His example can inspire us to persevere, especially when we begin to feel worn down, physically or spiritually.

Abraham: A Friend of God

Jesus said to his disciples, "I no longer call you servants, because a servant does not know his master's business. Instead, I have called you friends, for everything that I learned from my Father I have made known to you" (John 15:15). Abraham lived long before Jesus said those words. Abraham is the only person in the Hebrew Bible called a "friend of God" (Isaiah 41:8; James 2:23).

The label fit. Abraham had regular conversations with God. God talked with Abraham, and Abraham talked back. Over and over, we read words like, "The LORD said to Abram . . ." (Genesis 12:1, 7; 13:14; 15:9, 13; 17:1, 3, 9). Sometimes he seems to have spoken directly (whether audibly or inaudibly, Scripture doesn't say), other times through visions, dreams, or messengers (Genesis 18). There seem to be periods of silence (when their communication isn't recorded), but by Genesis 15, it's clear the relationship had grown more dynamic.

When God told Abraham to do something, he usually obeyed. But Abraham wasn't perfect. He had moments of failure. At one point it seems he got tired of waiting on God to provide him the child he'd promised, so Abraham took matters into his own hands and impregnated his servant, Hagar. Two decades later, when Abraham received the promised son (Isaac), his trust had evidently grown. When God asked him to do the unthinkable—to offer Isaac as a sacrifice—Abraham obeyed immediately. Think about this: this was the son he'd been promised, the son who would supposedly produce many offspring; yet, amazingly, Abraham hurried to obey. He trusted God *that* much. There's only one explanation for that kind of obedience: Abraham's walk with God had grown intimate, bound by a deep trust, through years of testing. Not only did he trust fiercely but he heard God's voice clearly. It had become familiar to him over years of walking in relationship with him—just as Jesus promised would happen when we know the Father (John 10:27).

Abraham's relationship was real and filled with human emotion. The Bible shows him falling facedown when he realized he'd disappointed God, and laughing when God told him something he had a hard time believing. Do you feel this free to express your emotions to God, to show him your true self rather than putting on a pious front or hiding them with your own versions of fig leaves?

Abraham's first response when he met God was to obey. We don't know why, but it paid off. He continued to do what God said until they'd developed a close relationship, and Abraham was able to talk with God, to hear and follow him, to be called God's friend. Abraham became the father of a nation that was called to bless the whole world. Here's his commendation in Hebrews:

> By faith Abraham, when called to go to a place he would later receive as his inheritance, obeyed and went, even though he did not know where he was going. By faith he made his home in the promised land like a stranger in a foreign country; he lived in tents, as did Isaac and Jacob, who were heirs with him of the same promise. For he was looking forward to the city with foundations, whose architect and builder is God. And by faith even Sarah, who was past childbearing age, was enabled to bear children because she considered him faithful who had made the promise. And so from this one man, and he as good as dead, came descendants as numerous as the stars in the sky and as countless as the sand on the seashore. (Hebrews 11:8-12)

If we're in Christ, we can enjoy the intimacy of a deep and growing friendship with him. We have the privilege of walking both *with* and *in* him (Colossians 2:6). But before Jesus, the idea that men and women could be "friends of God" was uncommon. Abraham's relationship with God was exceptional.

Abraham kept going because he was "looking forward to the city" of God. This was how he kept his eyes trained on God, even while he lived on earth and all the promises God made him hadn't been fulfilled yet. He faltered sometimes, but he always got back on track, coming to God in humility, confessing his failures, realizing God had already seen them anyway.

Abraham may have lived millennia ago, but he was a human just like us, and we can take a lesson from his deepening trust in and friendship with God over his lifetime.

Moses: Face to Face with God

Although Abraham was the only one literally called "friend of God" in the Old Testament, Moses is described in similar terms:

> As Moses went into the tent, the pillar of cloud would come down and stay at the entrance, while the LORD spoke with Moses. Whenever the people saw the pillar of cloud standing at the entrance to the tent, they all stood and worshiped, each at the entrance to their tent. The LORD would speak to Moses face to face, as one speaks to a friend. Then Moses would return to the camp, but his young aide Joshua son of Nun did not leave the tent. (Exodus 33:9-11)

Moses was animated by an ardent longing to know God and see his glory. And the more time Moses spent with God, the more dramatic this aspiration grew. After a while, Moses *had* to have God's presence. No messenger would do. He wanted a direct encounter with the living God. If the rest of Exodus 33 is any indication, God seems to have largely met this desire.

Look how bold and how intimate this conversation was. Though Moses was well aware of God's glory, this isn't a worship service. It's a conversation between close friends who knew each other well:

> Moses said to the LORD, "You have been telling me, 'Lead these people,' but you have not let me know whom you will send with me. You have said, 'I know you by name and you

have found favor with me.' If you are pleased with me, teach me your ways so I may know you and continue to find favor with you. Remember that this nation is your people."

The LORD replied, "My Presence will go with you, and I will give you rest."

Then Moses said to him, "If your Presence does not go with us, do not send us up from here. How will anyone know that you are pleased with me and with your people unless you go with us? What else will distinguish me and your people from all the other people on the face of the earth?"

And the LORD said to Moses, "I will do the very thing you have asked, because I am pleased with you and I know you by name." (Exodus 33:12-17)

Moses was known to God. Now he wanted his nation to be known to others *as* God's. He wanted the nation to be recognized as a separate, special people who reflected God's presence—which is exactly the promise God made to Abraham. By spending time with the Lord, not only had a relationship deepened but Moses' longings had come to align with God's.

In this very personal relationship, Moses was known to God by name and desperately wanted to be more closely led by him. He wanted confidence that God was going with him—with all the Israelites—as they went forward. In fact, if God's presence didn't go with them, Moses said, it wasn't worth going. To him, life without God's presence is a meaningless existence.

Moses got even bolder as this encounter continued:

Then Moses said, "Now show me your glory."

And the LORD said, "I will cause all my goodness to pass in front of you, and I will proclaim my name, the LORD, in your presence. I will have mercy on whom I will have mercy, and I will have compassion on whom I will have compassion. But," he said, "you cannot see my face, for no one may see me and live."

Then the Lord said, "There is a place near me where you may stand on a rock. When my glory passes by, I will put you in a cleft in the rock and cover you with my hand until I have passed by. Then I will remove my hand and you will see my back; but my face must not be seen." (Exodus 33:18-23)

Moses' request was a heady one: "show me your glory"! God knew Moses didn't fully understand what he was asking. Not one of us will see God as he really is until we are in our glorified, resurrected bodies; only then will we "see his face," Revelation 22:4 says, and only then will we be able to endure perfect intimacy with God. Nevertheless, God answered Moses. When he did, he had to literally protect Moses from himself—from the full extent of his glory and power—or else Moses would have been overwhelmed to the point of death. So God manifested himself in a partial vision, through the beauty of his attributes:

Then the Lord came down in the cloud and stood there with him and proclaimed his name, the Lord. And he passed in front of Moses, proclaiming, "The Lord, the Lord, the compassionate and gracious God, slow to anger, abounding in love and faithfulness, maintaining love to thousands, and forgiving wickedness, rebellion and sin." (Exodus 34:5-7)

Moses dropped to the ground to worship as soon as God's glory passed by. (That's the only thing a person *can* do, voluntarily or not, when encountering the holy God this closely.) When he got up and returned to the camp, Moses didn't realize how much of God's glory had remained with him:

When Moses came down from Mount Sinai with the two tablets of the covenant law in his hands, he was not aware that his face was radiant because he had spoken with the LORD. When Aaron and all the Israelites saw Moses, his face was radiant, and they were afraid to come near him. (Exodus 34:29-30)

Isaiah, Daniel, and others in the Bible had responses similar to Moses'. None of us can endure the fullness of God's presence while we're alive on this earth. God knows that. But we can still try, like Moses did, to get as close to him as possible, trusting he'll give us as much of himself and his glory as we can handle! When we pursue God like this, our growing intimacy with him energizes our activity. Our outward life starts to reflect that inward relationship and, like Moses, we begin to emanate his glory and love to others around us, often in ways we don't even realize.

David: A Man After God's Own Heart

God called King David a "man after his own heart" (1 Samuel 13:14). He beautifully exemplified what we've been talking about, but not just because he sought and lived in God's presence. His life also demonstrated how sin hinders us from walking with God, diminishing our experience with him. The pattern is familiar: we sin; we try to hide it from God (and usually from others too); and if confession doesn't come quickly, the sin grows—becoming a barrier to our developing relationship with him.

There's a deep backstory to David's great fall that began with his adultery with Bathsheba. We don't have time to trace all the details, but you can read (or skim) 1 Samuel 16–31 and 2 Samuel 1–10 for most of it. To start, we find a loyal, faithful, deeply admirable man of God, a shepherd who becomes a great military leader and then a king. That man sought to do what was right in the eyes of the Lord, showing kindness and mercy even to his enemies. But in 2 Samuel 11, David reached a critical time in his reign. The first verse hints at the fact that something unusual was going on: "In the spring, at the time when kings go off to war, David sent Joab out with the king's men and the whole Israelite army. They destroyed the Ammonites and besieged Rabbah. But David remained in Jerusalem" (2 Samuel 11:1).

It wasn't against God's law for a king to stay home while his men went to war, but it was unusual. David was a radically loyal person, and for him to send his men out to fight while he lounged around the palace was not normal for him. Something was already wrong, though we're not told what. He was restless—a good sign he'd gotten away from God. Something the law *did* require was for every king to make his own copy of God's book and keep it with him (Deuteronomy 17:18), meditating on it and leading by it. David had done that, but he clearly wasn't meditating on God's law when he wandered up to the roof of the palace and peeped at Bathsheba:

> One evening David got up from his bed and walked around on the roof of the palace. From the roof he saw a woman bathing. The woman was very beautiful, and David sent someone to find out about her. The man said, "She is Bathsheba, the daughter of Eliam and the wife of Uriah the Hittite." Then David sent messengers to get her. She came to him, and he slept with her. (2 Samuel 11:2-4)

It wasn't a single thought that led David to such an egregious sin. Bathsheba was probably not his first temptation. It's more likely he'd let idle thoughts turn into lustful ones that had accumulated for a while. And finally, tragically, he succumbed.

David's adultery with Bathsheba was the tip of an iceberg. Sin breeds more sin, which breeds lies to cover up. Within a very short time, David had violated many of the Ten Commandments, including murder. In a desperate attempt to avoid being found out, he intentionally had Bathsheba's husband, Uriah the Hittite— one of David's thirty mighty men—placed on the frontlines of battle so he'd be killed. This act of treachery apparently hung in the palace air for a year before David did anything about it. Meanwhile, he married Bathsheba, who bore him a son (who eventually died). What David had done displeased the Lord (2 Samuel 11:27).

God sent Nathan the prophet to confront the king. Kings in those days had great power. All David had to do was say the word and the prophet would've been imprisoned or killed. But, being obedient to God, Nathan approached David at the risk of both his own life and his relationship with David.

His approach was creative. He didn't come right out and accuse David. Instead, he told the king a story containing some parallels to David's own wrongs:

> There were two men in a certain town, one rich and the other poor. The rich man had a very large number of sheep and cattle, but the poor man had nothing except one little ewe lamb he had bought. He raised it, and it grew up with him and his children. It shared his food, drank from his cup and even slept in his arms. It was like a daughter to him.
>
> Now a traveler came to the rich man, but the rich man refrained from taking one of his own sheep or cattle to prepare a meal for the traveler who had come to him. Instead, he took the ewe lamb that belonged to the poor man and prepared it for the one who had come to him. (2 Samuel 12:1-4)

When David heard the story, he was livid: "The man who did this must die!" (2 Samuel 12:5). Now, the man wasn't worthy of death according to the law, but the offense did require restitution. But David's ability to discern right from wrong was still intact (at least as it concerned others), and his sense of justice stirred. No sooner had David unleashed his fury at the man in the parable than he was nailed for his own guilt: "You are the man!" Nathan declared to him (2 Samuel 12:7).

Nathan's storytelling reminds me of my late friend Ed Dudley. We called Ed the Velvet Hammer. Ed would tell stories, and as soon as you began laughing at them, you'd realize it applied to you. One of his favorites to tell was when someone tried to take credit where credit wasn't due: "A lot of people are like the guy who was born on third base, and woke up and thought he'd just hit a triple." Ed's stories were a little like the parables Jesus told. While our guard was down and we were still laughing, suddenly—whack!—he'd nail us. Nathan was also like that, and we all need a Nathan in our lives, someone willing to confront us about our sin, lovingly but firmly.

David faced a choice: would he succumb and submit to the prompting of God's Spirit mediated through Nathan? Or would he rebel against that word of truth and continue trying to cover up his tracks, as he'd been doing for so long? The illegitimate child had been born, and considerable time had gone by with no consequences. He might've even begun to wonder if he'd gotten away with his tangled web of sins. Now, he discovered, that wasn't the case at all. God was onto him, and Nathan was too.

This decision point was one of David's great moments. On the spot, he confessed to Nathan: "I have sinned against the LORD" (2 Samuel 12:13). He repented and fasted, and his child with Bathsheba died. Eventually, he had another child with Bathsheba, a child who went on to become the wisest king ever to live, and is also in the line of Christ in Matthew's genealogy—powerfully demonstrating how God can redeem even our worst failures! God's grace is beyond all human comprehension and certainly beyond our deserving. David's sin was great, but his response when he felt convicted showed he still had a heart for God. And thankfully, God loves to give second chances. Though sin diminished David's experience of God's presence for a time, that intimacy returned after he repented.

I like David because his heart was so much like ours. He's evidence that the best course of action is to confess, rather than cover up; to draw near to God in humility, rather than pride and self-justification. David's plea for mercy and restoration is enshrined in Psalm 51:

> Have mercy on me, O God,
>   according to your unfailing love;
> according to your great compassion
>   blot out my transgressions. (Psalm 51:1)

Later in the psalm, David acknowledged there was no sacrifice he could make that could cover his sins. This was very insightful:

> You do not delight in sacrifice, or I would bring it;
>   you do not take pleasure in burnt offerings.
> My sacrifice, O God, is a broken spirit;
>   a broken and contrite heart
>   you, God, will not despise. (Psalm 51:16-17)

David was right. Though he lived before Jesus walked the earth, it's clear from Psalm 51 and other Scriptures that he knew the only way to be saved from the mess he'd gotten himself into was to fall on the mercy of God. He appealed to that mercy and to

God's "unfailing love." What a wonderful example he provides of how we can regain a sense of God's presence in our lives after we've failed, even grievously so!

■ ■ ■

We haven't even scratched the surface of people in the Bible whose lives show what it means to walk in God's presence through our twisted and often difficult lives on earth. The stories of Joseph, Ruth, Jeremiah, Daniel, Mary, John the Baptist, Peter, John (the apostle), James, Barnabas, Paul, Timothy, and so many others live on as a cloud of witnesses to the fact that we can live in the presence of God no matter what our lives are like.

Listen to God in His Word

Spend some time reading the following three verses. Take your time reading them a few times. Pray while you read (using your mind on two levels at once), asking God to draw you in to spend so much time with him that you begin to radiate his glory to others, just like Moses did—so that others will "take note" that you've "been with Jesus."

- Exodus 34:29
- 2 Corinthians 3:18
- Acts 4:13

Practice His Presence
Role Models

You've read about several Old Testament examples who walked in God's presence. Now, think across your own life. Who has modeled walking with God for you? It may be a person you know (or once knew) well or someone you only know at a distance (like an author or a pastor). What are the person's practices or habits for sustaining an intimate relationship with God? If you're not sure, and the person is available to you, ask them! Then pray God will help you grow in this area and that you too can become an example for someone—not a perfect example but someone with a willing and humble spirit who hungers for and pursues him.

Part 2

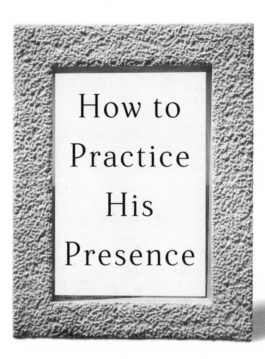

How to
Practice
His
Presence

5

Training

Train yourself to be godly.

1 TIMOTHY 4:7

I learned to drive a car with a stick shift. It was a 1954 MG TD (now my age shows). It was a hard car to drive. It had a rod with a roller ball for an accelerator, and there was little room for the other two pedals. To make matters worse, the first gear was not synchronized, and the car was difficult to shift. In my first attempts, the car bucked forward, and shifting the gears made the sound of grinding meat. My father was a bus driver. You can imagine his frustration, trying to teach me on that awful thing.

One horrific moment in that learning process stands out. I will never forget it. I was getting better by that point. No longer confined to a vacant lot for practice, I was finally allowed out on the streets. One day, I had to stop at a red light at the top of a hill. Anyone who knows anything about a stick shift knows why that presented a challenge. My car was at an angle. The car in my rearview mirror was not just behind me but *mere inches* behind me.

What was I going to do? I had to keep the MG from rolling backward, so I used the hand-pedal emergency brake while giving it extra gas and slowly releasing the clutch to keep from rolling when the light turned green.

I managed to do just that. I thought I had ruined the clutch when I heard a loud "reeee!" as I pulled out. But at least I didn't roll back.

Weeks later, the trial-and-error period with my MG was over, and shifting had become habitual. I no longer had to consciously think about the gearshift or the clutch. Driving became fluid and effortless. Today, it's hard to even imagine *not* being able to drive a stick.

Learning by Doing

All of us have skills we've learned by doing—skills so ingrained, so habitual, that they've become second nature: walking, running, riding a bicycle, playing a musical instrument, dribbling a basketball, writing, reading, typing, painting, singing, and so on. All of these skills were difficult when we were learning, but after hours of practice, sometimes with the help of a coach or teacher, now they come naturally. Many of them we can even do *while* doing other things simultaneously (eating while reading, marching while playing an instrument, walking while talking).

Most things we learn by doing. The academic world has caught on to this fact, which is why so many schools now tout experiential-learning opportunities. Book learning is essential, but its purpose is application. It's no different with spiritual things: we learn godliness by *practicing* godly skills and habits. For example, we learn to pray by praying, to meditate on God's Word by reading and meditating on it, and to love and serve others by getting out and doing it.

We can't train ourselves in godliness without first trusting God; without faith it's impossible to please him. But the next step is putting that faith into practice. In fact, faith that *never* gets put into practice isn't true, saving faith at all (James 2:14-26).

In his book *The Presence*, Alec Rowlands talks about earning his flight certification by taking an exam, but he hadn't yet flown a plane. He was a pilot on paper, but not in practice. Eventually, after hours of flying with an instructor, he became a pilot *in practice*. A lot of believers are like pilots with certification and no experience; they've prayed a prayer to accept Christ, maybe even been baptized—"but that distinction is pretty meaningless if our moment of salvation isn't simply the front door leading into an *ongoing* and *growing* experience of the Christian life."[1] Of course, authentic saving faith should lead to a life marked by growth, but Rowlands is right: we aren't only saved *from* something (sin, death, and hell), but *for* something, an eternal life that begins right here, right now. And embracing that life means gradually becoming in practice the person God has made us in position through Jesus Christ: a child of God, being conformed more and more to his likeness.

While there's certainly an emphasis on action in the Christian life—living out our faith in deed—there's perhaps an even greater emphasis on *being*. It's not that *doing* is unimportant, but our actions flow from who we are at our core (Proverbs 4:23; Matthew 15:16-20). "The most important thing in your life is not what you do; it's who you become," author Dallas Willard once said. "That's what you will take into eternity. You are an unceasing spiritual being with an eternal destiny in God's great universe."[2] This emphasis on *being* over *doing* may seem contradictory to the idea of training and practicing, but it's not. Activity is energized by intimacy, and intimacy with Christ is cultivated through day-to-day practice. Spiritual life is a dynamic process, not a measurable product, and every follower of Jesus is always in that process of *becoming* who we're meant to be.

Part of who we're meant to be involves that amphibious nature I talked about earlier. Though we're wired to live on two levels simultaneously, our natural disposition is to focus on what we experience by our senses. *We don't have to train to be aware of what we already see, feel, smell, hear, and touch*; it happens by default. But people were made with a capacity to be aware of the supernatural too. God has set eternity in our hearts. This capacity is just as great as our capacity to know the natural realm, but it needs to be tapped into and developed. Because it's invisible, it's too often overlooked, and our enemy, the devil, works hard to make sure we keep overlooking it.

There are practices we can engage in that will help us build this capacity—habits that will help us "carry the sanctuary frame of mind out into the world, into its turmoil and its fitfulness," as author Thomas Kelly put it. These practices increase our inward turning toward God *while* we go about our external lives: "secret habits of unceasing orientation of the deeps of our being . . . so that we are perpetually bowed in worship, while we're also very busy in the world of daily affairs."[3]

Building Skills and Forming Habits

Just like you can train to run fast or play an instrument, and like I trained to learn to drive my MG, we can all train to make ourselves more aware of God's presence. *Practicing* God's presence simply means we're taking what we already have—the Holy Spirit in us and our standing as children of God—and living it out more and more each day.

In any form of training, it's one step, one skill, at a time, and then practice, practice, practice. Runners don't start with a marathon.

They start small, building up both distance and speed incrementally over time. Eventually, repeated practice leads to a growing capacity, and a more natural, perfect exercise of that capacity. And just like with a car, a musical instrument, or our legs, the more we train, the more strength and freedom we have to not only succeed in what we're doing but to *enjoy* it.

If you're not a runner, and you went outside right now and ran around the block as fast as you could, you'd probably feel terrible. But ask trained runners what running is like for them. Ask someone like ultramarathoner Scott Jurek, and you'll see his eyes light up.

Scott was a gangly kid whose early years were painful. His mom struggled with multiple sclerosis, and Scott helped run his home and care for his mom while his dad worked. He liked skiing and ran to cross-train, but he wasn't fast. Other kids on the cross-country team called him "the Jerker." They threw mud at him and left him behind. He trained, but it didn't seem to help. His family experiences had given him a strong work ethic, though, so he kept training.

The fastest kid on his team was Dusty Olson, who said he couldn't figure out why Scott was so slow when he trained harder than anyone. After high school, he asked Scott to train with him for a fifty-mile race. Scott agreed. Race day came, and when Dusty's shoe came off in the mud, he saw Scott run past him. The slow kid who'd never even run a marathon ended up coming in second overall in a fifty-mile race. After the race, Scott swore he'd never do it again. Hours later, he'd changed his mind.

Many years and a long list of victories later, Scott Jurek is now considered one of the greatest runners in the world. And he still trains and helps others to do the same. When he finishes a long race, he wraps himself in a sleeping bag, hops over to the finish line, and cheers until everyone's finished.

Scott Jurek didn't start out trying. He started out training—that's what running was to him. He didn't expect to be fast; he just found out he *could be*. That's what training did for him. He ran, not because he loved it. He ran *until* he loved it.

Spiritual training is a lot like athletic training. For one, it's ongoing; there isn't a level we reach when we don't have to train anymore. It also requires time. An infant doesn't come out of the womb knowing how to walk, and a person doesn't learn to run fifty miles overnight; it takes months, even years, of training. Our capacity to experience God also grows slowly and steadily. This is normal. But over time, if we keep training, our capacity for relationship with God can grow and lead us to a love for and an enjoyment of him that we didn't expect.

What Training Is and Isn't

There's a big difference between *trying* and *training*, and it's the difference between success and failure in the area of spiritual training. I'm indebted to the writings of John Ortberg and Dallas Willard for calling my attention to this distinction.[4] Whereas *trying* is focused on applying our own (limited) power, spiritual *training* is focused on *gaining skill* in living life by *God*'s power. The difference is critical, because without the proper energizing source, our efforts will quickly fizzle, discouraging us and tempting us to give up. On the other hand, if we *train* instead of simply *trying harder*—and let our actions follow—then by the power of the Spirit, we can live the kind of unified, spiritually rich life we're meant to live. An easy life with smooth sailing? Not necessarily. A deeply fulfilling life that reflects how God made us and prepares us for eternity in his presence? Absolutely.

There's also a big difference between training and *earning* (*working for*) our salvation. While we were still sinners (God's enemies), Christ died for us (Romans 5:8). The Bible is clear that we bring nothing to the table for our own salvation, other than belief (and even that is a gift!); we are saved by grace through faith alone (Ephesians 2:8). Once we're believers, we also *grow* by grace—by his working in us: "for it is God who works in you to will and to act in order to fulfill his good purpose" (Philippians 2:13).

So training *isn't* trying, and it's not *earning* points with God. So what *is* the point of training? Why do we do it if all aspects of our salvation are a work of God, by his grace?

The Bible is clear that spiritual training is supremely valuable. Take a look at these words of Paul to his young mentee Timothy:

> Train yourself to be godly. For physical training is of some value, but godliness has value for all things, holding promise for both the present life and the life to come. This is a trustworthy saying that deserves full acceptance. That is why we labor and strive, because we have put our hope in the living God, who is the Savior of all people, and especially of those who believe. (1 Timothy 4:7-10)

Training in godliness—practicing God's presence—has value for "all things," in this life and the one to come. *This training is important, and it's worth it!* In his letter to the Corinthians, Paul also emphasized training, and its ultimate purpose: "Do you not know that in a race all the runners run, but only one gets the prize? Run in such a way as to get the prize. Everyone who competes in the games goes into strict training. They do it to get a crown that will not last, but we do it to get a crown that will last forever" (1 Corinthians 9:24-25).

In other words, spiritual training helps us know God better and grow closer to him. It encourages and aids us in the act of surrendering more of our lives to him and serving as a witness to others of the value of doing the same. This kind of training leads up to the day when we'll be in God's presence for eternity.

We can't forget that knowing God is the end goal; any practices, habits, or disciplines are the means to *knowing him better*, to growing in fellowship with him (just as we do certain things to cultivate a relationship with any person). This is a dynamic process, resulting in a transformation of our souls (Romans 12:2), a new attitude toward the world.

Maybe you've noticed that habits shape a person. They come to define someone's character and overall disposition. When we develop habits of godliness, they shape our attitude and our approach toward the world. The habits of our sinful nature get replaced by habits in keeping with our new, redeemed nature— giving us a whole new disposition. We reflect more of God in our everyday attitudes, thought patterns, and actions through the unique prism of our own personality.

The Jesus Prayer and Beyond

There's a well-known prayer called the Jesus Prayer that goes something like this: "Lord Jesus Christ, Son of God, have mercy on me, a sinner." In the book *The Way of a Pilgrim*, the main character—an anonymous pilgrim in Russia—prayed this short prayer thousands of times a day in response to Paul's exhortation to "pray without ceasing" (1 Thessalonians 5:17 NASB). The idea isn't just to utter words repeatedly but to meditate on them while we're doing our daily activities, and become aware of both our identity as sinners and Christ's identity as a merciful Savior.

In his book *How Dante Can Save Your Life*, author Rod Dreher wrote of some value he found in this prayer. Rod was suffering from depression, and his mentor advised him to pray the Jesus Prayer five hundred times a day (equating to about one hour).

Initially, he thought it a ridiculous exercise, but after doing it for a period of time, he says that one night while lying in bed he had a breakthrough. Several hundred prayers in, God suddenly impressed his love upon Rod. It was a message just for him, still written on his heart today, and much more personal than anything Rod had ever felt. The Jesus Prayers, he explains, helped still his restless mind, "chipping away at the ice encasing [his] heart."[5] Rod's practice was to breathe in with the first half of the prayer ("Lord Jesus Christ, Son of God") and exhale on the second ("have mercy on me, a sinner").

I'm personally more inclined to pray a prayer like this: "Lord Jesus, thank you for loving me, dying for me, and making me a child of God." I prefer this prayer because it encompasses the full message of the gospel (mercy and forgiveness for those who repent) rather than "laying again the foundation of repentance from acts that lead to death" (Hebrews 6:1). This prayer does not continually ask for mercy, but acknowledges the grace and new life we now enjoy in Jesus.

I've suggested some other breath prayers you might use (see next page)—Scripture-based prayers that can call our awareness back to God in moments when we're especially worked up or anxious. These short prayers are perfect in moments of heightened stress, so long as they don't become mindless mantras uttered without thinking. But most of the time we need more than one-liners if we're going to develop a whole new habit of thinking and living. We need a robust *variety* of practices that train us to invite God into every "last crevice" of our lives, as Frank Laubach put it.[6]

All-encompassing, day-in-and-day-out spiritual training may sound difficult and daunting. Especially in a fast-moving culture saturated in visual imagery and stimulation, the invisible world can quickly fade to the back of even the most spiritually inclined minds. Who can hope to maintain this kind of a mindset? Who has *time* for it? Yet, unless the habits of our minds and hearts change, we'll never step off the spiritual roller coaster. We'll always swing like a pendulum, from the secular to the sacred sphere and back again.

How do we get to the point of living *all of life* out of a steady center—with every aspect of our lives fanning out from that one hub (life in Christ)? Let's look at a few examples of how we can harness our amphibious nature and, with the Spirit's help, develop habits that enable us to live *and find joy* in God's presence even during life's busiest moments.

Practice Tip: Breath Prayers

When you're particularly stressed or anxious, short prayers to God, in combination with slow inhaling and exhaling, can help us gain a sense of calm—reminding us that he is with us, we are his, and he is in control.

Breathe In	Breathe Out
Abba	I belong to You
Lord	You are my Shepherd
Be anxious	for nothing
Taste and see	the Lord is good

Brother Lawrence: Retiring to God

Brother Lawrence's writings popularized the phrase "practicing the presence of God." Born Nicholas Herman in Lorraine (northeastern France) around 1611, he was raised in a poor family. He served as a soldier and later worked as a footman. In 1666, around age fifty-five, he entered a religious community, the Carmelites, where he took the name he's now known by.

Brother Lawrence had a life so obviously saturated with God's presence that people came to him wanting to learn to have this presence too. It seems he enjoyed this chance to mentor, and he wrote letters to encourage and counsel those people. Although he didn't plan for these letters to make up a published work, by the grace of God, they were compiled (along with some other recollections about his life), and now we can listen in to these great insights that otherwise might have been overlooked.

Brother Lawrence spent twenty-five years in the Carmelite community, until his death at age eighty. He served mostly in the hospital kitchen and became known throughout the community for his quiet and serene faith, as one who modeled a life lived in and with God. The book of his sayings is short and worth reading, though I wish it offered more in the way of practical advice about what he called "the method by which I arrived at that habitual sense of God's presence."[7] Still, there are a few key points we can glean.

First, Brother Lawrence made a point early in his spiritual journey to make loving God the end of all his actions.[8] How? A central motif in his explanation emerges: resignation. This was not passive, but a conscious, active surrender to God's purposes: a "[giving] ourselves up to God, with regard both to things temporal and spiritual." He added, "For my part, I keep myself retired with Him in the fund or center of my soul as much as I can."[9]

In this retired state, Brother Lawrence was actively forming and nurturing "a habit of conversing with God continually." He sought to bring God into all of his work—not changing *what* he did but *how* he did it: "doing that for God's sake which we commonly do for our own."[10] This ongoing dialogue with God was only possible through humility and yielding to God and his purposes, even in the most mundane tasks.

It's easy for our skeptical antennas to go up at this point and think this can't possibly work for us, that our lives are too complex. But think for a moment about your routines, the annoyances of your day. Isolate just one of them and ask yourself, can I bring God into *that*? Is the problem that your life is too complex or that you're always worried about the next hour or day instead of focusing fully on the moment at hand? In most cases, I think the answer is probably the latter. And that *whatever* we're doing (unless it's blatantly sinful and immoral), we *can* bring God into it—whatever and wherever *it* is.

God has brought me a long way in this area, but I still catch myself ignoring my amphibious nature far too often. One recent incident comes to mind, and it involves computer troubles. This particular day was going just fine until my Mac operating system had a run-in with Microsoft Office, causing Office to crash twice. The precise problem and solution are not worth recounting, but let's just say I was immediately tempted to gripe. And that's exactly what I did—internally, mostly, along with a little muttering under my breath at the aggravations of technology.

But what if, instead, I had stopped, and rather than listening to myself complain, I started a new dialogue, a conversation with God? Can God show up even in *those* moments, those small but angst-producing situations? I believe he can. Of course, we normally don't bring him there. We'd usually rather whine. But if we could welcome him there, how different might the situation be? We could pause, step back, and resist the temptation to get granular in focus. We can talk to the lover of our souls, our ever-present Father and Friend, in an eternal messaging thread: *Lord, you've promised to work all things together for good. I don't see how you can work these stupid computer problems for good, but I'm giving them to you. Please help me to believe you.*

Please rework this situation according to your plan, and help good to come out of this.

On another day recently I was teaching about a film when technology struck again. From the slides I planned to show to guide the presentation to the video recording connection to the speaker system for projecting my voice, nearly every little thing that could've gone wrong technologically did go wrong that night. As a result, my assistants and I sat wrestling with cords and devices, my presentation started a half-hour late, and I never did get several video clips to play during the talk. Resisting the temptation to fret, I calmly explained the frustrations to my waiting audience, asking God silently to make good to come out of the situation. The understanding among my audience members was palpable, and as they listened to me talk through the situation—giving it to God out loud—I became aware that my purpose that night may have been larger than simply delivering my prepared talk. For this reason, I always try to pray before any speaking engagement, "Lord, help me trust in you, abide in your Son Jesus, and be sensitive to the Spirit as I speak." In this way, it's easier to be more open to God's higher purposes for any given situation.

Another incident recently encouraged me to see how truly *possible* it is to embrace awareness of God at any moment. I was meeting a friend for lunch. After our food arrived, our waitress, McKenzie, asked if we needed anything. We didn't, but one of us replied, "We're about to bless the food; is there anything we can pray for you about, McKenzie?" With a look that mingled both surprise and gratitude, she proceeded to tell us of a difficulty in her life that she would like us to pray for. We did, and we also prayed for two others in the restaurant that the Spirit prompted us to pray for.

This exchange took no extra time on our part. It only happened because of a conscious effort—after years of training—to become more fully alive to the present moment. And believe me, I fail in this area plenty of times. That's why reviewing your day (as I suggest in the exercise at the end of this chapter) can be very valuable; the point is not to dwell on past mistakes but to learn, for the future, how we can better rely on God, adjusting our spiritual antennas so we can "pick up" his still, small voice, in the most mundane and annoying situations. He's *that* intimate, and *always* present, if we'll only recognize him. When we do, we'll realize a peace and a contentment beyond anything this world offers.

Frank Laubach's Experiment

Frank Laubach spoke of the importance of recognizing the divine omniscience in all of life, and he sought to cultivate an ongoing awareness of God. Here's what he wrote about the nearness of God: "All day I see souls dead to God look sadly out of hungry eyes. I want them to know my discovery! That any minute can be paradise, that any place can be heaven! That any man can have God! That every man *does have God* the moment he speaks to God, or listens to Him!"[11]

What was Laubach's discovery, and how did he come upon it? It occurred during his time serving as a missionary among the Moro people in the Philippines, when he tried to think about God once every minute for a year. This was godliness training to the extreme, and I don't recommend repeating it exactly the same way. The number of minutes is beside the point. The important lesson for us is his goal to *keep God in mind as often as possible*. His goal was continual improvement, becoming more consistent in 1930 than he was in 1929. He also focused on each hour in front of him, not whole days, weeks, or months: "My part is to *live this hour in continuous inner conversation with God and in perfect responsiveness to His will, to make this hour gloriously rich.*"[12]

Laubach knew he couldn't live in *perfect* responsiveness to God's will, and he was honest in his writings about many failures. But that doesn't mean he didn't aim high.

A few months into his experiment, Laubach spelled out the question we're all wondering by this point:

> Can we have that contact with God all the time? All the time awake, fall asleep in His arms, and awaken in His presence, can we attain that? Can we do His will all the time? Can we think His thoughts all the time? Or are there periods when business, and pleasures, and crowding companions must necessarily push God out of our thoughts?[13]

Laubach went on to "make the rest of [his] life an experiment in answering [that] question."[14] This was a serious endeavor; to have written it down was brave. But it shouldn't strike us as odd if we take Scripture seriously. There's a clear biblical basis for pursuing a life of wholehearted devotion to God. And he'll reward it (Hebrews 11:6), as he did for Laubach: "The most important discovery of my whole life is that one can take a little rough cabin and transform it into a palace just by flooding it with thoughts of God."[15]

Laubach's experiment was a little unusual, but his focus on cultivating habits of the mind, of a continual returning to God, is like an answer to Romans 12:2 (to renew the mind) or John 15 (to abide in Christ). The way Laubach dialed in on small increments of time shows that small moments can count, accumulating to something much larger. How many of us want time with God so much that we'll make up games to try to engage him? God honored Laubach's game by giving him a deeper sense of his presence, and by that presence huge joy and a bigger faith, which produced profound accomplishments in his work.

Habitual Versus Actual Recollection

Laubach's experiment focused on *actual recollection*: a *conscious* turning our thoughts to God at various times of day. We can do this in solitude or while we're busy, but it's conscious. Another type of awareness of God's presence is *habitual recollection*. This is the ongoing meditation and contemplation of God in our hearts, whether we're actively thinking about him or not. Habitual recollection involves a constant but less-than-conscious awareness of the world we live in, and is often defined by our relationships. For example, as a husband, I'm aware of being married all the time, though my wife, Karen, may not always be physically present or the subject of my conscious thoughts. Habitual recollection occurs with the parts of our nature or identity which are so deeply ingrained that they are *always there* in the background of our lives, even when they're not at the front of our minds.

Training ourselves to walk in God's presence entails *both* kinds of recollection, habitual and actual. As our relationship with God becomes more fully integrated into who we are and how we define our mode in this world, both kinds of recollection naturally increase. God's own thoughts (from his Word) will be brought to bear more quickly on our situation, as he is closer to the surface more often. This kind of recollection is how we "pray without ceasing," not only with our lips but as we live our lives.

Small Things Are Big

We have to start small. Tiny actions add up, and if we can't see it this way, we may never start. Practice starts somewhere! Laubach resisted the tendency to put off getting to know God and started right in, without any experience: "I do not have to wait until some future time for the glorious hour. I need not sing, 'Oh that will be glory for me'—and wait for any grave. *This hour* can be heaven. *Any* hour for *any* body can be as rich as God!"[16]

Walking in God's presence is a day-by-day, moment-by-moment journey. As much as we'd like to be glorified at the snap of God's fingers, the progress of growing nearer to God happens gradually over time. We can't wait and cram for the final exam. But we don't *want to* do that either. The beauty of a life lived in God's presence is that it's imminently *rewarding*, and Laubach noted that those rewards grow richer with time.[17]

Thomas Kelly commended readers similarly, urging us not to wait for some momentous occasion to obey or surrender: "Begin where you are. *Obey now.* Use what little obedience you are capable of, even if it be like a grain of mustard seed. Begin where you are. Live this present moment, this present hour as you now sit in your seats, in utter, utter submission and openness toward Him."[18]

Kelly's words remind me a bit of my friend's athletic trainer whose refrain to people just starting to run is this: "It doesn't matter how fast or far you go. It's still faster and farther than sitting on the couch!" The point is that smaller acts of obedience add up, accumulating to create a life marked by godliness.

This process can't be outsourced. Just like coaches can't make their athletes more fit and muscular, no one can make us grow closer to God. We have to put in the practice. Then, gradually, what we once did awkwardly and inconsistently becomes more natural and consistent:

An inner, secret turning to God can be made fairly steady, after weeks and months and years of practice and lapses and failures and returns. It is as simple an art as Brother Lawrence found it, but it may be long before we achieve any steadiness in the process. Begin now, as you read these words, as you sit in your chair, to offer your whole selves, utterly and in joyful abandon, in quiet, glad surrender to Him who is within. . . . Keep it up throughout the day. Let inward prayer be your last act before you fall asleep and the first act when you awake.[19]

Whether we find this easy or hard isn't important; the important thing is to begin—to take that first step.

The Glad Surrender

Richard Foster—a pastor so affected by Kelly's book that he wrote an introduction for a later edition—began with one simple commitment, a concrete step he could wrap his mind around: he made a commitment to God that he would set aside Friday nights to rest with his family and turn down any requests that would interfere with that commitment. When the first test of his decision came via a phone call from a church wanting him to speak, he successfully guarded his evening, and later wrote:

As the phone hit the receiver I jumped out of my chair shouting, "Hallelujah!" I had yielded to the Center, and the result was electrifying. That simple "no" coming out of divine promptings set me free from the tyranny of others. Even more, it set me free from my own inner clamoring for attention and recognition and applause.[20]

Foster's language is telling. He "yielded" to God internally— similar to the language of Brother Lawrence, Kelly, and Laubach. This is no surprise. No athlete develops new skills without yielding to the advice of the trainer. Neither will we learn to live this life of faith without yielding to our heavenly Trainer. Paul called it "beating" or "disciplining" his body into submission, a boxing metaphor (1 Corinthians 9:27).

Hannah Whitall Smith wrote eloquently of this "glad surrender":

> The maturity of Christian experience cannot be reached in a moment, but is the result of the work of God's Holy Spirit, who, by His energizing and transforming power, causes us to grow up into Christ in all things. And we cannot hope to reach this maturity in any other way than by yielding ourselves up utterly and willingly to His mighty working. . . .
>
> In order for a lump of clay to be made into a beautiful vessel, it must be entirely abandoned to the potter, and must lie passive in his hands.[21]

In this yielding of our whole selves, Smith added, it's generally "much less difficult for us to commit the keeping of our future to the Lord than it is to commit our present."[22] But now is all we have, and it's all we can yield. We can determine to commit the future to him, but the real test is what we do with the present. Will we recognize him or go about our day as though he's not with us? Maybe we start our day with him, but what about the end?

Much of this is about habit—what we're accustomed to doing.[23] We *can* train ourselves to put God more at the center every day, so that we live out our new identity in Christ by forming new habits and killing old ones (Colossians 3:5). This takes effort and persistence. It also takes a new mindset.

Martin Laird, in his book *Into the Silent Land*, illustrates (through a story about four dogs) how important our mindset— and the power of ingrained habit—can be in how we move through our lives:

When pummeled by too many thoughts a long walk would cure me of the punch-drunk feeling of lifelessness. The normal route led along open fields, and not infrequently I would see a man walking his four Kerry blue terriers. These were amazing dogs. Bounding energy, elastic grace, and electric speed, they coursed and leapt through open fields. It was invigorating just to watch these muscular stretches of freedom race along. Three of the four dogs did this, I should say. The fourth stayed behind and, off to the side of its owner, ran in tight circles. I could never understand why it did this; it had all the room in the world to leap and bound. One day I was bold enough to ask the owner, "Why does your dog do that? Why does it run in little circles instead of running with the others?" He explained that before he acquired the dog, it had lived practically all its life in a cage and could only exercise by running in circles. For this dog, to run meant to run in tight circles. . . . This event has always stayed with me as a powerful metaphor of the human condition. For indeed we are free. . . . But the memory of the cage remains. And so we run in tight, little circles, even while immersed in open fields of grace and freedom.[24]

We may have placed our trust in Christ, but many of us are like that fourth dog. We walk around in invisible cages, bound by false ideas, false narratives, false identities. Though these lies shouldn't hold power over us because of the new life of freedom we've been given, we forget to pull them off—or barely even notice them.

We're wired to find God. Laird said, "God is our homeland. And the homing instinct of the human being is homed on God. As St. Augustine put it 'we must fly to our beloved homeland. There the Father is, and there is everything.'"[25] Do you believe that? Our Father is good, and he calls us to his banqueting table, but have you arrived and forgotten to eat? The food is there, but have you picked up the utensils and tasted the meal? Have you embraced him in the details and realities of your life, not just theoretically in your mind? If you haven't, you're leaving the table starved. But if you have, he promises you'll "delight in the richest of fare" (Isaiah 55:2).

Listen to God in His Word

Read Hebrews 12:7-11, homing in on verse 11: "No discipline seems pleasant at the time, but painful. Later on, however, it produces a harvest of righteousness and peace for those who have been trained by it." Think about your view and experiences with training in general (e.g., physical, musical, artistic). How has your training in other areas of life led to a reward of some kind—akin to the "harvest of righteousness and peace" promised in verse 11? Then think about your spiritual training—how you view it and how you currently train to grow in godliness. Do you believe spiritual training will bring tremendous reward and freedom to your life? What ways might God want you to grow in this area?

Practice His Presence
First and Last Things of the Day

The beginning of the day and the end of the day set the tone of our day and our lives. Most of us have habits or routines at these times that we do without even thinking—whether it's reaching for the phone to check messages, browsing the news, frantically dressing so we can get out the door on time, or watching television. This week, focus on making time to acknowledge God's presence at these key times. Use these moments to help you initiate a conversation with him about your day, so he's the first and the last thing you think about each day. Choose *one* of the suggestions under each of the following headings (adapting them as you wish), using each to cultivate a habit of inwardly orienting toward God at the bookends of your day—and hopefully, the rest of the day as well! (Note: For the reading exercises, don't merely read but use the words in conversation with God—talking *and* listening to him!)

First thing in the morning, preferably before rising from bed (pick one):

- *Read a psalm.* I like to use Psalm 23, but other good options include Psalms 16, 34, 62, 91, 100, 103, 139, or 145. You can also progress chronologically through the book of Psalms.

- *Sing a song.* Listen to, sing, or read the lyrics to a praise chorus or hymn, making it a prayer to God.

- *Submit and depend.* Submit the day to God, asking him to help you accomplish *his* agenda and *his* purpose for you this day; consciously resolve to depend on him this day—trusting the Father, abiding in the Son, and walking by his Spirit (as discussed in chap. 2).

Last thing at night, while sitting or lying in bed (pick one):

- *Pray Psalm 63:6.* "On my bed I remember you; / I think of you through the watches of the night."

- *Review the day with gratitude.* I like to use four categories of gratitude to thank God, either at night or in the middle of the day: (1) the glory of God's creation; (2) material blessings; (3) relational blessings (people in your life); and (4) spiritual blessings.

- *The Lord's Prayer.* Pray the Lord's Prayer slowly, taking time to digest the meaning of the words Jesus gave as a *pattern* for our prayers:

My Father in heaven,

Your name is holy,

your kingdom come,

your will be done,

on earth as it is in heaven.

Give me today my daily bread.

And forgive me my sins,

as I also have forgiven those who have sinned against me.

And lead me not into temptation,

but deliver me from the evil one.

Amen.

(adapted from Matthew 6:9-13)

Rewiring Your Mind

[We are] fearfully and wonderfully made.

PSALM 139:14

You've heard the saying "It's like learning to ride a bike." After a little practice and training, bike riding is a skill that, once learned, can never be forgotten—even if you go decades without touching a bicycle.

Of course, that was before the Backwards Brain Bicycle.

A couple years ago, some high-tech welders challenged Destin Sandlin (their coworker and an actual rocket scientist) to ride a special bicycle they'd created. The bike was just like any other, with one alteration. The handlebars were engineered to work in the opposite way bicycles usually work: turning the handlebars left actually pointed the bike to the right, and vice versa. In other words, to ride this bike, Destin had to steer precisely the opposite way he'd learned at age six.

Because Destin's a rocket scientist, he could explain the complex algorithm behind how a bike works—from the downward force on the pedals to weight shifting to the gyroscopic procession in the wheels. In theory, he knew how these welders had tinkered with the bike's design. And he, like most people who saw the bike at first, assumed he could figure out the trick in a few tries.

As it turns out, all his engineering knowledge did no good. He just kept crashing every time he tried to ride it! Destin was determined to conquer it, though. So he committed to practice it five minutes every day. One day, after eight months of practice, he finally rode it successfully.

How did it happen? "One day I couldn't ride the bike, and the next day I could," he explained. "It was like I could feel some kind of pathway in my brain that was now unlocked."

In fact, any brain scientist will tell you that's exactly what happened: his brain had rewired, creating a new neural pathway that had finally superseded the earlier path created. His mind, through a combination of knowledge and practice, had established a new algorithm for bike riding.

Interestingly, Destin's six-year-old son, who'd only been riding a bicycle for three years, was able to ride the backwards bike after just two weeks! The experiment demonstrated how much more plastic (trainable or malleable) a child's brain is compared to a fully developed adult brain.[1]

This experiment tells us two important things about the human mind. First, knowledge doesn't equal understanding. Even though Destin knew the physics of the backwards bike, it didn't mean he could ride it; his knowledge was totally theoretical until he practiced—a lot. Second, the combination of the brain's capacity for change (also known as "neuroplasticity") and *repeated practice* led to a real, physical change in his brain and his actions. He was able to do something he was completely unable to do eight months before.

The Dynamic Human Brain

For a long time it was believed that our minds were limited. Sure, we could accumulate new information and learn some new skills, but our aptitudes and IQs were thought to be largely static from birth.

In fact, according to psychologist and neurologist Norman Doidge, the old idea that our brains don't change much over a lifetime wasn't just a belief, it was doctrine, and scientists belittled those who were making discoveries about the plasticity of the human brain.[2]

But soon, as research continued and technology advanced, there was no arguing that our brains are constantly transforming. In the past forty years, science has turned that old idea about the human brain on its head. As it turns out, intelligence is fluid, not fixed; and our brains have an astounding capacity for growth even as we get older.[3] This isn't to say certain people aren't born with specific proclivities or innate talents, but those gifts aren't everything. In general, our brains have an incredible capacity for adaptation and change, either positive *or* negative.

What does this have to do with living in God's presence? A lot, actually. As Christians, we're called to be always growing—drawing nearer to him and becoming more like Christ. We're never supposed to plateau, spiritually; never to retire from growth and learning, even in old age (Psalm 92:12-14). Now, neuroscience is producing evidence that our brains *are specially wired for ongoing growth.*

When Paul said of believers, "We have the mind of Christ" (1 Corinthians 2:16), he didn't mean we think all the exact thoughts of Jesus, but that we have the same Holy Spirit teaching us—the same source of thinking. Our mindset, or mode of thinking about the world, would literally (biologically) change to be more like Jesus'. This is possible because God built into our brain's anatomy this ability to "be transformed by the renewing of [our] mind" (Romans 12:2). It's a real process, but it's also still very mysterious, and I don't want to oversimplify our complexity as humans. We're fearfully and wonderfully created, with a sophistication even the best scientists and doctors will never fully comprehend. Neither do I want to gloss over the spiritual influences beyond our bodies' chemical processes, nor suggest that any bad habit is easily dispensed with. Believers in Christ have the Spirit of God dwelling in us—we're more than our biological contents! But this doesn't mean we can't gain something from understanding the organic basis for how our brains operate and change. He *made* these physical processes in us.

The bottom line is this: all the training and habit formation that I talked about in the last chapter is imminently possible, and science offers solid proof of that. It's feasible to *train* our minds to be more open to God. To *adapt* our thinking to see the world like he sees it. And to reorganize our lives around practices that help us become more aware of his presence. We can cooperate with God as he roots out the old ways and brings in the new through the power of his Spirit working *in us*, using our physical bodies as the vehicle or mechanism (2 Corinthians 5:17; Philippians 2:13).

Of course, God knew all of this before the neuroscientists did. But the science helps us to know a little about how our brains work, so we understand how God uses intentional training (and repeated practice) to help us grow in godliness and awareness of his presence.

What Is Neuroplasticity?

Neuroplasticity is the brain's ability to reorganize itself, functionally *and* physically, especially in response to learning and training or following an injury. The human brain is made up of about a hundred billion neurons (nerve cells), which communicate with each other over connections called synapses. The number of synapses in the brain number in the hundred trillions! Electro-chemical charges cause our neurons to fire, and the more frequently one communicates with the next, the stronger the synapse or connection between them. As these connections strengthen, they transmit messages more quickly, forming a pathway. Connections that aren't used as much weaken, while those used frequently strengthen.

Think of it like this: imagine a beautiful field of tall green grass, a blue sky, and a line of trees in the distance. After one time across the field toward the trees, you won't see much evidence that you crossed. Retrace that path ten times, and you'll start to see a path forming, a slight break in the grass. After a hundred crossings, a rough path forms. Thousands of crossings later, the path is beaten—clear and distinct. By analogy, the more you do something, the stronger and faster you get at doing it; the pathways in the brain are being beaten, so that, eventually—whether it's hitting a golf ball, driving a car, playing the piano, or thinking biblically—that activity becomes second nature.

The brain is like a collection of muscles. The more you exercise and strengthen those muscles, the stronger they get. Activities you do more, and thoughts you entertain more, become established patterns or habits. This is good news, because it means we are eminently trainable and retrainable beings! With training, *we can* change our negative habits of thinking and doing, whether it's believing lies you've heard over and over since childhood, an ungrateful attitude, or a habit of gossiping. We can even change our *desires*, since our brain is involved in shaping not only our intellect but also our emotions and appetites.

Neuroplasticity is involved in all forms of learning and training: physical, spiritual, and intellectual. It's the scientific explanation for how we acquire new skills and perfect old ones, whether it's mastering a backwards bike or playing an instrument. Its power has even proven helpful to people who train to overcome learning disabilities, depression, and substance addictions.

Neuroplasticity research has given the world a new way of seeing human potential. The brain isn't fixed as we once thought. It's dynamic. Norman Doidge described it this way in his book *The Brain That Changes Itself*: "The brain . . . is not an inanimate vessel that we fill; rather it is more like a living creature with an appetite, one that can grow and change itself with proper nourishment and exercise."[4]

For this growth and change to take place, repetition is a key. Scientists have a cleverly phrased rule for this idea that consistently repeated actions produce long-term changes in our mental patterns: "Neurons that fire together, wire together." A repeated thought or activity creates new pathways that ultimately change our minds, and our behavior, either for good or for ill.

Rewiring and Renewing

The applications to our spiritual lives are countless. For one, the Spirit uses our repeated exposure to God's Word to harness the power of our unfathomably complex brains and actually *change* our thoughts, attitudes, and actions for *his* good purposes. He uses our times of solitude to make us more peaceful. He uses our fasting to build self-discipline. He uses our praying to make us more dependent on him.

If we show up with truth every day and offer ourselves up to God for the renewing of our minds (Romans 12:2), our minds *will be renewed*. If we set our minds and hearts on things above

(Colossians 3:1-3), we *will be rewired* to think and desire the things of God. If we practice fixing our eyes on the life and example of Jesus, we *will* become more like him. If we make a habit of actively rooting out a certain sin the moment we become aware of it—instead of dealing with it only when we're caught or when it brings personal disaster—we'll find ourselves less prone toward that sin. And if we repeatedly take seriously the call to love our neighbors (and even our enemies), treating them with kindness, gentleness, and respect, we'll find that we have an increasingly genuine love for them.

None of this happens overnight, and much of it remains mysterious. Beyond the chemical explanation, *how* exactly does God change us? Just as the Bible isn't a science book, neither can science fully explain the invisible, supernatural forces at work in us—it can only point to the evidence of them. But we do know that, after we've trusted our lives to Jesus, our abilities are enhanced by his grace and the power of his Holy Spirit at work in us. The spiritual and the organic work together to make those things we train for effortless and pleasurable.

Needful Redundancy

The idea that the brain can adapt and reprogram itself has been around since the late 1800s, but now, functional neuroimaging (fMRI) is being used to actually see what happens to the brains of people who make changes in their lives. But we don't need fancy technology to see how extremely resilient the brain is. Just look at people who've had strokes or debilitating brain injuries, and then learned to walk and speak again.

Kerry Livgren, founder of the rock group Kansas, is one of those people. Kerry is a friend of mine. You might know him from a song he wrote during his Buddhist phase, called *Dust in the*

Wind. Later, though, he came to faith in Christ, and in 1991 we wrote a book together about the radical changes God made in his life. A few years ago, Kerry suffered a near-fatal stroke that rendered him unable to play a guitar or keyboard. He also lost much of his knowledge of Scripture. But Kerry recovered. He got both his music and his knowledge back for one reason: neuroplasticity—in particular, neural redundancy.

Neurologists have discovered that human brains have redundant coding built into them, not unlike (but much more complex than) the redundancy encoded into modern computers. It appears our Creator anticipated that we would need some reprogramming in case of sickness or injury (like a stroke). In recent years science has advanced to the point that we now know our brains' neurons are filled with *needful* redundancy. (The same is true of our DNA!)

Another friend of mine also suffered a severe stroke and had to relearn how to speak and walk. Over time, with training, his brain rewired itself, rerouting information-processing functions and creating new neural pathways. This process is called neurogenesis and actually changes the shape of the brain!

Needless to say, the whole system of the human brain, including its ability to remap, reprogram, and recircuit, is utterly astounding and profoundly sophisticated. A computer is built with a capacity to reconstruct memory if and when a failure in its operating system arises, but that's child's play compared to the vastly more complex capability of the human brain to assemble and reassemble memories after a portion of the brain has died.

Savants and Hints of Heaven

A 2016 report by the Salk Institute indicates that the brain's *memory* capacity is also astonishing.[5] Some have compared brains to computers, but scientists now believe that the brain has a capacity more in the range of the World Wide Web. And contrary to the popular myth that says we use only about ten percent of our brains, science now indicates that people are using less than that—only a fraction of one percent. The patterns of electrical and chemical activity in our brains, which include billions of synapses between neurons, are not only numerous but extremely precise. Our two-and-a-half pounds of gray matter use only twenty watts of power—barely enough to run a dim lightbulb—while concealing an underlying precision and capacity that make it the most efficient and most complex thing in the universe. Nothing even approximates it.

Though we don't yet know the real capacity of the human brain, there are hints of it in a rare group of people with astonishing cognitive abilities: prodigious savants. These people—though limited by things like low IQ, brain injury, or Asperger syndrome—exhibit incredible skill in other areas. One of the most well-known savants was Kim Peek, who was the inspiration behind the main character in the 1988 film *Rain Man*. Peek began memorizing books before he was two years old (though he couldn't walk until he was four), and as an adult he could read two pages at once, in three seconds, with perfect recall. He memorized thousands of whole books. You could ask him to recall the first line at the top of page 458 in *War and Peace*, and he could quote it verbatim. The tragedy was that he couldn't *understand* what he read. Like many savants, he was severely lacking in practical skills. The sheer feat, though, shows that this kind of recall is possible.

Savants' special skills differ. Leslie Lemke, for example, can play any song, even a complex classical piece, after hearing it only once. Alonzo Clemons can see an image of an animal once and sculpt it perfectly, down to the muscle fibers. Some savants can tell you the exact time, down to the second, without the aid of a clock. Then there's Stephen "The Human Camera" Wiltshire, who can be flown over a city he's never visited for one hour and afterward produce a massive mural of the place with perfect accuracy.[6]

Another savant, Daniel Tammet, is sometimes called a "Rosetta Stone" of the brain. He's able to recite more than 22,000 decimal places of the number pi from memory and can calculate any equation with his eyes closed. But unlike other savants, Tammet has a very high IQ and can communicate about what's going on inside his head. His book *Born on a Blue Day* gives us a glimpse into a world most of us could never imagine. Tammet tells of his efforts to overcome the limitations of Asperger syndrome, training himself in things most of us take for granted—like how to make eye contact, when to smile, or how much distance to allow for personal space. Meanwhile, things that seem astonishing to us come easily to him, like learning a foreign language. Tammet learned Icelandic (one of the ten languages he knows) in less than a week. His amazed teacher later commented: "I will never get . . . a student as gifted as he is, because it's almost beyond. It's not human."[7]

She's right, and she's wrong. Though savants are fully human, they, like all of us, are made in the image of a divine being who has built into us immeasurable capacities to know and be like him. My hunch is that, as a result of sin, our human capacities are diminished in three areas:

1. longevity (further diminished after the flood in Genesis 8)

2. cognitive capacity

3. capacity for pleasure

Savants, I believe, offer a *hint* of humans' true cognitive capacities, which were only radically changed because of the fall

(Genesis 3). Likewise, we get whispers of the deep pleasure we were meant to enjoy, but even the greatest pleasures on earth can't rival the delight that resides only with God (Psalm 16:11). Only when we're living in his presence can we tap into this eternal source of pleasure and wisdom. And when our bodies are resurrected, the Bible suggests that all of our capacities will be restored to a level we can't even imagine now. Heaven will be a continuation of a dynamic process that only began on earth. In our limited, fallen minds, we can't fully conceive of how great this destiny is (1 Corinthians 2:9). But one day we will: "These are but the outer fringe of his works; / how faint the whisper we hear of him!" (Job 26:14).

The Negative Side of Neuroplasticity

William James observed,

> The drunken Rip Van Winkle in [the play of the same name] excuses himself for every fresh dereliction by saying, "I won't count this time!" Well! he may not count it, and a kind Heaven may not count it; but it is being counted none the less. Down among his nerve-cells and fibers, the molecules are counting it, registering and storing it up to be used against him when the next temptation comes.[8]

The science of neuroplasticity brings good news for healing, learning, and forming good, new habits. But neuroplasticity also has a dark side. Norman Doidge calls this the "plastic paradox." The same power that renders our brains "more resourceful [also renders them] more vulnerable to outside influences," Doidge explains.[9] The same wiring that helps us become experts at something (through practice), or more like Christ (through spiritual discipline), can also help us "become permanent drunkards . . . by so many separate drinks."[10] And if our minds are left untamed and untrained, the negative habits are often our default.

Here's a simple, nonspiritual example: A young boy suffers a bad bite from a pit bull. As an adult, he has a difficult time trusting any dog. He continues to play the scene of the vicious pit bull in his mind every time he sees a dog, making himself less and less able to interact with any dog. Another example is how we view our heavenly Father. People who've had negative experiences with distant, harsh, or abusive earthly fathers have a difficult time viewing God as a loving heavenly Father who wants to bless them even when they don't deserve it. A rewiring in their minds, by the power of the Spirit and God's Word, has to happen for them to begin associating good feelings instead of negative or fearful ones with the heavenly Father.

Four factors have a heavy hand in influencing the formation of these pathways that become the foundation of our thinking and doing. One is *experience*. Our personal experiences etch much stronger neural pathways than listening to a lecture. Another—which is the case with our dog-fearing friend—is *emotional arousal*. When we feel extreme emotion about something, it leaves a much more indelible mark on our minds. And when we experience very negative emotional experiences, we develop some of our most harmful and stubborn patterns. Some of these bad habits, once established, can become so strong that they can easily override our attempts to form new, good ones.[11]

When we think of bad, ingrained habits, smoking is one of the first that comes to many people's minds. Say a girl smokes a cigarette to impress her friends when she's thirteen. Forty years later, she wants to quit smoking by the time her first grandchild is born, but her attempts have all failed. Why? Through a combination of emotional arousal (caused by the euphoria from the nicotine) and *repetition*—a third factor in neuroplasticity—she's gone beyond just making new neural pathways and forming a habit. She's actually altered her body's chemical balance, creating a craving that demands to be satisfied.[12] The girl grows up to be a Christian woman, and she wants to trust God, but when she feels upset, it's the cigarette she goes to first.

The final factor influencing neuroplasticity is *focused attention*. It's difficult to believe that simply focusing your attention could be as powerful as numerous repetitions or emotional arousal, but it's a fact. When our attention is focused on a certain thought or behavior pattern, and we don't allow our thoughts to move away from a particular subject or task, synaptic connections become stronger and pathways are formed. Perhaps the most disturbingly negative way focused attention works is in our ability to write scripts for ourselves (or to accept those written for us by others):

- *I'm ugly.*
- *I'll never be like my brother.*
- *I'm stupid.*
- *I always mess up—I'll never measure up.*
- *I'm not the kind of person people like to be around.*

These scripts, when we meditate on them enough, not only damage our self-image but, most importantly, can lead us to believe lies that directly oppose God's truth about us. And when we can't see ourselves as God does, it's pretty difficult to see him for who *he* is.

Practice Tip: Your Identity in Christ

Do you struggle with seeing yourself correctly—through God's eyes? One way to rewire your brain in this area is to meditate on what his Word says is true about you. Review some of the following statements (more are available at kenboa.org/who -does-god-say-I-am), and pick one or more that you struggle with believing. Write it down, put it by your bedside, and read it every day until it starts to sink in. When you read it, turn it into a prayer, asking God to help you see yourself as he does. Only when we see ourselves correctly can we follow his command to love others compassionately.

- I am a child of God. (John 1:12)
- My old self was crucified with Christ, and I am no longer a slave to sin. (Romans 6:6)
- I have been set free from the law of sin and death. (Romans 8:2)
- I have been accepted by Christ. (Romans 15:7)
- My body is a temple of the Holy Spirit, who dwells in me. (1 Corinthians 6:19)
- I am a new creature in Christ. (2 Corinthians 5:17)
- I am no longer a slave but a child and an heir. (Galatians 4:7)
- I am redeemed and forgiven by the grace of Christ. (Ephesians 1:7)
- I am God's workmanship, created to produce good works. (Ephesians 2:10)
- I have been made complete in Christ. (Colossians 2:10)
- My life is hidden with Christ in God. (Colossians 3:3)

Technology: Servant or Master?

One summer day last year, I took my grandson, Kenny, to a park. He went willingly and moved quickly because he was playing Pokémon GO, a virtual scavenger hunt game that took the world by storm in 2016. Kenny knew this particular park had a lot of these virtual creatures. As we were walking around, it struck me that probably nine out of ten people there were looking at their phones. They weren't talking to each other or looking around, admiring the trees and gardens. Wholly unaware of their surroundings, their eyes were glued to their screens. I've grown used to seeing this kind of behavior when I'm out, but it's scary to see the fixation continue even when people get out into nature. When our imaginations become reduced to what we can see in a several-square-inch rectangle, we're in trouble!

When I go to a conference, the times between sessions are essentially silent breaks now. These times used to be for meeting new people or catching up with those you hadn't seen in a while. Now, everyone avoids eye contact and spends time catching up on email or social media—"connecting"—while utterly disconnected to the people standing right beside them.

The whole world system that we're supposed to try so hard *not* to allow to shape us now comes in a compact, pocket-sized device, and it's fundamentally changing the nature of human character and relationships. The alienation that resulted from the fall has been amplified. The authenticity of our connections with God and other people is diminished to the point that many younger people no longer have the skills or confidence needed for genuine conversation. A teen will text a friend in the same room, afraid to say a word to that person face-to-face. We have an illusion of community, but we're losing the real thing. When we barely know how to communicate with people we *can* see, how in the world can we expect to communicate with the One we *can't* see? Don't get me wrong: I'm no Luddite. I use a smartphone and other technologies. What I've found, though, is that technology makes a great servant but a very bad master. And although the verdict's still out on the long-term impact of smartphones, it doesn't take much to see that too many people are allowing their technology to rule them. These devices consume significant amounts of our time (several hours a day, on average, and more if you're a teenager) and have come to dictate many people's relationships instead of helping to deepen and enhance them.

One of the saddest effects of technology is the explosion of pornography. Studies have shown that repeated viewing of sexual images on a screen—because of the power of emotional arousal and focused attention, compounded by repetition—is actually rewiring people's minds *and desires.* Instead of finding pleasure in a single spouse within the boundary of marriage, as God designed, countless people (most often men) are caught up in addictions to cheap substitutes. The result is a loss of the capacity for real intimacy and a distorted view of true beauty. The good news is, this kind of rewiring can be undone—the addiction *can* be broken.[13] But it takes training and trust in the One who made you.

Practice Tip: Spiritual Training and Neuroplasticity

You can apply the four principles of neuroplasticity to spiritual practices. Here are a few ideas of how to do that.

Focused attention. Fix your mind on God! Find a place free of interruptions and distractions, away from your phone or email. Pray as you read your Bible—a physical one.

Experience. God's Word isn't meant only to be read but to be cherished, hidden in our hearts, *and applied* to our lives. Talk to God about what you're reading, asking him questions about it. Find a creative way to help you remember what you read: etch part of the verse in a tree, shout it aloud, make a song out of it, or paint a picture. Then go and *do.* What you do will depend on the verse: some Bible verses offer a truth or promise to believe; others command and stir us to action; and some ask us to forsake a particular sin. Whatever the verse says, it's not meant to stay on the page but to be put into practice!

Emotional arousal. What kinds of things do you love to do, drink, or eat? Where's your favorite spot to be? Do you have a favorite kind of music? Think about how you might tie together these things that arouse your emotions as contexts for getting closer to God. If you'd ask your best buddy to go fishing with you, then go on a fishing trip with the goal of connecting to God! If you'd invite your best friend over for tea on your porch, do the same with Jesus. (You might even pull up an empty chair as a visual reminder that God is there with you.) Some people like to take prayer walks—praying to God as they admire his creation. None of these things should be a crutch, something you *have* to have to feel close to God, but they can make your time with him that much more joyful, memorable, and inviting.

Repetition. Make daily time for God—even just five minutes to start—and over time your hunger for more *will* grow! Put this time on your calendar, regarding it as official, even more important than other appointments. It helps if it's at the same time every day, and if you schedule it when you're at your best.

The Life We've Lost in Living

Nicholas Carr, in his Pulitzer Prize–winning book *The Shallows*, cited numerous studies showing diminished reading comprehension among those who read online; this is because of the greater pressure the Internet (with all its hypertext and distracting content) exerts on the working memory, which is necessary for learning and remembering what we read.[14] "What's the big deal," you may ask, "since I can always Google it?" The big deal is that memory, and how much it's taxed in the short term, directly affects our ability to concentrate, stay calm, and remember things in the long term. This in turn affects our capacity for deeper and creative thinking, contemplation, reflection, and even for compassion and empathy—skills we desperately need for spiritual practice.[15]

It's no coincidence that God constantly reminds his people to "remember" him, what he's done, and his Word. He knows what happens when we *don't*: we forget who and whose we are, and the purpose of life. It should therefore frighten us when Carr says that the Web—the place many of us spend hours of time per day—leads to the tendency to forget, to retain what we read for only "a few seconds at best" before "it's gone, leaving little or no trace in the mind."[16]

Carr isn't saying that technology and the Internet are evil (he affirms their positives), but he *is* saying that excessive use of them, to the exclusion of other types of activities, is changing how we perceive, think, and relate. He (along with other researchers) offers evidence that these changes aren't incidental. They're *biologically* based, corresponding to real changes in our brain's structures and pathways that can occur if we allow Web use to almost entirely *replace* "old ways" of thinking and learning (for example, reading physical books or having longer face-to-face discussions).[17]

The state of our world today reminds me of T. S. Eliot's poem *Choruses from "The Rock"*:

The endless cycle of idea and action,
Endless invention, endless experiment,
Brings knowledge of motion, but not of stillness;
Knowledge of speech, but not of silence;
Knowledge of words, and ignorance of the Word.
All our knowledge brings us nearer to our ignorance,
All our ignorance brings us nearer to death,
But nearness to death no nearer to GOD.
Where is the Life we have lost in living?
Where is the wisdom we have lost in knowledge?
Where is the knowledge we have lost in information?[18]

The more wrapped up we get in the world and our own agendas over pursuing God, the more we'll see a slow degeneration of our minds and hearts. Lost in a sea of information and data, we'll miss the flourishing lives we were meant to live, both individually with God and in community with others.

Leveraging Your Brain for the Good Life

Spiritual transformation, Dallas Willard wrote, "is achieved by the ministry of the Spirit in the midst of necessary and well-directed efforts."[19] Sure, our brains can become wired for profoundly bad and hard-to-break habits by small surrenders to sin. But their malleability can also be leveraged in good and productive ways. Those same four factors that influence our neural pathways and lead to habits can be used to our advantage.

Jesus promised us an abundant life, full of the source of all good things: himself. He promised we would live in him, and he would live in us. He's invited us into God's kingdom—a whole new way of living in a more rewarding manner than any other vision of life ever offered, and one that lasts forever. It's a kingdom we enter by grace through faith, and that we live and grow in through grace-empowered training and practice.

For centuries, people have engaged in plenty of practices (spiritual disciplines) to bring them closer to God—things like prayer, solitude, Bible reading and study, meditation, self-denial, rest, and worship. Some of these don't get much attention anymore, because they don't appear to work as well in a culture that wants everything quick. But now you know better: good things take time, and developing a relationship with God is no exception.

With all this talk about our brains and practice, it's important not to miss one thing: we *need* the Holy Spirit in us for this training to work. Yes, there are chemical processes, but somehow, God's at work in and through them! If we're rallying every force in our power to rewire our minds and develop new, godly habits, we have to first remember our most critical ally—God's Spirit. His Spirit isn't a magic formula, but he is our ever-present Helper—the One Jesus promised every believer could count on for strength. The Bible even says his Spirit makes available to us the same power that raised Jesus from the dead (Romans 8:11)! We don't lack strength. We just need to ask for it, this day, this hour, whenever we need it.

Let's look at a little more science to help us understand the Holy Spirit. This time, instead of brain science, we're going to look at ornithology (birds) and aerodynamics (flight).

Lift Force

God seems to like eagles. Thirty-three Bible verses mention them! Eagles are true flying birds, meaning they get off the ground by flapping, but they soar by thermals. Eagles begin flight training around four months old. But even before that, at about two months, they stand up in the nest and spread their wings when they feel gusts of wind. They're training to *know* the thermals! Thermals are the columns of air formed as heat rises from the ground. Because heat rises, these air columns push up and up, displacing the cold air around them. By staying in the warmth of the thermal, the birds continue to soar. Eagles become experts in this!

In this magnificent aerodynamic action, gravity isn't deactivated—it's still at work—but the higher principle overcomes gravity. Eagles drop down when they step off a branch. Then, they start flapping like crazy. Once they're in the air, though, their wings don't have to work very hard, and while soaring, they use a small fraction of the effort required to rise. They're almost at rest and can just enjoy the pleasure of flight.

When we first begin training our minds to abide in Christ—by dwelling on Scripture, fixing our minds on higher things, and praying—we're like eaglets spreading our wings. Once we start flapping, though, we lift up. Maybe after a few tries we're back down on the ground. But through repeated practice, we finally soar. And here's the amazing thing about this metaphor: in Greek, the Holy Spirit is called *pneuma*, which means "current of air."[20] Think about what this means for us! We flap and flap, but eventually we catch the current of air, and we soar. This is how the Holy Spirit works with our training. He's not only our coach; he's the power behind everything we do! And over time, life in him truly brings *pleasure* in the deepest and purest sense.

Although I've been experimenting for years to live more in God's presence, I've found more of this "soaring pleasure" lately. What used to be more difficult has become easier.

You can experience this lift force too, when you draw near to the God who says he'll also draw near to you (James 4:8). And instead of finding yourself among a bunch of earthbound turkeys squabbling around, you'll be like an eagle, soaring on the wings of the Spirit of God.[21]

Listen to God in His Word

Read Philippians 4:8: "Finally, brothers and sisters, whatever is true, whatever is noble, whatever is right, whatever is pure, whatever is lovely, whatever is admirable—if anything is excellent or praiseworthy—think about such things." Use the verse this week to help you set your mind on the things of God. Place it somewhere visible where you'll see it often during the day. Better yet, memorize it, hiding it in your heart (as Psalm 119:11 says we should do with God's Word). Use the verse to help you monitor your thought patterns, paying special attention to moments when your mind tends to shift into neutral (e.g., while waiting at traffic lights or standing in line) or when you may be tempted to complain. Ask God to use these words to draw your thoughts upward.

Practice His Presence
Read a Good Book

Reading a physical book engages all of the senses. It encourages you to slow down, think deeply, and make inferences or connections. It also aids our memories, especially if you underline or mark text while you read. This week, pick up a hardcopy book, preferably a somewhat older piece of literature (maybe one that smells and feels old!). Choose one that will "bite and sting" (as James Houston put it)—a book that will challenge your thinking and outlook. Some suggestions follow:

- *Sense and Sensibility* by Jane Austen
- *Jane Eyre* by Charlotte Brontë
- *The Brothers Karamazov* or *Crime and Punishment* by Fyodor Dostoevsky
- *Middlemarch* by George Eliot
- *Les Misérables* by Victor Hugo
- The Chronicles of Narnia series, *The Screwtape Letters*, or *The Great Divorce* by C. S. Lewis
- *The Lord of the Rings* trilogy by J. R. R. Tolkien
- *Anna Karenina* by Leo Tolstoy
- Poetry by T. S. Eliot, Emily Dickinson, or George Herbert

If you look at your phone often, put your phone in another room while you read and eliminate as many distractions as you can. After a month or so, notice whether the increase in print reading has affected your ability to concentrate when you read God's Word, contemplating its truths and their application to your life.

7

Reseeing the World

A new set of eyes (so to speak) will develop within us
enabling us to be looking at God while our outward
eyes are seeing the scenes of this passing world.

A. W. TOZER, *THE PURSUIT OF GOD*

It was the European Theater of World War II.
One day in early April 1943, a B-24 Liberator called "Lady Be
Good" had successfully completed a bombing mission in Italy
and was heading back to its airbase in Libya. On the return flight,
the crew realized it needed to be very careful not to fly too low,
where it would be vulnerable to anti-aircraft guns. Because of its
flying altitude, the plane had to rely completely on its instruments
to tell when it was time to descend. What the crew didn't know,
however, was that on that particular night, an unusual tailwind
was propelling the aircraft farther, faster. When the instruments
alerted it was time to begin their descent, the crew members
balked and decided there was no way they could have arrived so
soon. Because they didn't want to make themselves vulnerable to
attack, they all agreed to ignore the instrument panel, go with
their hunches, and continue flying.

As it turns out, their instruments were correct. Because of the tailwind, the plane overshot its mark. By the time the error was discovered, it was too late. The plane never found the landing strip and ran out of fuel over the Sahara Desert. The remains of the crew members were eventually found at varying points north of the wreckage. They'd wandered to find help but died before they found it.[1]

Our minds and senses are *so* reliable *so* often that we come to trust them completely. Even when we have the option to double check ourselves against something absolute (like an instrument panel), we don't, because we *just know*. Much of the time, we're right. But we aren't *always* right. What we see isn't always the reality of what's there.

I'm fascinated by optical illusions because they give us insight into this fact. I'll resist the temptation to give too many examples, but let's look at a couple.

The first is called Shepard's tabletop illusion (see fig. 7.1). The tops of these two tables are identical in size and shape! Perspective cues from the edges and legs influence how you interpret the shapes. These cues are why one tabletop looks wider than the other.

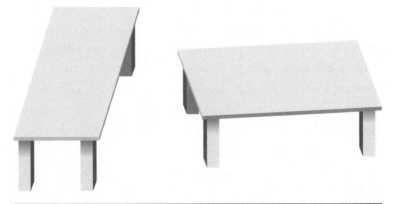

Figure 7.1. Shepard's tabletop illusion

Figure 7.2 is another one, called the twisted cord illusion. The vertical lines appear to bend, even though they're all perfectly straight and parallel to each other.

Figure 7.2. The twisted cord illusion

These simple illusions make an important point: what you see isn't always what you get. Sometimes, we're not seeing the world clearly. Many times our gut hunches will tell us something's wrong or doesn't make sense when in reality it's our hunches that are the problem. Other times, we may be 100 percent convinced of our own closely held belief and still be wrong. Our brains are processing and interpreting in a way that doesn't match reality. Our lens is bad.

A perfect example of this is in the Bible in the book of Numbers. Moses sent a dozen spies into the Promised Land on a reconnaissance mission. All twelve came back and said the land was everything God said it would be, but ten of them didn't believe the Hebrews could take it. Only Joshua and Caleb believed God's promise to give it to them. Though they were all right about what they *saw*, ten of them weren't *right*. Only Joshua and Caleb saw the land through the lens of God and his faithfulness. And guess which spies got to enter the Promised Land?

A New Lens

If we want to orient the everyday rhythms of our lives toward God, we have to trust him to navigate our course and teach us to see the world *his* way. The main way he does this is through his written Word. The Bible works like a lens, helping us to see everything from God's perspective. The lens doesn't always come into perfect focus the first time we look through it. The lens of Scripture is more like glasses we grow accustomed to over time—the longer we wear them, the less we notice they're there. Over time, with practice, his thoughts and perspective become our own—though they're reflected through the prism of our unique personalities and lives.

Most of us need more than a slight adjustment. We need a complete recalibration of our whole system of thinking, a total paradigm shift. Author Thomas Kelly called it "a mass revision of our total reaction to the world."[2]

Revising our view of the world is about more than our cognitive thoughts. It encompasses conscious and unconscious assumptions, instincts, affections, and reactions. It's a new, unified, harmonious vision of life through the only perfect lens: God's Word. Scripture brings everything into sharp focus, so we see clearly—as things really are—rather than as a fuzzy, upside-down picture in a thousand fragments.

Kelly wrote a lot about this God-shaped vision, and it goes back to that two-level living I mentioned earlier:

> There is a way of ordering our mental life on more than one level at once. On one level we may be thinking, discussing, seeing, calculating, meeting all the demands of external affairs. But deep within . . . we may also be in prayer and adoration, song and worship and a gentle receptiveness to divine breathings. . . .
>
> For the religious man is forever bringing all affairs of the first level down into the Light, holding them there in the Presence, reseeing them and the whole of the world of men and things in a new and overturning way, and responding to them in spontaneous, incisive and simple ways of love and faith.[3]

Kelly was proposing that we stop seeing life as divided into separate spheres (sacred and secular) and, instead, resee every activity, encounter, and experience in light of God's truth. We bring the spiritual to bear on the visible world. *Kelly got it*: all of life is lived in the presence of God; there's no part of it, nothing too mundane or ordinary, that isn't permeated by him.

But Kelly didn't see the world like this his whole life. He arrived at this understanding only after much internal struggle, and just a few years before he died.

Kelly spent most of his adult life trying to accumulate academic degrees and earn invitations to colleges and universities.

He was a restless man, never satisfied. He vacillated between striving in science and philosophy, and a clear call on his life to missions and ministry. His ambitions and obligations grew "overnight, like Jack's beanstalk"—and crushed him.[4] He discovered in himself a problem common to many of us (especially Westerners): we're "apt to think our great problems are external, environmental," rather than realizing it's "the inner life . . . where the real roots of our problem lie."[5]

One day, around age forty-three Kelly made a sharp turn, and no one can put their finger on the reasons why. Suddenly, he became happy with where he was, teaching at a small college in Pennsylvania. He became gentle and encouraging. People described him as having a new sort of authenticity. He said God's presence was becoming more and more real to him as he focused on the "Divine Center." This Center, he said, was an "absolute orientation in God . . . where you live with Him and out of which you see all of life, through new and radiant vision."[6]

Kelly's new "singleness of eye" (or purpose) led to a simplicity in his outward and inner life that, before, had always eluded him.[7] For the next four years he continued to formulate his ideas while teaching and ministering in churches. He wrote about his new spiritual discoveries and finished the last of these writings on vacation and then sent them to a publisher. He died of a heart attack at age forty-seven, the day after he accepted the book deal.

God has given us tools to use for his glory. One of them is the writings and experiences of godly people like Thomas Kelly. If we submit our hearts and minds, souls and wills, to God for training, we *will* be changed, and he *will* enable us to see everything with fresh eyes. It took years for Thomas Kelly's brain to finally adjust to God's lens, but it doesn't always take that long. For some people this change happens much more quickly—more like the way

Destin Sandlin woke up one day and was able to ride the Backwards Bicycle. I experienced this sudden rewiring about a year and a half after my conversion. I'd been clearing my head of the Eastern mysticism, occultism, and other non-Christian ideas that had infiltrated my thinking, and was undergoing a conscious worldview transition during my first year of seminary (which I entered as a six-month-old in the faith). In this period of intense exposure to the Bible and to writers like Francis Schaeffer and C. S. Lewis, one day it suddenly clicked. In an epiphany moment I saw all of life as one integrated whole, revolving around God and his truth. Of course, my view has developed since then, but it's as though the framework all fell into place in an instant. The lens suddenly focused, and the fuzzy picture became crystal clear. The good thing is, once learned, the practice of seeing through God's lens becomes second nature and deeply satisfying.

So let's look at some of the adjustments that will happen in our vision as we begin to see through the lens of Scripture and walk more closely with God.

Everything Is Integrated

Human beings straddle two worlds. We can't escape this fact, no matter how hard we try. The most obvious intersection of the natural and the supernatural is when Jesus came to earth in human form (known as the Incarnation) more than two thousand years ago. But collisions between the two realms are actually happening all the time, if we have eyes to see them.

Have you ever met someone new, and the moment you met them you had an immediate sense that they knew God? There was just something about them you couldn't account for any other way? The apostle Paul talked about "spread[ing] the aroma of the knowledge of [Christ] everywhere" (2 Corinthians 2:14). Have you met someone who was like Jesus in such a way that you could almost smell it wherever the person went?

The book of Acts offers a great example of this: "When they [the Jewish leaders] saw the boldness of Peter and John, and perceived that they were uneducated, common men, they were astonished. And they recognized that they had been with Jesus" (Acts 4:13 ESV). There was something about Peter and John—beyond even the miracles themselves—that bore the mark of God's presence. These men carried the fragrance of Christ. This will begin to happen with you too as you spend time with Jesus. As you're learning to pray without ceasing, taking Scripture in, allowing God to rewire your brain for peace, looking for God in everyday encounters, and aligning your thoughts to his, his aroma will become palpable on you. It won't grow strong in an instant, and probably not even in a month, but eventually his sweet fragrance will be discernable to those around you.

Jewish people recite the Shema every day. Its words come from Deuteronomy 6, and it starts like this: "Hear, O Israel: The LORD our God, the LORD is one. Love the LORD your God with all your heart and with all your soul and with all your strength" (Deuteronomy 6:4-5). When Jesus added the words translated "all your mind" (Matthew 22:37), his inclusion was consistent with the Hebrew imagery of a person's entire heart and soul. When you love God, you love him with everything. There's no "God life" and "me life," no sacred and secular, no division between who I am on Sunday and who I am the rest of the week. Just like Thomas Kelly learned, we have only one life, and God is the Master of all of it. Everything is integrated and overlapping. Factory workers who assemble just one piece all day every day can do sacred work if the focus of their hearts and minds while working is on God. If they do their work with excellence and diligence, honoring God in their arena of influence, they are spiritual, reflecting Christ to the people around him.

It's critical that we see *all* of life, as Martin Laird puts it, as "shot through with God," full of divinely given opportunities in whatever we're doing.[8] God is not a spoke in the wheel of our lives; he's the hub! He's the divine Center we live out of, as Kelly said, as present with us during Monday Night Football as he is at nine o'clock Sunday morning. No place or time is beyond his reach.

This truth is throughout the Bible:

The LORD your God will be with you *wherever* you go. (Joshua 1:9)

So whether you eat or drink or *whatever* you do, do it all for the glory of God. (1 Corinthians 10:31)

Whatever you do, work at it with all your heart, as working for the Lord, not for human masters. (Colossians 3:23)

This means that our lives cannot be lived to impress or please others, but to please God and him alone. He is our audience, all week long. His daily agenda is our agenda, his business is our business. We are stewards of what he's given us, down to the last penny, talent, and second. The exact kind of activity we're engaged in isn't important (as long it's not illegal or immoral), only that it's done for the glory of God. Here are a few examples from real people's lives:

- An insurance salesman prays before he goes into his appointments, and sometimes during them, with his customers. Why? "The decisions they're making about things like long-term care can affect not only their pockets, but their lives and futures—theirs and their families," he explains. "And if I'm a Christian, I'm a Christian all the time, including when I'm on the job; I can't just set that identity aside when I'm at work."

- A physical therapist takes time to pray for—and if the person's open to it, *with*—each patient she sees; she acknowledges God made that person and knows what's wrong in their body, and asks for God's strength and insight, so she can be an agent of *his* grace and healing.

- A busy mother weekly takes her children to the library after school; they take a homemade loaf of bread, with a note of thanks and blessing attached, and give it to the librarian they've come to know well.

As God works in us using our training in his Word, we'll start to see this unity, this integrated life, and our default to dividing our lives—so often reinforced by our politically correct culture—will be superseded by a vision of *one* life, all lived in God's presence. We'll still see and live in the visible world, but we'll be seeing from a different perspective—God's perspective. With this view, theologian Matthew Henry says, we'll discern the "real beauties of holiness, but the power of discerning and judging about common and natural things is not lost."[9] We won't become so holy that we can't see normal things for what they are. On the contrary; we'll see them more clearly.

Everything Is Temporary

The natural and supernatural worlds overlap, but they're not the same. This world isn't our home, and it makes false claims to us. Its demands are constant and loud and visible, so it's easy to forget that though we live and learn here, we don't belong to it. Christians are owned by God—doubly owned, because he both created us and redeemed us from the slavery to sin that had taken us captive. We belong with him, in his presence, now as well as in eternity. The deepest, most real part of us, as Paul said, is "hidden with Christ in God" (Colossians 3:3).

Poet George Herbert spoke about these false claims that the world tries to place on us. His metaphysical lyric poems are a little difficult for modern readers (they were penned around the same time as the King James Version of the Bible). But they're worth taking time to understand. In his poem "Man's Medley," he wrote: "To this life things of sense make their pretense."[10] Part of our problem, he's saying, is that we put too high a value on the things we experience using our five senses. Often, this value is so high that we actually begin to become skeptical about the realness of anything we *can't* see, hear, touch, taste, or smell.

Since the time Herbert wrote, naturalism—the idea that the material world or cosmos is *all* there is—has become even more prevalent. In the 2000s, especially, the importance we place on visual and other sensory experiences is far greater than it was in the 1600s. We've come to instinctively trust the things we can measure or quantify, and distrust everything else—especially things we can't see. It's a tragic view, because it misses *both* the supernatural *and* the beauty of God in nature.

How do we refute this claim the world tries to make on us, not just with words but with our lives? There's another line in Herbert's "Man's Medley" that sounds a lot like C. S. Lewis's explanation that we're amphibious. Herbert said we live "with th' one hand touching heav'n, with th' other earth."[11] Unlike the animals and the angels, we're part of both worlds, the material and the spiritual. God made us to simultaneously exist in *each* of these worlds at the same time. Both are equally real, but if we're not careful, we'll start to treat the visible world like it's our permanent home, not realizing there's much more for us than our five senses pick up.

One way we live like Herbert said—one hand touching heaven, the other earth—is by seeing everything we have and are as a gift from him, given to us out of his grace. We see our stuff as *his*, not *ours*, and our time, talents, relationships, and opportunities as belonging to him. As long as we're in this life, we're stewards, though one day we'll be heirs of riches far greater than any on this earth (Romans 8:17). Holding loosely to our earthly belongings can be difficult, whether we have little or much; it's not a matter of quantity but of heart and mindset. But walking through life in a stewardship posture is one way we live in God's presence and manifest his presence to others.

Another way we remind ourselves of our pilgrim status is to realize that, no matter how old or young we are, our bodies are wearing out. Poet William Butler Yeats described our condition this way: "Sick with desire / And fastened to a dying animal."[12] What an image of our instinctive longing for another country, of our inner homesickness! The physical decay and death we'll all experience are outward symbols of an inward disgrace. We're not as we were meant to be. We were meant to live forever, and we all desire that destiny. It's a destination we may long for more keenly as we age, or when we undergo suffering (more on this in chap. 9).

The good news is, the destruction wrought by sin and death isn't permanent. Jesus made a way out of this pit. He made a way for us to get back to our real home. He promised to prepare a place for us, if we belong to him (John 14:3), and that is where we will live. That home is immeasurably more wonderful than any of our imaginations, and when we get there we won't have to think twice about how to walk in his presence. Our fellowship with him will be restored and complete:

Look! God's dwelling place is now among the people, and he will dwell with them. They will be his people, and God himself will be with them and be their God. "He will wipe every tear from their eyes. There will be no more death" or mourning or crying or pain, for the old order of things has passed away. (Revelation 21:3-4)

Practice Tip: Two Eternal Things on Earth

All on this earth is temporary except two things: (1) the Word of God (Isaiah 40:8; 1 Peter 1:25), and (2) people. The most worthwhile activities involve investing the former in the latter by sharing the gospel or building up fellow believers. Look at your weekly agenda and ask yourself how you're investing in these two eternal things. How can you invest in them more?

Everything Is Inverted

In his book *The Divine Conspiracy*, Dallas Willard told a brief story: "Recently a pilot was practicing high-speed maneuvers in a jet fighter. She turned the controls for what she thought was a steep ascent—and flew straight into the ground. She was unaware that she had been flying upside down." "This," Willard said, "is a parable of human existence."[13] I agree. In this world, God's principles are often the exact opposite of the ones we're accustomed to living by. In God's kingdom, the last are first, the meek become powerful, the humble are exalted, those who serve are the true leaders, and those who lose their lives (for his sake) find them. In fact, the picture painted by Jesus of the flourishing life, in the eyes of God, essentially stands every value of the world on its head. So choosing to live in God's presence means we choose to let the world think we're upside down.

In 1960, Moody Science released a film that documented an experiment with a man who wore a special pair of goggles. These lenses inverted everything he saw. He would put these goggles on all day long and walk around with them, so that light which normally reaches the retinas upside down was now inverted. Because the brain is so adaptable, his mind eventually reinterpreted the images, so that he was able to see the world as before. He demonstrated this by riding a motorcycle and flying an airplane while wearing the light-inverting goggles. This experiment was done before some of the groundbreaking discoveries about the brain and its neuroplasticity in the later twentieth century, so it was fascinating to see what could happen.

Our eyes already invert every image we see onto the back of our retina. These images are turned upside down before our brains turn them right-side up. With these glasses the man became accustomed to seeing the entire world upside down. The experiment, evidently, was stopped because of the severe headaches the process caused. My theory, given what we now know about neuroplasticity, is that if the researchers had pressed on, the headaches would have diminished. The theoretical limit would have been for his brain to see correctly with or without the goggles. But the point is that the human brain is highly flexible, and this experiment in physical sight is a metaphor for spiritual seeing. The man became able to see upside down only by training in these goggles. If he could do this with his physical mind and eyes, what are the possibilities for our souls? By training, how much more closely can we come to see God, and the world he made, correctly?

Everything about the world's system—its values and perspective—is inverted. As followers of Christ, we have to turn these values right-side up again, and we do so through renewal in his Word. The Sermon on the Mount (Matthew 5–7) provides a vision of God's kingdom that is in direct contrast to the world's vision of the good life. The question is, will we believe what Jesus said is important, or will we believe what the world says is important? If you read closely, you'll see that the things God tells us to pursue are not the sorts of things people would pursue if left to their own devices. Who wants to pursue meekness, mourning, persecution for the sake of righteousness, or being poor in spirit? These aren't natural inclinations. If I were to promote a seminar on these values, it likely wouldn't draw a large crowd.

Everything in Scripture appears upside down to fallen human nature, but in reality the Scriptures are right-side up, and *we're* the ones wearing the crazy goggles. Our situation, and the choice we face in our lives, is not dissimilar to that in a pivotal scene in *The Matrix* (1999) with the two main characters, Morpheus and Neo. I won't relate the entire dialogue here, but the scene is too relevant to our point *not* to excerpt it in part:

MORPHEUS   You're here because you know something. What you know you can't explain, but you feel it. You've felt it your entire life, that there's something wrong with the world. You don't know what it is, but it's there. . . . Do you know what I'm talking about?

NEO   The Matrix.

MORPHEUS   The Matrix is everywhere. It is all around us, even now in this very room. You can see it when you look out your window or when you turn on your television. You can feel it when you go to work . . . when you go to church . . . when you pay your taxes. It is the

> world that has been pulled over your eyes to blind you from the truth.

NEO   What truth?

MORPHEUS   Like everyone else, you were born into bondage. Into a prison that you cannot smell or taste or touch. A prison for your mind. . . .

> Unfortunately, no one can be told what the Matrix is. You have to see it for yourself.[14]

Neo is essentially being told: "You've been deceived all your life. You're in a simulation. None of this stuff is real. Everything you've seen is upside down." We face a similar choice. Will we continue to live in an illusion or embrace our true identity as children of God? To embrace our true identity means we'll have to reverse our worldview—rewire our brains—so that we see as God sees. We'll have to start valuing and pursuing the things that matter to him.

Jesus said these chilling words to the Pharisees: "That which is highly esteemed among men is detestable in the sight of God" (Luke 16:15 NASB). These words are frightening. We value and esteem all the wrong things. And none of these can satisfy us. To a nation of people who had lost their love for God, the prophet Jeremiah said,

> This is what the LORD says:
> "Let not the wise boast of their wisdom
>   or the strong boast of their strength
>   or the rich boast of their riches,
>   but let the one who boasts boast about this:
>   that they have the understanding to know me,
>   that I am the LORD, who exercises kindness,

justice and righteousness on earth,
for in these I delight,"
declares the LORD. (Jeremiah 9:23-24)

Here, God has blown away the very things most people live for: power, wealth, wisdom, and respect. He's saying that everything is inverted, and the things the world says matter don't. Meanwhile, what really matters—knowing God—is the one thing the world keeps trying to distract us from. Pursuing him first may appear completely backward, according to the world's definitions, but in the end it's the world that is backward, blinded to the true source of lasting pleasure.

Everything Matters

Brother Lawrence said we tend to think of God as caring most about the big things: who we marry, where we go to college, or our profession. But training in godliness happens at a day-to-day level, in our regular lives. All of our *little* decisions and routines, many of which we do without thinking, collectively shape who we are.

Francis Schaeffer's explanation is that there are "no little people, no little places."[15] Everything, everyone, and everywhere are important to God. This is why Jesus emphasized the importance of faithfulness in small matters: "Whoever can be trusted with very little can also be trusted with much, and whoever is dishonest with very little will also be dishonest with much" (Luke 16:10).

Every circumstance and action is important. Each moment presents an opportunity to either yield to God or neglect or resist him. We can either focus on loving God and neighbor or become consumed with loving ourselves and this world disproportionately. We can either welcome him into this hour or ignore him during it. We can talk to *him* in continuous, silent conversation—as Brother Lawrence and others trained themselves to do—or we can go about our activities talking and listening to *ourselves.*

Seeing life this way—as composed of many *little* moments that matter to God—doesn't make it any easier to obey, but it focuses our attention on what's right in front of us, one of the keys to our brain's plasticity! When we focus on the one decision, situation, task, or opportunity before us, rather than worrying about the next one or a whole day of them, then obeying God and living in his presence becomes less overwhelming. We start to see as God sees. Part of how God teaches us to do this is through regular Bible reading, reading it not like just any book but realizing it's the living and active Word of God (Hebrews 4:12). With his Spirit and Word alive in you, God can enable even small bits of his truth to transform you one thought, one word, one action at a time.

Here's one thing I do now, because of my growing belief that the "little people" and "little places" are big things to God. I spend a lot of time traveling in the car. This could be dead time. Or I could listen to music and let my mind wander. I could spend it in negative ways, worrying or complaining (as I sometimes catch myself doing). But more and more, I've been trying to use this time to set my thoughts on God, to redeem that time and enter that two-level thinking. I'll elevate my thoughts, for example, by thinking of something I'm grateful for, or by running through a Bible verse I'm trying to commit to memory. If I'm driving with someone else, I listen to the person while praying for them, and ask God to inspire my response. These aren't things I *always* do, but they're things I sometimes do, so that I'm focusing my attention on what God says to focus on, the people he calls me to love.

Just a few days ago I was riding in a taxi from the airport to my hotel, where I was staying during an out-of-town speaking engagement. At first, I was reading in the back of the cab, but partway to my destination, I felt prompted to talk to the taxi driver. I struck up a conversation with the man, who I found out was a Muslim originally from Egypt. I requested to have him as my driver the next day, and we picked up where we'd left off. I wouldn't characterize the conversation as spiritual, though we talked a little about prayer, and he explained some hardships in his life. When we parted ways, though, I asked for his address, and later on, I sent him a note with a copy of my book *Rewriting Your Broken Story* along with a "Bread of Life: Gospel of John" tract.

I have no idea how God will use that interaction—I entrust that to him—but the point is that there are no ordinary people, no ordinary times. Right in the middle of that taxi ride, God awakened me to see an opportunity and to view that taxi driver as someone God loves and wanted me to reach out to. Afterward, I realized his purpose in my trip could've been as much about this interaction during what I saw as an in-between moment as my speaking at that conference. *Everything*, *everyone*, every moment matters to God!

Second Corinthians 4:18 calls us to "fix our eyes not on what is seen, but on what is unseen, since what is seen is temporary, but what is unseen is eternal." This kind of thinking seems crazy to the world. And if we fail to see through God's lens, it won't make much sense to us either. But if we'll trust the perfect instrument of truth and guidance God has given us, his Word, we'll have a safe landing. We'll see correctly. And when we see through

Practice Tip: Everything Matters

Brother Lawrence committed to doing "little things for the love of God, who regards not the greatness of the work, but the love with which it is performed." We can do the same, committing the most mundane acts of our lives to him. Choose one of the following ordinary tasks, or come up with your own. Each time you go to do that activity, say to yourself (even if you think it sounds funny), "I'm going to do this in Jesus' name," and then give thanks to him as you do it.

- getting the mail
- taking out the garbage
- doing dishes
- cooking and eating dinner (or another meal)
- picking up the kids from school
- another ordinary chore, errand, or activity that you do with regularity

the lens of the immortal, invisible God—the One of all wisdom, who sees and knows all things, past, present, and future—everything comes into sharper focus. That includes the way we see our time (chap. 8), suffering and sin (chaps. 9-10), and other people (chap. 11), as well as our eternal purpose and destiny (chap. 12).

Listen to God in His Word

Read 2 Corinthians 4:18: "So we fix our eyes not on what is seen, but on what is unseen, since what is seen is temporary, but what is unseen is eternal." Do a vision examination on yourself: do you tend to focus on the things of this world to the exclusion of eternal things? What are some ways you can fix your eyes (the attention of your mind and heart) on unseen things—the things God values?

Practice His Presence
Cultivate a Seeing Eye

Psalm 19:1 says, "The heavens declare the glory of God; the skies proclaim the work of his hands." Wonders in the physical world point beyond themselves to the presence and mind of our awesome Creator. While driving, walking, or even just observing from your window or porch, take a few minutes each day to notice at least one aspect of creation: flowers, leaves, trees (or plants in general), clouds, the colors of the sky, birds, or animals, and reflect on how their beauty and order point to the Creator. Don't merely see these things but savor them—revel in them—and rejoice with God, thanking him for his amazing artistry.

8

Reorganizing Your Time

In repentance and rest is your salvation,

in quietness and trust is your strength.

ISAIAH 30:15

Perhaps the single greatest threat to applying anything in this book is busyness. And though applying these principles may not require a complete overhaul of your schedule, it is going to take a great shift in how you see time. Although we can be aware of God's presence while doing other things, we need to make a habit of regularly devoting concentrated time to him if we're going to get to know him better (the end goal!). Many of us grew up without the around-the-clock technology we have today, yet we've allowed these always-on devices to slowly invade our time without stopping to take stock of their effects. If Nicholas Carr is right, smartphones—as helpful as they are when used in moderation—may actually be eroding our ability to reflect and contemplate.

The way busyness, even idle and trivial busyness, has taken over in our society reminds me of a passage in C. S. Lewis's book *The*

Screwtape Letters. In it, the narrator, a senior demon named Screwtape, is advising his understudy, Wormwood, on ways to "attract [the] wandering attention" of the person he is seeking to tempt. Screwtape speaks of causing the man to waste his time on "anything or nothing" and summarizes:

> You will say that these are very small sins; and doubtless, like all young tempters, you are anxious to be able to report spectacular wickedness. But do remember, the only thing that matters is the extent to which you separate the man from the Enemy. It does not matter how small the sins are provided that their cumulative effect is to edge the man away from the Light and out into the Nothing. Murder is no better than cards if cards can do the trick. Indeed the safest road to Hell is the gradual one—the gentle slope, soft underfoot, without sudden turnings, without milestones, without signposts.[1]

If we're not careful, busyness—even if it's from very beneficial activities—will edge us down that gentle slope.

The Problem of Busyness

Americans in 2016 spent an average of five hours per day—one-third of their waking hours—on a smartphone or other mobile device.[2] The figure is even higher among young people. And yet everywhere, people complain of "not having time" and being "busier than ever." The fact is, the vast majority of people have allowed technology, media, and entertainment to dominate their lives to such a great extent that we are the most distracted, hyperactive population in history. Time-saving inventions that were supposed to bring us more free time have only made our lives more frenetic and stress-filled, and our addictions to urgency and performance have made us externally driven rather than internally called.

Both drawing near to God and strengthening the neural pathways that train us to have the mind of Christ require focused attention for best results. But the time spent on our phones has caused neural rewiring that is now making us *less able* to focus our attention. I'm not suggesting that our phones *automatically* prevent us from getting close to God, but when used in excess and to the exclusion of deep-focus activities like reading a book or having a longer face-to-face conversation, they've been shown to damage the skills of our hearts and minds that help us do so. They *disincline* our brains toward a state of mind and heart that enables us to pray and meditate on his Word.

My associate Len Sykes relates the problem of busyness to five areas:

1. *In our homes,* which *should* be sanctuaries for spiritual and personal development in settings of love and acceptance;

2. *In our work,* which should be done for the glory of God and should not *replace* God as the source of our security and significance;

3. *In our recreation,* which should incorporate sabbath principles of restoration, rather than always taking hard-charging approaches that ultimately devitalize instead of revitalize;

4. *In our church work or ministry,* which can easily become a place where we are seeking to please others and meet expectations rather than taking on only those activities and responsibilities to which God is calling us; and

5. *In our walk with God,* when we engage in excessive activity at the expense of cultivating true intimacy with him.[3]

Taking time to rest requires trust, because it can seem unproductive from the world's viewpoint. We don't see immediate, tangible results when we invest time in a relationship. We can see it in retrospect, but while we're building the relationship we don't see the same rewards as we do from a week at work or six months at the gym. Relational rewards don't work that way. But intangible investments are necessary.

The answer isn't to become a hermit or to return to the past in how we do everything, but to recognize the problems busyness poses and take charge of our calendars and devices rather than letting them take charge of us. We need to consciously build into our schedules times of regular rest and reflection, and understand that it's impossible to waste time on God. He will honor the time we spend with him, and he'll use those moments spent growing in intimacy with him to energize the rest of our activity.

People with a growth mindset have an inclination to continue to grow and get better in many areas. But instead of trying to do everything, a wiser aim is to do most what we do best. Rather than multiplying mediocrity in a bunch of areas, we'll use our time most wisely if we focus on developing excellence and greatness in a few areas of strength instead of spreading ourselves thin or spending a lot of time trying to shore up our weaknesses.

I realize this is easier said than done. I too struggle to prioritize so many things I want to accomplish, and to make and *keep* my time commitments to God. When someone is in full-time (vocational) ministry, it's easy to think they will automatically stay in close connection with God, but that's not true. Even the most spiritually focused activity is no substitute for God himself, and all people, pastors or not, have to nourish their personal relationships with God to prevent them from getting strained. If we don't, our activity will be less fruitful, and fatigue will set in.

The Urgent Versus the Important

Stephen Covey, in his book *First Things First*, popularized an analogy for why we have to be careful to prioritize the most important things in our lives first, rather than leave them for the time that's left over. He said we can imagine a container in which we're supposed to fit a few large rocks, a collection of pebbles, and a cup of sand. If you first dump the sand and pebbles into the jar, you'll find there's no more room for the larger rocks. If, instead, you first put the rocks in the jar and *then* add the pebbles and sand, the smaller objects and finer grain flow around the larger, fitting without a problem. The analogy isn't perfect, because oftentimes, if we add the big rocks first (starting with the biggest Rock of all, God), some of the pebbles and sand may not fit. Jesus said that's okay, because we've chosen the one truly needful thing (Luke 10:42).

But Covey's main point is good: we either let the urgent flow *around* the important in our lives or the important flow around the urgent. The urgent clamors for immediate attention: "Do this, read that, focus on this, make that happen." In the process the important things—our relationship with God and others—can get deferred or postponed, sometimes indefinitely. We think, "I'll have time for that later, once I get this one urgent thing done." In that case, we're presuming on the future, which God clearly tells us is a foolish thing to do.

The wise person makes God and spiritual growth first priority, allowing the lesser priorities to flow around that one most important relationship. The foolish person continually puts off spiritual growth, with the result that it probably never happens, and the lesson of the parable of the rich fool is ignored:

> Then he said, "This is what I'll do. I will tear down my barns and build bigger ones, and there I will store my surplus

grain. And I'll say to myself, 'You have plenty of grain laid up for many years. Take life easy; eat, drink and be merry.'"

But God said to him, "You fool! This very night your life will be demanded from you. Then who will get what you have prepared for yourself?"

This is how it will be with whoever stores up things for themselves but is not rich toward God. (Luke 12:18-21)

None of us is guaranteed another day, hour, or minute (James 4:14). Yet how many of us live, especially when we're young, as though we have infinite time! The older we get, the harder it is to ignore the reality that we're mortal, and our body is wearing out. We *don't* have all the time in the world. Our lives are like withering grass, fading flowers, and vanishing mist (Psalm 103:15-16), here today and gone the next. It's in moments of reflection, either in physical or inner solitude, that we regain the right perspective on our lives, allowing us to wisely order our time and schedules so we don't omit the important at the expense of the urgent.

Numbering Your Days

The psalmist said, "Teach us to number our days, that we may gain a heart of wisdom" (Psalm 90:12). We're mortals with a limited time on earth. What if this day were our last? Knowing our time is limited should make us mindful of eternity and ready to live every day as if it were our last. But how do we actually maintain this mindset? Most of us, unless we live in a war-torn country, aren't exposed to death like people once were, and we don't make much of a habit of remembering our mortality. Death usually happens in hospitals or nursing homes instead of *our* homes. Painkilling drugs can make the end of life less dramatic in its approach. Capital punishment today is a far cry from Jesus' day, when the most gruesome form, crucifixion, happened in the public eye, for all to see. Advances in medicine mean infant and childhood death are less common.

Although we can't (and certainly don't want to) return to how things were before modern medicine, I do think the relative hiddenness of death now means we lack the frequent, visible reminders that help us live well each day, mindful of our mortality and our humble position before God. It's only when a close friend or family member contracts a serious illness, or a loved one passes away suddenly, that we get these reminders. For a moment, we're given a chance to reflect on our lives more deeply.

These reminders to reflect on our mortality used to be more common than they are today. Called *memento mori*—which means "remember you're going to die"—these practices are powerful ways for helping people to remember to "number [their] days," as Psalm 90:12 says.

One Sunday last fall, I was preaching on this psalm, which is a prayer of Moses, at a church in Connecticut. This "Meeting House" was built in 1761, and there are two objects beside the pulpit: a candle on one side and an hourglass on the other. Few in the congregation realized their purpose. Before I began speaking, without telling the congregation why I was doing it, I lit the candle and then turned over the hourglass. When I reached the verse about numbering our days, I explained that these visuals were *memento mori*, teaching us to live our brief sojourns on earth wisely and well, never presumptuously.[4] When I finished the sermon, I blew out the candle and turned the hourglass on its side—time out.

Memento mori may sound morbid to the modern mind, but these reminders have shown up in objects as well as art and music for centuries, serving as prompts for deep and important reflection.

Today, a more well-known ritual expression of *memento mori* is the observation of Ash Wednesday, a holy day set aside in liturgical churches to mark the beginning of Lent. During church services, ashes are often imposed on people's foreheads in the form of a cross, while the rector or priest says some rendition of these words: "Remember that you are dust, and to dust you shall return" (Genesis 3:19; see also Psalm 103:14; Ecclesiastes 3:20). For the last several years in my Wednesday Morning Men's Fellowship in Atlanta, we've done a variation of this practice on Ash Wednesday. Instead of limiting the statement to the curse of Genesis 3:19, I sought to combine this *memento mori* with a blessing. I looked into each man's eyes, held his shoulder with my left hand, and while imposing the ashes in the shape of a cross on his forehead with my right hand, I said, "Remember that you are mortal in this life, and eternal in the next."

Art is full of *memento mori*. A sixteenth-century anamorphic painting by Hans Holbein called *The Ambassadors* especially intrigues me. In the painting, two men, who evidently have just inked a treaty together, are shown at the height of their prowess. Each object in the painting has been carefully chosen to demonstrate their myriad earthly attainments, knowledge, and exploration. A lyre with a broken string hints at discord between the two men. But the object in the foreground is what grabs your attention. The anamorphic object is blurry and distorted, and is only brought into the correct perspective when the painting is viewed from a certain angle: it's a skull (if you have a chance to visit the National Gallery in London, go see it). The scene is a metaphor for the fact that even at the height of power and prestige, humans are still mortal and their lives fleeting. The question is, what will be the significance of that dash between our birth and death years on our gravestone? Will it be a legacy that fades like the grass or one that leads into eternity?

When Time Dilates

Believe it or not, I personally have had more than a dozen near-death experiences, and those are only the ones I know about. In many of these, time dilated (slowed down), to the extent that I became aware of everything, especially unfinished business with God, or I came in contact with my true hope at a deeper level. I'll share just one as an example.

In college, I was a member of a fraternity. I had a Chevy 409 at the time, and right after we installed a larger carburetor and made other modifications, I was in the parking lot at the back of the fraternity house with three guys I'd just met. I wanted to show them how fast that car could go. They got in the car with me, and I opened it up, gunning my way out of the long driveway. But I forgot about a little dip where the driveway merged into the street, and when we reached that dip, the car was going so fast that it went airborne. The car hit the road, and I shifted gears and went full throttle. It was impressive until it was time to hit the brakes at over 100 mph, since I was approaching a T-intersection in the neighborhood. To my horror, when I put my foot to the brake, it sank straight to the floor. The brake line had severed when the bottom of the car hit the street. At that sickening moment, everything was in slow motion. I became almost hyper-realistic, calculating that I had just enough time for one downshift before we careened into the yard in front of us. Each yard was full of old-growth trees and separated by hedges, and at that speed, hitting one of those trees would mean death. Somehow, I avoided the trees as we tore through multiple yards and hedges until I was able to get back on the street, push the wheels to the curb, and stop. My three passengers were absolutely silent—they thought I'd done the whole thing deliberately. We pushed the car to a gas station, and the following morning I walked that street to see where the car had torn through the hedges. The large trees were so numerous that it would take concentration to avoid them at 5 mph. How in the world had I done it?

The memory of this remarkable experience is so vivid because, during the few seconds it took place, it felt as though a lot of time had passed. That's what happens when time dilates—it's as though time pauses or life slows down considerably.

Time dilated for an acquaintance of mine a few years ago when he attempted suicide by jumping off the Mississippi Bridge. He was one of only two people who have survived that jump. As soon as he was in the air, he immediately knew he would go to hell. Just before hitting the water, he called on the name of Jesus. That process took only a few seconds, but to him it seemed like eons. This can happen to anyone before they die or come close to death—only God knows the heart at that point.

One more example is Ted Williams of the Boston Red Sox, who (allegedly) trained himself to be so focused on the moment at bat that he could see the stitches on the ball hurtling toward him. How that could be true, I don't know, but the point is that God gives us opportunities that will never come back to us, moments that cause us to see time differently and shape our vision of reality in new ways. These experiences help us realize the foolishness of presuming upon the future. Without these kinds of moments, God knows most of us will keep on blowing and going, plotting and planning, ducking and diving, scheming and dreaming. These unpleasant interruptions are divine invitations to reevaluate and recalibrate. They invite us to ask ourselves, *Am I putting my treasure and hope in this passing world, or am I living in light of eternity?*

The English writer and poet Samuel Johnson said, "Depend upon it, sir, when a man knows he is to be hanged in a fortnight, it concentrates his mind wonderfully." Similarly, the eighteenth-century Anglican priest William Law, in his book *A Serious Call to a Devout and Holy Life*, asked readers to imagine how a person's life might change if they knew they had five fixed years to live. Many of us have talked about this kind of exercise, but how many of us have actually dedicated time and attention to considering it and then lived accordingly?

Second Corinthians 6:2 says, "*Now* is the day of salvation," and we're never wise to put off matters of eternity for a day that we might never live.

Practice Tip: Avoiding Presumption

Presumption is a sinful attitude that assumes we have all the time in the world to prepare for the next world. This mindset affects how we treat others and God; it affects how we use our time, often putting off until later what could be done now. To avoid this sin and live more aware of the presence of God from moment to moment, pay attention to how you make and talk about long-term plans. When you start to presume either future success/accomplishments (resulting in pride) or future disaster (resulting in worry), call to your mind a few key words out of one of the following quotes. (Place it somewhere visible to you, if it helps!)

- Do not boast about tomorrow, for you do not know what a day may bring. (Proverbs 27:1)

- Now listen, you who say, "Today or tomorrow we will go to this or that city, spend a year there, carry on business and make money." Why, you do not even know what will happen tomorrow. What is your life? You are a mist that appears for a little while and then vanishes. Instead, you ought to say, "If it is the Lord's will, we will live and do this or that." (James 4:13-15)

- Wherever you are, be *all* there. Live to the hilt every situation you believe to be the will of God. (Jim Elliot)[5]

- Our grand business undoubtedly, is not to *see* what lies dimly at a distance, but to *do* what lies clearly at hand. (Thomas Carlyle)[6]

Living in Light of the Resurrection

It can help us to look at each day as a mini-life, with a birth, followed by growth, decline, and death (putting on our burial clothes and going to bed). When we see our lives this way, rather than always anticipating the future or dwelling on the past, we're more able to take up our cross *daily*, as Jesus said we're to do.

Like the formative early years of a human life, some of the most formative moments of our day are the earliest ones. These times set the tone of our day. Frank Laubach made a habit of lying in bed and refraining from starting the day's activities until his focus was on the heavenly Father: "My part is to live this hour in continuous inner conversation with God and in perfect responsiveness to His will," he wrote. "I determine not to get out of bed until that mind set, that concentration upon God, is settled."[7]

What if we took Laubach's approach? What if, instead of letting thoughts of our to-do list bombard us the moment we wake up, we direct our *first* thoughts toward God? Or, instead of reaching groggily for our phones or coffee cup, we reach *first* for God? Or what if, instead of rushing out of bed or out the door, we *first* rush into God's presence, submitting our day to him before our feet hit the floor? What if we wake up and commit to feeding ourselves not only physically, with breakfast, but with spiritual sustenance—God's Word? What if, instead of going into the day worried or afraid, we embrace it as one God has given, and then live it in light of eternity? What if words like these were the first ones on your lips?

> Awake, sleeper,
> And arise from the dead,
> And Christ will shine on you. (Ephesians 5:14 NASB)

How do you think *your* days would be different if you did even just one of these things at the beginning of your day? Paul followed that verse in Ephesians with these words: "Be very careful, then, how you live—not as unwise but as wise, making the most of every opportunity, because the days are evil" (Ephesians 5:15-16). What if we not only *start* our day with God at the forefront, but we *end* it with a reminder of our mortality and dependence on God, maybe with one of these verses?

> I lie down and sleep;
> I wake again, because the LORD sustains me. (Psalm 3:5)

> In peace I will lie down and sleep,
> for you alone, LORD,
> make me dwell in safety. (Psalm 4:8)

And what about everything in between, the middle of your day? No matter the condition of our bodies, every one of us can do three things during our days to "redeem the time" (Ephesians 5:16 KJV):

- love people
- pray for others
- serve others

If we do these three things, in whatever context God has placed us, we'll be living out our mission to be "living epistles" to the world (2 Corinthians 3:2 KJV). As we do, it helps to be mindful of the distinction between *chronos* (chronological "clock time"— time as we think of it) and *kairos* (special opportunities and occurrences), realizing that the most significant thing we do in a day may not be on our calendar at all. If we hold a loose grip on that daily plan, as well as our long-term plans, we'll be more open to the *kairos* moments when they come. We'll see those daily interruptions as invitations rather than annoyances.

Whether we're young or old, we can all see our days this way, as mini-lives to be lived to the fullest, making the most of the *chronos* and *kairos* times we're given. Then we'll live that united, integrated life Thomas Kelly talked about: "Living from the Center is a life of unhurried peace and power. It is simple. It is serene. . . . We need not get frantic. He is at the helm. And when our little day is done we lie down quietly in peace, for all is well."[8]

Solitude: Tethering Ourselves to Christ

We'll never have this clear vision of the present, or of each of our days, without moments of quiet, away and apart from the noise of the world. Solitude has always been one of the most fundamental spiritual disciplines, because it moves us away, for a time, from the lures and aspirations of the world, into the presence of the Father.[9]

In solitude, we remove ourselves from the din of the culture, even from our peers and family, and allow God to examine our hearts and minds, and to teach and speak to us through the quiet prompting of the Spirit. These moments may be short or long, but preferably they should be daily. With some extra planning and resolve, we can also take more extended times of solitude, which

I've personally found very beneficial. The key is to schedule these personal retreats as you do other appointments, blocking out a whole afternoon, day, or longer time far in advance. It also helps to set a place that takes you away from your usual routine, whether it's a rented cottage in the country, a condo on the coast, a monastery, or another place that offers a personal retreat.

Many people are uncomfortable with solitude and silence, especially if they're not used to it. Now, even if we're technically alone, because of technology, we almost never have to sit quietly anywhere, unless we choose to. With the world at our fingertips, we hardly know what it's like to go an hour being quiet. Yet the Bible, especially Jesus' example, makes it clear that solitude is an indispensable practice in the life of a believer.

Solitude can mean physically removing ourselves from the presence of others, and it can also refer to an inward posture (wherever we are) of listening to God's voice—sitting at Jesus' feet like Mary did (Luke 10:39). Far from wasting precious time, solitude catalyzes and enhances our activity, enabling us to better live out of his power and strength. Too many of us are more closely tethered to our phones than we are to Christ. When we take time to draw near to him, the turmoil of this world "grows strangely dim." We become more fully alive to God, and as a result, to the people he has sovereignly placed in our lives. Our souls will thrive and enlarge rather than be diminished. We'll find life-giving energy in the simplicity of living for him alone, instead of leading a divided life that drains us and produces an undercurrent of anxiety.[10] This kind of rootedness can occur only through solitude, which includes silence, praying (talking *and* listening to God, or moments of wordless[11] or contemplative prayer), studying, meditating, hearing his Word read or taught, and even fasting.

Roots and Wells

Our culture hates stillness and does everything possible to keep us from pursuing solitude. Two metaphors illustrate well the importance of solitude—especially in today's era of nonstop, noisy gadgets and quickening pace of life.

The first image is a tree's root system. Underneath the ground's surface is this system that cannot be seen and yet is essential and life giving. Without it, a wind would quickly topple the tree. Similarly, only Christ, through time spent with him in solitude, nurtures our souls, rooting us deeply in God's love. These moments of rest enable us to become more alive to others when we *are* with them, as well as less distracted and less self-focused. Why? Because we're attached to a greater root system, drawing our strength like branches from a vine, and that gives stability and security.

The second metaphor is an artesian well. This is a well that, because it was created by drilling deep enough, never stops flowing. The pressure inside allows it to keep flowing outward. Likewise, if we draw from the eternal spring of Christ's presence in times of solitude, "rivers of living water will flow from within" (John 7:38). With our ultimate needs for security, significance, and satisfaction met in him, we're freed to approach relationships not out of need but out of the overflow of fullness and wholeness of Christ in us.

Contemplatives of the Past

Some of the most well-known saints of the church were like artesian wells—real people who lived long and often in God's presence, and also emanated him to the world through vibrant ministries (to the poor and others). Jesus himself struck the perfect balance; he was the ideal contemplative in action, taking the solitude of God with him everywhere he went, whether in a boat with his disciples, alone on the Mount of Olives, or in a crowd.

Many men and women in the early church took seriously the image of spreading the fragrance and presence of Christ to the hurting world around them. Basil the Great, from the fourth century, is little known to Protestants but revered in the Orthodox tradition. St. Basil led a monastic lifestyle that emphasized brotherly love in contrast to the usually austere, hermit-like lifestyle of a monk. He founded institutions to aid the poor, the sick, and travelers. The Basiliad, a large complex outside Caesarea he had built, featured a poorhouse, hospice, and hospital, serving people with leprosy. St. Basil established a soup kitchen that fed the hungry during a famine, and he worked to help thieves and prostitutes reform their lives. He believed our life and work should be integrated: "Thus wilt thou pray without ceasing; if thou prayest not only in words, but unitest thyself to God through all the course of life and *so thy life be made one ceaseless and uninterrupted prayer.*"[12]

Another person who combined a contemplative and others-focused lifestyle was Catherine of Genoa. An Italian Roman Catholic saint and mystic before the Protestant Reformation, she led a life of deep devotion and prayer (praying for as many as six hours a day); yet she became most admired for her fervor for helping the poor and the sick during the devastating plagues at the turn of the sixteenth century. Initially, she visited the slums of Genoa, but eventually she and her husband, who were childless, moved to the heart of the city to establish, and live next to, a hospital for the poor. Working without pay, she became the hospital's director and stayed there full-time until her health declined. Canonized in 1737, Catherine wrote in her *Life and Teachings*:

When God finds a soul that rests in him and is not easily moved, he operates within it in his own manner. That soul allows God to do great things within it. He gives to such a soul the key to the treasures he has prepared for it so that it might enjoy them. And to this same soul he gives the joy of his presence which entirely absorbs such a soul.[13]

Notice how Catherine's outward works were energized by a soul at rest in God, a soul reflecting and centered on him. Her intimacy with God, like that of St. Basil, animated her earthly activities.

Practice Tip: Balanced Schedule

We all have to seek a balance between rest and work, recharging and discharging. Examine your schedule for the coming week or month. Ask yourself if you've been overdoing it lately. Is there margin in your agenda to allow you to embrace those *kairos* opportunities that God brings into your days, or do you barely leave enough time to get from one activity to the next? Do you often accept requests that flatter you but end up draining your time and energy? Take this week to ask God to help you set *clear criteria* for accepting new invitations or requests. Run every new request through these criteria. *This is important even if you're not overcommitted right now*, because it will help you guard against unnecessary busyness in the future. It will ensure you pursue excellence in a few things instead of doing a shoddy job on numerous tasks. *Hint: If you're married, consider involving your spouse. For example, give your spouse veto power over a new activity that he or she feels will overcommit your time or be dissonant with your life calling.*

An Unhurried Life

We can't draw life from Christ daily if we're constantly frantic and hurried. Our fretfulness chokes out his Word, and God made us to need moments for contemplation and reflection. Without it, we wither and our souls shrink. We need margin—time outside our scheduled activities. If our lives are overscheduled, there's little chance we'll take time for solitude; the urgent will almost always take precedence. We'll also miss those special, divinely appointed *kairos* moments, as we'll be too hurried to see the opportunity of the precious present.

Andrew Sullivan, a contemporary commentator, recently captured the state of our current situation in a *New York Magazine* article about the slower pace of life we've lost gradually, almost without realizing it:

> [The] Judeo-Christian tradition recognized a critical distinction—and tension—between noise and silence, between getting through the day and getting a grip on one's whole life. The Sabbath—the Jewish institution co-opted by Christianity—was a collective imposition of relative silence, a moment of calm to reflect on our lives under the light of eternity. It helped define much of Western public life once a week for centuries—only to dissipate, with scarcely a passing regret, into the commercial cacophony of the past couple of decades. It reflected a now-battered belief that a sustained spiritual life is simply unfeasible for most mortals without these refuges from noise and work to buffer us and remind us who we really are. But just as modern street lighting has slowly blotted the stars from the visible skies, so too have cars and planes and factories and flickering digital screens combined to rob us of a silence that was previously regarded as

integral to the health of the human imagination. This changes us. It slowly removes—without our even noticing it—the very spaces where we can gain a footing in our minds and souls that is not captive to constant pressures or desires or duties. And the smartphone has all but banished them.[14]

Of course, without such spaces for "gaining a footing in our minds and souls," we've crowded God out of our lives as well, giving him nary a thought as we swipe and tap away.

Another author, Dr. Richard Swenson, wrote about the subject of margin in his book *Margin: Restoring Emotional, Physical, Financial, and Time Reserves in Overloaded Lives.* Though dated, the book's observations are perhaps even truer today, and many of the principles are timeless. His idea of building "reserves" into our lives, so we're not always pushing ourselves, has important implications for followers of Jesus. These time reserves (or our lack of them) affect every aspect of our lives, including our relationships with God and others. Not only that, but, as Swenson argues, our ability to face problems in our lives is greatly diminished. The less time margin we have, the more emotionally stressed we get, and the more prone we become to overreacting or snapping at small irritations.[15] Over time, a lack of margin in our lives can result in anxiety or depression, which, not coincidentally, have become much more rampant lately.[16] Ironically, our "time-saving" devices have led to an increasingly complex, hurried lifestyle that is, on the whole, *not* happier or easier.

The late Dallas Willard was famous for his unhurried manner. People who spoke to him would notice how, like Jesus, he'd reduce his entire world to only them, speaking to them, listening to them, not showing any indication of needing to be somewhere else more important. He was not the kind who'd have been caught looking at his phone or text messages while with another person;

you wouldn't have found yourself competing with virtual friends in his physical presence, as we often do today.

Willard lived very simply. He used to say, "Hurry is the great enemy of spiritual life in our day. You must ruthlessly eliminate hurry from your life."[17] In other words, to truly take care of our souls and grow in awareness of his Spirit dwelling in us, we can't be constantly living for the future and rushing into the next moment. We need to be present in this one. If we don't hurry into the next hour, there's a much greater chance we'll welcome and enjoy God's presence in *this* one. We'll avoid living in the future, the past, or some other fantasy world, heeding missionary Jim Elliot's advice: "Wherever you are, be *all* there. Live to the hilt every situation you believe to be the will of God."[18]

Listen to God in His Word

Read the full context of two of the key verses discussed in this chapter: Ephesians 5:1-16 (with a focus on the last two verses) and Psalm 90 (with a focus on verse 12). Review what these two passages say about how we view and make use of our time on earth.

Practice His Presence
Rest and Solitude

Many people think of solitude and rest as the same things, but they're not. And we need some of both, preferably daily. *Rest* is when we're doing something leisurely and there's *no* goal to produce anything. It's passive downtime to be enjoyed for its own sake. *Solitude* is time away from the world, except we're in a receptive mode—making an active, conscious effort to focus on getting with God and receiving what he wants to give and teach us. Both rest and solitude require faith because they both appear nonproductive from the world's point of view. However, there is no *shalom* (deep peace in our lives and relationships) without *shabbat* (sabbath rest), and no growth without dedicated time with God!

Consider whether you have times of rest and solitude built into your regular routine. If you don't, look for a time when you can build a few minutes of one (or both) into your schedule. See these times as nonnegotiable so you don't let something urgent crowd them out. You might be surprised at how even just a few minutes of rest or solitude make a difference!

Daily solitude/silence. To start, set aside ten minutes each day to get alone and intentionally embrace the precious present. Use these minutes for (1) adoration (offering a brief word of praise to God for one or more of his attributes or works) and (2) thanksgiving (thanking God for the good things in your life). Beware of the world encroaching upon this time—it will try! As you get used to this practice, you might want to lengthen the time and include additional prayers or Bible reflections.

Mini-sabbath (weekly rest). Schedule a mini-sabbath for all or part of a day (it doesn't have to be Sunday) every week. During this time, you're in a receptive mode, not an active push mode. Choose some *leisure* activity to do during this time: reading, painting, taking a walk, doing a crossword or jigsaw puzzle, listening to music, or simply sitting on a bench outside. Whatever you do, it should be something you do as an *end in itself*, not because of anything it produces. The activity can be with another person, but avoid involving someone who tends to drain or stress you. Also try to leave all electronics at home (or put them away in off mode) to avoid distraction. Once you've built rest into your weekly routine, try increasing to at least ten minutes of daily rest time.

9

Rejoicing amid Suffering

Let me learn by paradox . . . that the
valley is the place of vision.

PURITAN PRAYER

Kara Tippetts was a young mother of four when she was diagnosed with advanced-stage breast cancer. Before passing away fewer than three years later, she courageously faced life as she underwent treatment, and made an indelible mark on the world through her blog, *Mundane Faithfulness*. Her embrace of God's sovereign plan for her life—whatever the outcome—led to her book's title, *The Hardest Peace*. In the foreword, Joni Eareckson Tada says, "suffering is a strange, dark companion; but a companion, nonetheless. It's an unwelcome visitor, but still a visitor. Affliction is a bruising of a blessing; but it *is* a blessing from the hand of God."[1]

As a friend of Tippetts summarized, "[Kara] believed cancer was not the point, but Jesus was; how she responded and trusted Christ in the midst of this hard was where she would find Grace."[2] Tippetts found an intimacy with Jesus through her suffering that was "impossibly *sweet*."[3] Here are her own words:

I come to you in these pages as a broken woman, realizing that my brokenness may be my greatest strength—that it may be the greatest strength of us all. In the depths of my illness, I have been able to set aside my striving and look for God's presence in my suffering. My season of weakness has taught me the joy of receiving, the strength of brokenness, and the importance of looking for God in each moment. . . .

Learning the gift of each breath and spending it all in big, BIG love is the greatest calling of my remaining days— yours, too.[4]

That is exactly the calling Tippetts lived out. And her words will reverberate into many others' lives, calling them to find, as she did, not a program or a three-step solution, not even a good idea, but a Person: "the Jesus who humbly washes the feet of His disciples."[5]

While she was still alive, Tippetts connected with Joni Eareckson Tada, whose story of suffering is much better known and includes not only a recent battle with breast cancer but fifty years in a wheelchair due to a diving accident at age seventeen. When that incident rendered her a quadriplegic, Tada struggled mightily with her condition and God's purpose in it: "Most of the questions I asked, in the early days of my paralysis, were questions voiced out of a clenched fist," she recalls.[6] After a lot of grieving, wrestling, and searching, however, she came to see the gift God had given through her life-altering injury. Rather than seeing it as a curse, she began to see that her daily suffering had been God's "severe mercy," drawing her into a deeper trust in and relationship with him.[7] Today, she's a living example of 2 Peter 1:6-7, having added perseverance and godliness to her faith.

Tada's condition resulted—as it did for Kara Tippetts and so many others—in her values getting "turned from wrong side down to right side up." She began to find beauty and gratitude in small things, like the leaves blowing in the wind outside her hospital window, and to understand what really matters in life. This is how Tada describes it: "And though others may receive gifts of healing, I believe that He has given me a gift beyond compare. For heaven is nearer to me and at times it is all I can see."[8]

In This World . . .

Jesus guaranteed that *all* of us will have trouble in this world (John 16:33). Suffering is no elective, but a required course, in the university of life. It's a tool God uses to shape us. It's a connection to Jesus, who suffered to save us. And it's the place where many of us enter most fully into the presence of God.

There's no way *around* suffering, but there is a way *through* it that helps us come out better on the other side. And it's with him (Psalm 23:4; 1 Peter 5:10).

God uses pain, struggle, and suffering to give us a better vision of our desperate condition—and to set our sights beyond this world. The fact is, all of our lives are held together on the thinnest of threads. Scripture talks about this a lot, that our lives are like the grass, glorious today, withered tomorrow (Psalm 103:15; 1 Peter 1:24). Not only can we not guarantee another day of life (James 4:14), but God gives us no guarantees of a life of ease and comfort (Acts 14:22; 2 Timothy 3:12). Of course, physical suffering is only one type of adversity, the most visible kind. But mental, emotional, and spiritual anguish are also very real. Missionary Nik Ripken's story encompasses all of these.

Ripken is perhaps best known as the author of *The Insanity of God*. In this "true story of faith resurrected," he writes, "I was unaware of our destination at the time. No one had written 'Hell' on our official flight plan."[9]

That was how Ripken's mission work in Somaliland began. His pilot had told him, "I can take you in, no problem. I just can't promise when we might be able to get you out."[10] Ripken had no idea what this place, where he was sure God had called him, would be like. When he landed in the bombed-out capital of this self-declared nation on the northeast edge of Ethiopia, everyone was carrying automatic weapons, and mothers and their children worked together digging through the trash for food. He saw drug-dealing soldiers traveling in tanks, taking money from the poor in exchange for narcotics. He saw believers taking Communion for the first time who were also taking it for the last time. Later, the terrorist group Al-Shabaab would hide their bodies, so they couldn't be mourned or praised for their courage. Ripken had never witnessed oppression like he felt in that place.

Six years later, he left. He'd accomplished little in Somaliland and lost his son, Tim, in the process. Despondent, his family returned to America: "I couldn't see the relevance or the power of Jesus' resurrection in Somaliland. I couldn't point to any evidence of good overcoming evil. I couldn't see where love was overcoming hate."[11] He thought he'd walked into Somaliland in the center of God's will, which, he'd been taught, was the safest place to be. Now that belief was being challenged. His life and faith were shaken:

> It might . . . be safe to be in the center of God's will—but we would be wise to stop and think about what it means to be safe. I felt that I had lived a life in response to the call of God. Instead of effective ministry, measurable results, and what might pass for success, I felt mostly loss and heartache and failure.[12]

Everything Ripken believed about obedience had been brutally challenged, and all his concerns ultimately boiled down to one hard question: Is Jesus worth it?

That was twenty years ago. Since then, Ripken, his wife, and their missions team have taken this question into seventy-two countries—interviewing hundreds of believers who've endured severe persecution, as well as the children and grandchildren of martyred believers who didn't live to tell about it. In his book Ripken presents these stories to the Western church with the same question: Is Jesus worth it?

If, or rather *when*, suffering comes to you, how will you answer this question? Suffering isn't a good thing *in and of itself.* But it's sometimes the only force with enough strength to release the death grip we have on our lives and the idols we've built them around. God uses suffering to get to the core of what we really believe, to sharpen our faith and deepen our trust. Only when we release the idol in our hand do we see it for what it really was—a worthless piece of tinfoil compared to the diamond he wants to give us. That diamond is his grace, and it's life in his presence.

He Meets Us in Our Suffering

Suffering is difficult because it causes pain, whether physical or some other form. And it can be difficult for our faith because God sometimes doesn't take away or even dull the pain (or the thing causing it), even when we ask him. Instead, he tells us to fix our eyes on Jesus and endure (Hebrews 12:1-2). That's what those persecuted believers Ripken's team interviewed did, because Jesus understands suffering better than anyone. He's the Suffering Servant (Isaiah 52:13–53:12), who endured the cross for our sake, undeservedly but in full submission to God's greater purposes. And when we suffer for our faith, we share in the "fellowship of his sufferings" (Romans 8:17; 2 Corinthians 1:5; Philippians 3:10). When we're betrayed, he's right there with us, saying, "I know how this feels" (Hebrews 4:15). He weeps and mourns *with* us

(John 11:35). And he's with us when people hate us, reminding us, "If the world hates you, keep in mind that it hated me first" (John 15:18).

Suffering, like nothing else, can focus our life purpose and our vision of the good life. Those who have experienced deep suffering will tell you that they felt God to be the nearest when they were "in the valley." There our hunger pangs for the presence of our heavenly Father can be the sharpest, where our longing for heaven grows because the things of earth and the hopes of this life have let us down. The place of suffering is where we identify most clearly with Christ, if we *choose* to trust God and his goodness in the middle of it, rather than succumbing to the very human tendency to grumble or see ourselves as victims.

Our suffering can cause us to feel our need for God more intensely. Psalm 34:18 tells us he's "close to the brokenhearted." This doesn't mean he's *not* close to others, but somehow, in our pain, where we're at our most vulnerable and weakest point, he's most able to come alongside us, comfort us, and reassure us *he is here.* He sees and he knows.

Hardships show us both that God "rewards those who earnestly seek him" (Hebrews 11:6) and that *he himself* is our greatest reward (Genesis 15:1). In the middle of our own lack or pain, we feel most keenly the truth that only God satisfies (Psalm 145:16), and only in *his* presence is there *full* and permanent joy (Psalm 16:11).

Our suffering is never in vain if we are in Christ. He can *always* redeem our troubles for our good and his glory—using them to teach us to walk in full reliance on him, with one chief goal: "*I want to know Christ*—yes, to know the power of his resurrection and participation in his sufferings, becoming like him in his death" (Philippians 3:10, emphasis added).

Bitter or Better?

There's a catch: suffering doesn't *automatically* result in a more God-focused life. It *can* result in despair and a sense of alienation from God. Kara Tippetts easily could've spent her last days on earth bitter and angry, shaking her fist at God. Joni Eareckson Tada could have spiraled downward into a pit of depression instead of making her life about Christ and sharing his message with the world. Nik Ripken could have quit ministry instead of traveling the world to prove God is worth it. Examples abound of people whose suffering led them to turn their backs on God, rather than to run into his presence.

Our suffering will either make us bitter or better. If it shapes us negatively, we'll reap a harvest of bitterness. But if we embrace it—like Tippetts, Tada, and Ripken did—we give God the chance to use it to forge in us a quality of character that we wouldn't otherwise have. James wrote about this response to suffering, and the good fruit that comes from it: "Consider it pure joy, my brothers and sisters, whenever you face trials of many kinds, because you know that the testing of your faith produces perseverance. Let perseverance finish its work so that you may be mature and complete, not lacking anything" (James 1:2-4).

There's a mystery in suffering, and these verses in James hint at it. Our natural inclination is not to welcome suffering, and God knows it. But there's something in our suffering, however painful it may feel at the time, that produces joy: not joy *because* of the pain but *in spite of* the pain. It's a joy that comes from knowing that, if we unclench our fists, God will give us the internal healing and rich spiritual blessings that can only be found in him (Ephesians 1:3-5). And then we'll know, without a doubt, Jesus *is* worth it.

Our painful experiences are God's invitation to us to cling to his character and power more fully than we would if things were going well. And the way we cling to him is by seeking and living in his presence, walking by his Spirit, and seeing through his lens instead of our own limited, out-of-focus lens. If everything is going our way, we tend to become self-sufficient. Not sensing our radical need to depend on him, we tend to fall out of awareness of his presence, toward self-reliance and an illusion that *we* have everything under control. But we *don't* have everything under control, and we *can't* see the future; only God knows what's coming our way. And he knows that sometimes the only way we'll learn moment-by-moment trust and confidence in him is in a desperate state, when the things and hopes of this world have failed us.

A Living Hope

We all hope in something. And a loss of that something in our lives—through death, unfulfilled dreams, chronic illness, a material loss, or whatever else—compels us to cling to and hope in the one who is the same today, yesterday, and forever, rather than the things that are temporary. He uses our suffering and pain to transfer our *hope* from things that won't last to things that will.

The biblical character Job was stripped of nearly every earthly blessing in one of history's most well-known accounts of suffering. His reaction determined his destiny. After taking up his case directly with God, he repented and humbled himself (Job 42:1-6). His experience of God's presence seems to have been greater afterward: "My ears had heard of you, but now my eyes have seen you" (v. 5). Before his suffering, Job knew *about* God, but now he *knew* God. And God knew Job. In the end, God restored Job's earthly fortunes beyond what he'd even had before, twofold (Job 42:10)! This isn't a promise for us, but God can work that way. It's likely, though, that Job clung to those fortunes less tightly than before, realizing that the *real* riches he'd gained were the intangible ones: wisdom, humility, contentment, and a greater sense of God's presence that were produced in his "furnace of affliction" (Isaiah 48:10).

In the past year, several of my friends have received devastating news about loved ones. One person's daughter, a mother of three in her late thirties, was diagnosed with an advanced stage of an aggressive brain cancer. Another friend's son committed suicide. A third friend had a son who died in his sleep from an unusual tracheal condition. There are few words that can offer comfort in these situations, when the pain of loss—or fear of possible loss—is so huge. No trite words will do.

But in these moments, when we receive bad news about ourselves or others, there's an opportunity. It's a chance to invite God's presence into our relationships and our lives. How do I pray for my friends? What in the world can I possibly say to them? Mortality hits us in the face, and we'd probably rather run than sit in the middle of it and wait with someone. But the Holy Spirit *can* direct us, and we can sit there, inviting his presence into that very moment when we're with our friend, or spouse, or other family member. Sometimes, that's the best thing we can do, rather than filling the silence with our own words.

A few years ago, a friend suffered public humiliation in a small town because of something someone else had done to her. I'll spare you the details, but there came a moment when the sins were announced publicly, and she had to stand and face them. At the moment this happened, she had three women praying around her, two local friends and one who had driven twelve hours to be by her side. They literally surrounded her in prayer at one of the most horrific moments of her life, interceding for her when she didn't have the strength to ask God for anything. She says she'll never forget the pain and utter disgrace of that moment, but she will also never forget how God was present to her through those friends, and to this day she feels incredible gratitude toward them.

We'll all suffer something, and we'll have the choice to embrace it as an opportunity to experience God more or to get angry and turn from him. If we embrace him as our "living hope through the resurrection of Jesus Christ from the dead" (1 Peter 1:3), then we have something that never fades and dies. When we're suffering, or enduring suffering with someone we care about, we have to grab hold of that hope and hang onto it for dear life.

The book of First Peter is sometimes called the "Job of the New Testament." In the letter, the apostle Peter was writing to Christians in the early church who faced increasing suffering and persecution. Through Peter's writing, God didn't downplay the pain of their trials but instead encouraged them toward that "living hope" by taking the long view—*his view*—of their suffering: "The God of all grace, who called you to his eternal glory in Christ, after you have suffered a little while, will himself restore you and make you strong, firm and steadfast" (1 Peter 5:10).

This verse shows us two important things about suffering. First, it's inevitable—"*after* you have suffered." Everybody suffers in some way, at some point. Second, although the suffering may *feel* long-lasting, in the context of eternity it's only "a little while." Suffering is temporary, even though, when we're in the middle of it, it can be awfully hard to see the light at the end of the tunnel. Christian faith doesn't ignore or make light of the reality of suffering, but it offers hope in it. If we're comforting someone who's enduring pain, we can bring Christ, who's alive in us, into that pain. We can lead that person into God's presence by praying for them and asking that the "God of all comfort" (2 Corinthians 1:3) give them exactly what they need in their pain. When I'm comforting friends or family, I often borrow from these words of Paul: "Brothers and sisters, we do not want you to be uninformed about those who sleep in death, so that you do not grieve like the rest of mankind, who have no hope" (1 Thessalonians 4:13).

It's okay to grieve, but as Christians we don't grieve as those who have no hope. Our final destination is secure. Our end prospect is joy (Proverbs 10:28; John 16:20). This kind of outlook doesn't downplay the present pain, but it puts it into proper perspective. And sharing this view can be, in a very real sense, God's way of coming close to those who are suffering and brokenhearted.

Responding to Suffering

When pain arouses our attention, it prompts lots of why questions: "Why is this happening?" or "Why would God allow *this*?" All of us ask these kinds of questions, and we're right to take these questions straight to God. But how we respond when he doesn't give us the answer we want in the time frame we're expecting, or when he doesn't seem to answer at all, reveals a lot about us, and also determines whether our suffering will lead us to become bitter or better—to enjoy more of God's presence in our lives or less.

Jesus said God would respond when we ask, seek, and knock (Matthew 7:7). But he didn't promise we'd always get the answer we want and hope for. The whys we ask tend to fall into four basic categories, and some are more helpful than others.

The *whys of grumbling* are not helpful: "Why me? What did I ever do to deserve this?" or "Why not him instead of me?" These questions are often our first instinct, but we must move on from them quickly, or we'll find ourselves in a sea of self-pity and misery.

The *whys of grief* aren't necessarily bad questions. They can lead us to seek God rather than fall into a pit of hopelessness. The book of Psalms contains laments that we can read for great comfort. Their authors are like kindred spirits for those going through hardship. These songs don't deny God's goodness but allow us to join the psalmist in crying out with the full range of our emotions, which God already knows anyway, and invite us to steep in his ways and promises.

The *whys of guidance* are more about God's greater purposes, less about the reasons for our circumstances. These questions are more focused on the good God wants to bring out of our suffering, but they can still be self-focused: "God, why is this happening to *me*—what do you want *me* to learn from this?" Ultimately, God's intention is for us to comfort others with the comfort we ourselves have received from God (2 Corinthians 1:4). As with Job, suffering and pain can give us a redemptive life message that is experiential rather than merely theoretical, increasing our capacity to speak truth with great love and compassion.

The *whys of gratitude* are the best kinds of whys. They're often evidence of God doing a great work through time spent in his presence during our suffering: "Why have you been so good to me, God?" "What have I done to deserve this?" This reaction to suffering is the least common, and it reveals a heart of humility. When my friend's thirty-eight-year-old daughter was diagnosed with cancer recently, I tried—without downplaying his pain—to help him move from grief to gratitude. I asked him something like this: "If you could go back in time, before your daughter was born, and you were told you could either have a daughter for thirty-eight years or no years at all, what would you choose? Would you still want to have that time with her?" When framed this way, my friend, though still grieving, has had an easier time giving thanks to God for his daughter's life, even though it will probably be much shorter than he imagined.

Practice Tip: Psalms of Lament

In the midst of suffering, many godly people have used the book of the Psalms—especially the psalms of lament, which make up one-third of the entire book—as a way to draw near to God. You can use these when you're going through a hard time, or suggest them to others enduring difficulties. It's helpful to read them slowly, pausing often, and turning them into prayers to God. Be sure to notice the transition from lament to praise!

- Psalms of individual lament (just a sampling): Psalms 3; 6; 13; 22; 28; 44; 56; 57; 142.

- Psalms of corporate lament (for times of communal distress, such as natural disasters or national oppression): Psalms 44; 60; 74; 79; 80; 85; 90.

Turning Outward

Suffering is intensely personal: "Each heart knows its own bitterness" (Proverbs 14:10). But it can give us a fresh perspective and vision of life, one that brings God's bigger purposes into sharper view. It's one way he teaches us that the truly worthwhile life is not one spent on ourselves, trying to secure the best life that we would choose *now*. The best life is one poured out to God as an offering to him. And as we take our minds off ourselves and place them on God and his plan, we find ourselves more able to focus on serving and loving others. In fact, the best way to get our minds off our own problems and pain is to look around and find others, even just one person, in need. Then we can serve that person as though we are serving Christ himself.

As hard as it is to stop feeling sorry for ourselves, we have many promises from God. If we love him, he will work all things for our good (Romans 8:28), and our hardships won't permanently overcome us (John 16:33). Even in our suffering, then, we can move on to obeying his commandment to love others. In this way, our suffering becomes part of our life in his presence, and often even a tool of his redemption, for ourselves and others.

In his book *A Different Kind of Happiness*, Larry Crabb homes in on how God has made this soul-forming world, with all its brokenness and suffering, a context for forming relationships. He urges Christians not to let their pain sidetrack them from the high calling of living and loving like Jesus. The goal of spiritual practice, Crabb says, is not only for our benefit, but also for others: "It is easier, and therefore more talked about, to practice spiritual disciplines in an effort to feel God's presence than to practice them in order to draw on the Spirit's power to love well."[13]

The prophet Isaiah said the Messiah would be a man of suffering (Isaiah 53:3). The night before he was put to death by the most brutal form of capital punishment invented, he was on his knees washing feet. He wasn't paralyzed with fear at the coming betrayal and rejection, but serving his friends in love.

Loving like Jesus means loving others like Jesus did—even in the middle of our own suffering, our own rejection and pain—and drawing on his strength to do it. When we help others, sharing in *their* suffering, we're also becoming closer to Jesus by sharing in *his* sufferings (Philippians 3:10). Crabb says this (loving like Jesus) is the route to the only "real and sustaining joy" in life, and it's a path few take and that even fewer remain on for long.[14]

Julian of Norwich took that route more than six hundred years ago. She was on the brink of death at age thirty, and a priest came to administer her last rites. When he held up a crucifix and began to pray, she had visions of Christ and ended up recovering miraculously. But Julian was never the same again, and she devoted the rest of her life to prayer, writing, and mentoring and counseling others.

Joy and love became hallmarks of her writings, which are still read centuries later: "With all the will of my heart I assented to be wholly God's," she wrote of her commitment after her near-death experience.[15] Her most famous saying is a lesson for us all: "All shall be well and all shall be well, and all manner of things shall be well."[16]

We all struggle with "drinking the cup of suffering." And everyone's cup is different: a chronic physical ailment, painful emotional experiences or abuse, an unfulfilled dream, a spiritual emptiness we can't explain—the possibilities are endless. Thomas Kelly pointed out that even the great saints had periods of dryness when they felt a "smaller sense of his presence" than in other seasons. The key is to keep coming, keep returning to him, no matter our circumstances or feelings. In the process, spiritual good *will* come in time: "The heart is stretched through suffering, and enlarged. But O the agony of this enlarging of the heart, that one may be prepared to enter the anguish of others! Yet the way of holy obedience leads out from the heart of God and extends through the Valley of the Shadow."[17]

Practice Tip: The Least, Last, and Lost

Jesus was always willing to stop everything and take time for the people others looked down on, avoided, or didn't notice: little children, a demon-possessed man, a woman who'd been hemorrhaging for twelve years. This week, take time to notice these overlooked people. Maybe it's an administrative assistant at work, a cashier at the grocery store, the person who delivers your mail, or just a person nobody talks to. Take time to speak to these people. Ask how they're doing or make it a point to thank them if they're serving you somehow. Look for an opportunity to show them Christ's love and mercy, remembering Jesus' words in Matthew 25:40: "Truly I tell you, whatever you did for one of the least of these brothers and sisters of mine, you did for me."

The Way of the Cross

The qualities we most admire in heroic and noble people are never forged in ease. They come from experiences of pain and adversity. God prunes us through these experiences, not because he wants to see us suffer but because he knows sometimes it's the only way to strip us of our pride and bring us closer to him, so the authentic cry of our hearts isn't "just give me relief" (or healing or anything else) but "just give me Jesus."

One of the most powerful lessons of suffering is that God is God and we are not. It's the lesson Job learned, and the one Kara Tippetts, Joni Eareckson Tada, and Nik Ripken learned. It's also the lesson my wife, Karen, who suffers from chronic pain, is learning, and I along with her, as I ask God's wisdom for how to best comfort, serve, and sympathize with her. We won't always understand why God is allowing us, or those we love, to suffer. Sometimes he lets us see the reasons later, but sometimes we never really know. Our best response is not to demand answers but to ask for more of him.

A key to suffering well, as Jesus did, is to never view God in light of our changing circumstances, but to view our changing circumstances in light of God's unchanging character. When we do the first, filtering our vision through the lens of our circumstances, we'll find ourselves on a spiritual roller coaster, swinging like a pendulum. When things go smoothly for us, we think, *Look at how God has blessed me—how great he is!* But when things appear to be going badly, we'll wonder, *What happened to God? I can't trust him—he took away my [fill in the blank]!* If, instead, we view our circumstances through God's perfect love and goodness, accepting that our understanding is limited, we'll more clearly see the one who "[does] everything well" (Mark 7:37). We'll come to believe that all things are filtered through his grace—and he can use *anything* in our lives for a redemptive purpose.

No two journeys are the same. Your path is different from mine. As a result, as the French Jesuit priest Jean-Pierre de Caussade wrote, there's no formula for how your life will go, only the guide of God's Word and his indwelling Spirit: "divine action is ever fresh, it never retraces its steps, but always marks out new ways. Souls that are conducted by it never know where they are going; their ways are neither to be found in books, nor in their own minds; the divine action carries them step by step."[18]

Kara Tippetts understood this at her core. That's why she was able to trust God in the midst of her own unique experience of suffering—suffering that many of us would label as unjust—embracing it to the end:

> Grace is worth the effort. . . . Grace is what meets me after I run to the bathroom to be sick when I think on my reality. Grace is what will meet my children when I'm not here. I don't know how, but I know it will. . . . Jesus didn't have to extend His love. He didn't have to think of me when He went up on that cross. He didn't have to rewrite my story from one of beauty to one of brokenness and create a whole new brand of beauty. He simply didn't have to do it, but He did. . . . He bought me that day He died, and He showed His power when He overcame death and rose from the grave. He overcame my death in that moment. He overcame my fear of death . . . and the fruit of that death, that resurrection, and that stunning grace is peace. It is the hardest peace, because it is brutal. Horribly brutal and ugly, and we want to look away, but it is the greatest, greatest story that ever was.[19]

Listen to God in His Word

Hebrews 11 refers to people in the Bible who endured suffering. Read the chapter (yes, all of it; it's worth it!). As you read, notice two categories of people that emerge: (1) those who were delivered from suffering and saw God's promises fulfilled in this life, and (2) those who died without seeing that deliverance. What's the difference between these two groups? *Is* there a difference? Did one group have more faith than the other? Now, read Hebrews 12:1-11 (or just skip straight to that final verse, if you prefer). What's the connection between Hebrews 12:11 and Hebrews 11? What about the connections of all of these verses to the things you just read in this chapter?

Practice His Presence
The Hard Thanksgiving

Paul, in 1 Thessalonians 5:18, says we're to give thanks in all circumstances. Not some, not most, but *all* circumstances. The word he uses for thanksgiving is *eucharisteō* (where we get the word *Eucharist*, which is one term for the Lord's Supper or Communion). Sometimes *eucharisteō* comes easily, like when we get good news or something exciting happens to us. But there's also a *hard thanksgiving*. This is what we do in circumstances that, in our limited view, seem difficult or less than desirable. Think about your life right now. Do you need to offer God a hard thanksgiving for something in your life right now? If so, do it now, asking him to help you see your circumstance as a temporary part of living on this earth. Ask God to use this situation to help you lean on him more, draw closer to him, and welcome his presence into more of your life.

Repenting of Sin

We deceive ourselves by the smallness of our surrenders.

DEREK KIDNER

Though he was in his early thirties, Andrew already had a lot going for him: a godly wife, three children and a fourth on the way, a four-bedroom house in a suburb of Dallas, a decent-sized savings account, a recent promotion to senior manager at a Christian-run business, and regular vacations at the beach in Galveston.[1]

But one day, all of it collapsed. The crisis appeared to come out of nowhere at first. Andrew was active in his church, a youth leader with his wife, and regarded by all who knew him as a godly husband, dad, and friend. In reality, though, he'd been living two lives for years. He'd hidden his secret life well. But after his wife discovered an affair with an old high school friend—a relationship that had begun as an emotional affair online—she came to realize that it was only the tip of the iceberg, a culminating event in what had been a long progression into sexual sin.

Andrew had been indulging in pornography on and off since he was a teenager, and after seven years of marriage, he realized that his addiction problem wasn't solved, as he thought it might be, by being married. The tangled web he'd woven in his life by not dealing with sin early, and by letting it grow and fester, almost cost him his marriage. It did cost him his job.

Sadly, this story isn't uncommon; in fact, I know several similar stories. Many of these tragic situations haven't ended as well as this one. By God's grace, Andrew's life got back on track. He confessed and asked forgiveness from his wife, and then did the same before his entire church family. His wife forgave him, though the bonds of trust are still healing. He stepped back from his ministry role at church, set up a one-on-one mentoring and accountability relationship, and for the first time in his adult life faced the duplicity in his heart. He recommitted his life to Christ and began living, day by day, in God's presence, not perfectly but faithfully.

Looking back, Andrew can see the lies that held him captive for so many years, including the lie that it's safer to cover up sin than to confess. But he couldn't see any of this while it was happening. He believed his wife would leave him if she ever knew the extent of his sin. He believed "what she didn't know couldn't hurt her" and chose to live a divided life instead. He ignored the warnings he knew were in the Bible, choosing to focus instead on the Scriptures he liked, and became very adept at lying and covering up.

But sin always brings consequences, one of which is that it blinds us and distorts our thinking. Worst of all, it leads us to hide from God instead of enjoying the blessing of his presence in our lives. Though it seems unnatural to us, the best thing we can do with our sin, when we become aware of it, is to bring it (as quickly as possible) to God—fighting the desire to hide—and ask for forgiveness, as well as his help to turn from it. This process, called repentance, is the only way out of sin's bondage and back into a deep relationship with our Father.

Sin Doesn't Define Us

When we try to hide our sin from God, strange things can happen. We start to keep the sin close to us, almost like a pet, nurturing it, feeding it, hoping God somehow overlooks it. What we're doing, biologically, is reinforcing those neural pathways in our brain that are involved in that particular sin, with all the force of the four factors that strengthen a thought or behavior pattern (experience, focused attention, repetition, and emotional arousal), until they become habit. And habits, as we know, can be tough to break. Worse, we'll begin to allow that sin to define us. We'll start buying into the lie that our particular habit of sin or weakness is part of who we are, something we can't shake off and maybe shouldn't try to. We're like freed slaves who keep running back to our old master and again taking up residence in his household, thinking *that's* where we belong. But it's not; we're made to be free. That's why Jesus came (John 8:36; Galatians 5:1)!

Sin can never master a person who has committed his or her life to Christ, no matter how bad it is: "For sin shall no longer be your master, because you are not under the law, but under grace" (Romans 6:14). We may fail to use the power the Spirit gives us to overcome sin, but we *do have* this power available to us, and we can pray that God will help us to use it. This is no small thing: this power now available to us is the very same power that raised Jesus from the dead (Ephesians 1:19-20)!

When you're in Christ, your sin isn't the deepest you. It's not your identity. Sin is identified with the flesh, the part of you that was put to death when you were "crucified with Christ" (Romans 6:6; Galatians 2:20). Your reborn self (what Paul calls the "inner being") is alive in Christ and able to draw near to the Father. Your old self (the flesh) is still there and still sins as long as you're on this earth (Romans 7:22-23), but the penalty of sin is gone. The more you embrace God's Spirit, walking in *his* power, the more the power of sin is also overcome. This is a capacity you didn't have in your fallen state. And one day, the day you're made completely like Christ, not only will sin not have power but it won't even be present anymore (1 John 3:2).

These ideas, laid out by Paul in Romans 6–8, are important to grasp if you want to practice God's presence: the sin that hinders your relationship with God isn't even a small *part* of who you are anymore. You have a new identity—a new deepest you—if you're in Christ. The sin you commit is something to be thrown off (Hebrews 12:1) so you can fix your eyes on Christ and live in full enjoyment of the position and freedom you've been given in him.

Andrew went through a process of unlearning the habits of his old life and replacing them with new ones through training and trust. Similarly, when I first became a believer many years ago, I had all kinds of sins I had to root out from my old life before Christ. By God's mercy, he didn't make me aware of every one of these sins at once. But he slowly showed things to me that weren't pleasing to him and areas where I wasn't fully relying on him. (He's still showing me today!)

Throwing off the sins that "so easily entangle us" (Hebrews 12:1) isn't fun or easy, but it's always worth it. And God promises to join *his* strength with our willingness to do it (1 Corinthians 10:13). The best course of action is to do so immediately, as soon as God brings it to our attention. This process is gradual and lifelong, and it's the process of us becoming in practice what God has already made us in position: his beloved children, with all of the rights and privileges of heirs.

When we stumble (and everybody does), we have this promise: "If we confess our sins, he is faithful and just and will forgive us our sins and purify us from all unrighteousness" (1 John 1:9). It's for this reason that, whenever we become conscious of our sin, we can enter humbly but boldly into the presence of God (Hebrews 4:16), confident that he'll see us through the lens of Jesus' righteousness, forgive us, and empower us to change. Because of Jesus' sacrifice, we need not fear that we'll face the eternal consequences that our sin deserves.

King David: A Case Study

King David, the man after God's own heart, wasn't sinless. When he sinned, he sinned big, breaking at least half of the Ten Commandments in rapid succession. But when his friend and adviser, the prophet Nathan, confronted him, he immediately repented: "I have sinned against the LORD," he confessed (2 Samuel 12:13). David refused to eat, and he lay on the floor for days, begging for God's forgiveness. Listen to his words as he took his sin immediately to God:

> Wash away all my iniquity
>   and cleanse me from my sin.
> For I know my transgressions,
>   and my sin is always before me.
> Against you, you only, have I sinned
>   and done what is evil in your sight. . . .
> Create in me a pure heart, O God,
>   and renew a steadfast spirit within me.
> Do not cast me from your presence
>   or take your Holy Spirit from me.
> Restore to me the joy of your salvation
>   and grant me a willing spirit, to sustain me.
>   (Psalm 51:2-4, 10-12)

This is a beautiful request for God's forgiveness, but in it David prays for something you and I don't need to pray: "Do not cast me from your presence or take your Holy Spirit from me." In David's context (before Jesus' death and resurrection), the Holy Spirit's presence was selective and temporary. The Spirit could come on a person and later leave. (Read the story of David's predecessor, King Saul, to see. You can find it in the book of 1 Samuel.) That's why we see David asking God to allow him to remain in God's presence. But now, if we're in Christ, the Spirit's presence isn't selective anymore. *All* believers are baptized into the Holy Spirit, and his Spirit comes and lives in us forever. We can grieve the Spirit (Ephesians 4:30)—meaning we ignore or resist him by indulging in sin, resulting in our diminished enjoyment and awareness of his presence—but he's still in us. And he's here to stay.

David's prayer for God to restore to him the joy of his salvation and to be granted a "willing spirit" is a prayer for all of us when we don't feel God close to us. David knew what it was to soar with God, to thoroughly enjoy being in his presence. He desperately wanted to be near God again, but, like all of us, he stumbled (James 3:2), and he stumbled badly. He knew his egregious sin would continue to keep him from experiencing God if he persisted in it, so he did what he had to do to ensure God's Spirit would stay. And then, though his heart was still healing, he wrote with gratitude at the relief of being restored:

> How blessed is he whose transgression is forgiven,
> Whose sin is covered!
> How blessed is the man to whom the LORD does not
> impute iniquity,
> And in whose spirit there is no deceit!

When I kept silent *about my sin*, my body wasted away
Through my groaning all day long.
For day and night Your hand was heavy upon me;
My vitality was drained away as with the fever heat of
    summer. *Selah.*
I acknowledged my sin to You,
And my iniquity I did not hide;
I said, "I will confess my transgressions to the LORD";
And You forgave the guilt of my sin. *Selah.*
    (Psalm 32:1-5 NASB)

David had felt terrible pressure as a result of God's convicting presence. His whole being was affected as his sin weighed on him. This was a good thing. (If you can practice *conscious* disobedience *without* a feeling of alienation or estrangement from God, that's a bad sign. It may mean you don't have the Holy Spirit and need to trust your life to Christ.) But God's kindness calls our sin to our attention and leads us to repentance (Romans 2:4). His voice calling us to return to him never condemns and accuses without also offering us the hope of forgiveness and restoration through him.

Because we are whole, integrated beings, and not disconnected parts, sin impacts our minds and bodies, as well as our souls. So if we want to enjoy being with God, we can't hide anything from him. We all sin sometimes, but the shorter the time between the sin and genuine repentance, the better. (The same is true in human relationships: the shorter the time of the grudge or rift between us and another person, the easier it is to enjoy the relationship again.) And if we regularly ask the Holy Spirit to examine our hearts, we're much less likely to become enslaved to sin in the first place.

David was relieved after he confessed. As scary as confession is, it brings freedom, which we can't know without it, and it restores the relationship we so desperately want. David celebrated his rapidly restored relationship with God:

> You are my hiding place;
>> you will protect me from trouble
>> and surround me with songs of deliverance. (Psalm 32:7)

We were meant to hide *in* God, not *from* him! David understood this. Although he'd coveted and committed adultery and murder, among other sins, he experienced God's unmerited forgiveness and immediately rejoiced in it.

What do *we* need to do to recover a palpable sense of God's presence when it's been lost because of sin? The short answer is to stop hiding our sin and confess. Sin always creates a barrier between us and God. And disobedience, by its very nature, leads to separation and alienation. If we let it linger, we become *accustomed* to disobedience (just imagine those neural pathways getting cemented, one repetition of a sin at a time). But if we confess our sin quickly, trusting Christ to remove it, we put ourselves on a path that accustoms us to *obedience*—and our fellowship with God throughout each area of our lives deepens.

We have to be ruthless in rooting out sin (if you don't believe me, read Matthew 18:8-9), because if any sin becomes *habitual* and *persistent*, and we fail to repent of it, we damage our relationship with God. Hidden sin—that is, hidden to others, but never to God—hurts our intimacy with God more than we realize. It thrives in secrecy and darkness, and the only way to kill it is to drag it out in the open and expose it to the light. Sometimes this means confessing it openly to the people hurt by our sin, like Andrew did, but not always. Regardless, we can always do so without fear, because God *promises* to forgive and heal when we turn to him. We can run from our sin straight into his protection and his presence, knowing we'll be safe there.

Temptation and Sin: Five Stages

You've probably heard of the seven deadly sins. But you may not know that they have their roots in a list developed by an ascetic monk named Evagrius Ponticus in the fourth century AD. His list of eight patterns of *logismoi* (evil thoughts) included the temptations from which all sinful behavior springs. Loosely based on Proverbs 6:16-19 and other Scriptures, he intended the list to be a diagnostic tool to help people identify their own weaknesses and provide remedies to overcome them. More than two centuries later, Gregory the Dialogist (Pope Gregory I) revised the monk's list to the seven deadly sins we know today: gluttony, fornication, avarice, sloth, anger, pride, and envy.

Almost eight centuries later, another monk, Father Maximos of Mount Athos, wrote about these *logismoi* using five stages that show the progression from temptation to sin. A believer who seeks to understand these stages is like a soldier studying enemy tactics; if we know how temptations present themselves to us, we'll get better at recognizing when they're happening and at resisting their allure.

Father Maximos's stages, like Evagrius's and Gregory's lists, directly mirror truths in the Bible. The five stages are similar to how the apostle James talked about sin. Sin, James explained, doesn't appear out of nowhere; it originates from our own evil desires and wrong thoughts (James 1:14). Wrong thinking isn't innocuous: when cultivated, it can result in sin, even though that process may take seconds, days, or even years. The more quickly we recognize wrong thinking, the more quickly we can hold it up to the light of God's truth and ask his strength to eradicate it in our lives.

Father Maximos's five stages are as follows:

- Stage 1. Assault: The *logismos* (evil thought) first attacks a person's mind.
- Stage 2. Interaction: A person opens up a dialogue with the *logismos*.
- Stage 3. Consent: A person consents to do what the *logismos* urges them to do.
- Stage 4. Captivity: A person becomes a hostage to the *logismos*, finding it more difficult to resist.
- Stage 5. Passion or obsession: The *logismos* becomes an entrenched reality within the person's mind.[2]

Stages one and two are temptation. No sin has yet been committed. Stage three is the decision to sin. Stage four follows and is the point when, having been defeated by the sin more than once, we've become its hostage. It'll be very difficult to avoid continuing in that sin. By the time we reach step five, the sin has become an ingrained habit, which is harder to break, especially if the behavior is addictive. With stage-five (habitual) sin, stages one and two are usually compressed. Breaking the sin pattern will involve recognizing the temptation in one of the first two stages so that we resist before again consenting to the sin. We fight sin patterns using God's Word—the "sword of the Spirit" (Ephesians 6:17)—in prayer and submission to God.

Think through how fast you can move through the first three stages with a phone in your hand. Someone does something to offend you, and without taking any time to think it over, you post a comment (let's say it's on Facebook). If you're really angry, you might even include names in your response. With one click of a finger, you've moved from stage one to stage three, completely skipping over the part where you stop and think. You weren't even aware of the wrong thought for five seconds before you consented to sinfully act on your anger. The person you offended responds on their Facebook page, and then other people begin commenting. The whole thing blows up and you don't know how to stop it. The Internet is full of reports of lawsuits, lost jobs, and even lost lives because of social media posts. As Christians, we're supposed to be slow to speak (James 1:19). That command applies even when our speaking is through our fingers in an age of instant communication. If more of us were aware of the temptation-to-sin progression, we might be less prone to downplaying the danger that the initial, frontal attack poses— heeding Peter's words: "Be alert and of sober mind. Your enemy the devil prowls around like a roaring lion looking for someone to devour" (1 Peter 5:8).

The Anatomy of Temptations

The enemy of our souls is on the prowl. He wants us to act too fast. He wants to catch us unaware and suck us in, to attack us when we least expect it. When we're not aware of this, then before we know it, we'll find ourselves giving in to temptation and feeling far from God. Here's how James describes this progression:

> When tempted, no one should say, "God is tempting me." For God cannot be tempted by evil, nor does he tempt anyone; but each person is tempted when they are dragged away by their own evil desire and enticed. Then, after desire has conceived, it gives birth to sin; and sin, when it is full-grown, gives birth to death. (James 1:13-15)

Self-deception plays a huge role:

> Get rid of all moral filth and the evil that is so prevalent and humbly accept the word planted in you, which can save you.

Do not merely listen to the word, and so deceive yourselves. Do what it says. Anyone who listens to the word but does not do what it says is like someone who looks at his face in a mirror and, after looking at himself, goes away and immediately forgets what he looks like. (James 1:21-24, emphasis added)

Why is it so important to fight sin? Because sin *always* alienates us from God. It always takes us farther from his presence, not closer. It's like we've temporarily stepped off the road and stopped following him. We're still headed his way—we can get back on the road anytime—but to do that, we need to confess our sin openly to him and resume *his ways.*

When sin is habitual, it's especially alienating because it means we're "cherish[ing] sin in [our] heart," and as a result, our prayers are blocked (Psalm 66:18). There's a barrier. I'm not suggesting we have to be perfect and sinless before God ever hears us; none of us will ever be, on earth! But when we're complacent about our sin, and we don't hate it like God hates it, and we refuse to resist it, then we're cherishing it. And it's pretty hard for God to shape us when we're clinging to something (or things) that he hates.

What's the answer? The Bible says we don't avoid sin by focusing on it. We avoid it by fixing our eyes on Jesus and his perfect Word: "Whoever looks intently into the perfect law that gives freedom, and continues in it—not forgetting what they have heard, but doing it—they will be blessed in what they do" (James 1:25).

We can't and should never try to fight sin and temptation on our own. We need God's help, his weapons of spiritual battle. Here's James again: "Submit yourselves, then, to God. Resist the devil, and he will flee from you. Come near to God and he will come near to you. Wash your hands, you sinners, and purify your hearts, you double-minded" (James 4:7-8).

The sequence in these verses is important: *first*, we submit to God, *then* we resist the enemy. *We should never try it the other way around;* if we try to resist first, we will fail. Only people who submit and sacrifice themselves to God (Romans 12:1) are in a position to resist the enemy and avoid sin.

Seeing Through the Stages

Let's revisit the story from the beginning of this chapter—the one about young, successful Andrew. So much about his life looked picture-perfect from the outside: his beautiful, growing family; his activity in church; and his success at work. His was the kind of Christmas card you'd get and immediately think it could've come straight out of a toothpaste commercial. It was easy for friends to envy him, and by all appearances, things were fine.

Only Andrew knew that all was not well with his soul, that he was going through the motions, feeling far from God. Only he knew he'd explored "adult" sites every time his wife had been in the hospital with a new baby, plus a few more times at work when business was slow. He didn't know why he kept looking at the pictures, but he never examined the temptation much either. He kept skipping straight to stage three without much thought. And what started as a few isolated incidents, over time, became a habit, the "meditation of his heart." It's what he turned over and over in his mind. Deep down, something in him knew turning to the computer wouldn't help his nagging loneliness, but he did it anyway. He carried a lot of shame and felt like an imposter, but he hid it well.

Then came the day he was online and a Facebook notification pop-up appeared "out of the blue" (though we know better). His best (female) friend from high school had recently moved to a town less than an hour away. She just wanted to chat and catch up. Maybe because of what he'd just been looking at on the computer, he let his mind wander and started daydreaming about her.[3] In the middle of his fantasy, he recognized his thoughts were headed in what he considered a more serious wrong direction, so he shook it off, closed his laptop, picked up his keys, and walked out the door.

Where was Andrew at this point, according to Father Maximos's five stages? We know he'd been involved with pornography before, and he'd consented to viewing it intermittently since he got married. There's a neural pathway, first formed in his high school days, becoming a well-beaten path: he's at stage four. But what happened today was something new. The enemy isn't satisfied with us committing just one sin or even a bunch of them. He wants to take us hostage and cripple us from seeing ourselves—and living—as the children of God that we are. When Andrew shook off that first temptation to interact with his female friend, he dropped the enemy's ball on the field at stage two and left the game. We'd be cheering for him if we knew it wouldn't happen again. But Andrew hadn't learned to fight yet. He was still unprotected and open to assault. The stop in his mind was mostly related to the consequences he'd feel in his life if he got caught. He hadn't yet wielded the power of the Spirit to battle his sin. He was unaware of the enemy's tactics. It was only a matter of time before his opponent moved in on him again.

What if, instead, Andrew acknowledged God's presence before turning on the computer, submitted himself to him, and prayed:

May the words of my mouth
  and the meditation of my heart

be pleasing to you,

O Lord, my rock and my redeemer. (Psalm 19:14 NLT)

Of course that wouldn't solve everything, but it'd be a start. God's Word is powerful, more powerful than we usually realize. And because of what we now know about the way God uses our brain's anatomy to shape us, we know that the more Andrew trains his mind away from the source of temptation and toward God and his truth, the more he causes new neural paths to form and old ones to weaken. The greater Andrew's focus on, and time in, the Bible, the more his mind will form new habits of thinking, new sources of pleasure, good sources. He might still fail from time to time, but his intimacy with God would return because he was no longer trying to hide and keep his sin safe; he was drawing nearer to God, farther from his sin, and God *promises* to draw near to us when we do that (James 4:8).

Andrew also needed confession and community to heal. We all need regular examination in light of God's Word—to keep the devil from getting a "foothold" (Ephesians 4:27), as well as at least one friend we trust enough to tell the truth about ourselves to, someone who helps keep us from growing "hardened by sin's deceitfulness" (Hebrews 3:13).

The Way Out

Just like there's a way that leads into sin, there's also a way out of it. The apostle Paul said that for every temptation we face, God provides a way of escape (1 Corinthians 10:13). There's a secret door leading away from every sin; we just have to ask him to show us where it is. And because our enemy is not so creative (he only has a comparatively small handful of tricks), the temptations we face are common among us—whatever we're facing, there's someone else who's been there too. And sometimes, if we can find an escapee, that person can help us to freedom.

The ultimate death to sin, though, is light. Bringing our sin out into the open is like bringing a lit match to a bucket of lighter fluid. It may be rapid, explosive, and painful; but it's fast. You may only need to confess to God and one other person before you start to feel the incredible relief that comes from freedom from sin. If your sin has affected a group (your family, church, a community), then you may need to confess publicly before a larger number of people. James 5:16 makes it clear that confessing our sins to each other is part of God's design for his people, in part so we can pray for each other, and also because there's something about naming a sin aloud that makes it more real to us in addition to providing a measure of accountability going forward.

Even after you confess your sin to both God and others, and you're free from it, you may still face consequences. Sin, even forgiven sin, drags consequences along with it. (It's God's mercy that we don't always face sin's full effects, like we deserve.) But you'll face those consequences as a free person.

This is what Jesus bought for you—freedom from sin and a room in his house. When the Bible says you're no longer a slave to sin (Romans 6:18; 8:2), it's not some vague idea. You are *not* a slave to sin. You may have made yourself a hostage in that old master's house, but he doesn't own you. There's a way out, and you should ask God to help you find it as fast as you can, because the house being prepared for you is worth any lesser pleasure and sin that we have to give up (Psalm 84:10; John 14:1-4; 1 Corinthians 2:9).

Practice Tip: Confession

Everyone sins. When we do sin and become conscious of it, it's important to confess our sin to God right away, not try to conceal or justify it. The following Scriptures are good guides in how to confess our sins to God. While (or after) you read them, ask the Spirit to search your heart and reveal any areas of unconfessed sin. After you acknowledge these to the Lord, then *thank* him for his forgiveness! Thank him for loving you even when you were still a sinner. Ask him to help you treasure him above everything, and to seek and enjoy the greater, eternal pleasures he offers above the fleeting pleasure sin brings.

- This is the one You esteem: He who is humble and contrite of spirit, and who trembles at Your word. (Isaiah 66:2)

- The sacrifices of God are a broken spirit; a broken and contrite heart, O God, You will not despise. (Psalm 51:17)

- If I confess my sins, He is faithful and just and will forgive me my sins and purify me from all unrighteousness. (1 John 1:9, adapted from NASB)[4]

The Daily Fight

Oswald Chambers observes, "Our battles are first won or lost in the secret places of our will in God's presence, never in full view of the world."[5]

Resisting temptation is an ongoing, daily (sometimes minute-by-minute or hour-by-hour) process. We'll fail if our goal is to conquer sin once and for all at a single point in time. And we'll fail if we don't ask God's help. To fight sin, we have to surrender to God *this moment*. People who view sin this way usually find that when they resist once, resisting gets easier. That's our God-given neuroplasticity at work! By the same token, repeated consent to sinful thoughts makes temptation harder and harder to resist. Here's how Proverbs 6 illustrates the progression:

How long will you lie there, you sluggard?
    When will you get up from your sleep? [the sin is sloth
        or laziness]
A little sleep, a little slumber, [the pattern forms, little by little]
    a little folding of the hands to rest—
and poverty will come on you like a thief [laziness has
        consequences]
and scarcity like an armed man. (Proverbs 6:9-11)

Sinful patterns in our lives don't happen overnight; they're the culmination of many sins we've committed over and over (usually the ones we thought were small). If you wake up one day and wonder, *How did I get here?* the answer is that you surrendered to the enemy, one square inch of territory at a time. "So, by inches and minutes," the opportunity to resist temptation disappears, "a little, a little, a little," and before you know it, you've succumbed.[6] Once a sin becomes an entrenched habit, it can only be undone through confession and repentance, with accountability and training that teach us to replace bad habits and thoughts with good, God-honoring ones.

Scottish theologian Thomas Chalmers said an old sin habit is only driven away by "the expulsive power of a new affection." He wrote about two hundred years ago, so the language sounds a little different to us, but the way he describes this expulsion of sin by replacing it with a new love is excellent:

The world is the all of a natural man. . . . He loves nothing
    above it, and he cares for nothing beyond it; and to bid him

love not the world, is to pass a sentence of expulsion on all the inmates of his bosom. To estimate the magnitude and the difficulty of such a surrender, let us only think that it were just as arduous to prevail on him not to love wealth, . . . as to prevail on him to set wilful fire to his own property. This he might do with sore and painful reluctance, if he saw that the salvation of his life hung upon it. But this he would do willingly, if he saw that a new property of tenfold value was instantly to emerge from the wreck of the old one.[7]

If we don't treasure God's presence, we won't see the *need* to rid ourselves of sin. But if we *have* tasted what life is like when we walk closely with him, we'll give up anything else, because we'll know *he is worth it*. (Jesus talked about this; see Matthew 13:44-46.) When we grasp the sweetness of life in his presence, we'll not only be able to throw off sin with more ease, but we'll view sin more like God does—*hating it*—because it stands in the way of the thing we want most: fellowship with him.

Life in God's Presence

Failing to resist temptation and indulging in sin doesn't cause us to lose our salvation, but it *does* cost us intimacy with God. We regain that intimacy by running to him, right in the middle of the sin or temptation, and asking him to help us expel it from our lives. We don't need to clean up our act *before* we run to him; we can't do that anyway! But we do have to *want* to see the sin gone from our lives. We have to *want* to want him more than anything.

The Bible says Christ died for us even while we were still sinners (Romans 5:6, 8). It says he knows we're weak on our own (Psalm 103:14; Matthew 26:41). But even while our sin distances us from him, he's still there to be our strength. Though intimacy might be lost or diminished for a time, and although he may discipline us (Hebrews 12:11), he still loves us and is rooting for us to exchange the love of sin for a love for him.

Sin is the result of a disordered love. We want some good thing, but we want it more than we want God, and we give it his place. Whether it's a distorted desire for beauty, intimacy, love, or some material thing, these are only temporarily alluring; their satisfaction doesn't last! What does last is the new life we've been given, life in the presence of the One who is full of joy and holds all the pleasures of eternity in his right hand (Psalm 16:11). The best way to remember this is by frequently reminding ourselves (and each other) of what Scripture says about this eminently *good* and abundant life we have in him: "The thief comes only to steal and kill and destroy; I have come that they may have life, and have it to the full" (John 10:10).

Listen to God in His Word

Read the following verses:

- Psalm 36:8
- 2 Corinthians 2:9
- Hebrews 3:12-13

As you read, think about how you've fought sin in your life before, and how you're fighting it now. Do you believe that sin is the enemy's ploy to "steal and kill and destroy" the abundant life God wants to give you in his presence, or have you been captivated by the fleeting pleasure sin offers? Focus on all that he offers you in Christ first; then, go back to the parts of this chapter that you need to review to help you recognize temptations in your own life. Confess. Submit to God. And then, take up his "armor . . . so that you can take your stand against the devil's schemes" (Ephesians 6:11).

Practice His Presence
Monitor Temptations as They Arise

If we want to avoid distancing ourselves from God and becoming hardened by the lies the tempter tells us, it's important to monitor temptations as they arise and surround ourselves with people who will encourage us to value our relationship with God. Temptations come with an appeal to one of three lusts, according to 1 John 2:16: the lust of the flesh (e.g., sexual sins, physical violence, gossip, substance abuse, or gluttony), the lust of the eyes (coveting or envying), or the pride of life (e.g., a hunger for power for our own ego's sake or bragging rights, wanting credit/glory for something others did, desiring to be held in high esteem, or an obsessive desire to feel valued or more important than others around us). Here's a way you can be alert and submit to God every time you encounter temptation:

1. Identify the root source of the sin (where's it coming from?).

2. Look at 1 John 2:16 and name the category of temptation.

3. Find a way to focus on Jesus. We don't overcome sin by trying to avoid it. We do it by training our focus on Jesus. (Ask yourself: *What does Jesus offer that is lasting and better than the sin that is before me?*)

Remaining in Community

Once you were not a people,
but now you are the people of God.

1 PETER 2:10

"One of the worst things sin did . . . was to make [people] selfish," Andrew Murray said.[1] Christ enabled us to turn from our selfishness and love again. More than that, he came and *showed* us how, by setting the prime example of love: "A new command I give you: Love one another. *As I have loved you,* so you must love one another. By this everyone will know that you are my disciples, if you love one another" (John 13:34-35, emphasis added).

God knows we're relational beings; he made us that way. He wants us to live in his presence not only as individuals (although we have to do that too), but together, as a community. We're not just a bunch of self-contained "temples" of the Holy Spirit, but also *one body* of believers, living *together* in his presence (as we will for all eternity).

There are many clues in Scripture about the importance of community, but one we might not always think about, pointed out by

Charles Colson in his book *The Body*, is the scene with Peter, Jesus, and the disciples in Matthew 16. By this point they, and many others, have seen Jesus do many miraculous things—from feeding huge crowds with a tiny handful of fish and bread to walking on water and healing—as well as teach with amazing authority. There are rumors. Who *is* this man? Some think he's a prophet come back from the dead. When Jesus presses his disciples on who *they* think he is, Peter makes his bold declaration: "You are the Messiah, the Son of the Living God." To this, Jesus answers, "Blessed are you, Simon son of Jonah, for this was not revealed to you by flesh and blood, but by my Father in heaven. And I tell you that you are Peter, and on this rock I will build my church, and the gates of Hades [hell] will not overcome it" (Matthew 16:17-18).

We need to pay attention to Jesus' response, Colson pointed out, because it's a telling sign about what happens when we come to faith in Christ:

> When Peter made his confession, Jesus did not say, "Good, Peter. You are now saved and will have an abundant life. Be at peace." Instead, He announced the church and established a divinely ordained pattern. When we confess Christ, God's response is to bring us into His church; we become part of His called-out people. . . . And our commitment to the church is indistinguishable from our commitment to Him.[2]

Do Colson's words surprise you, maybe even make you a little uneasy? It's likely they do if you've had a bad experience with church, or if you grew up in the West, where the spirit of self-reliance and individualism is so strong.

The idea that we're committed to a bunch of people (most of whom we don't know) does sound a little scary, I have to admit. But here's the thing, and it's the point Jesus was making to Peter:

knowing God—and living in that truth every day—isn't just about "me and Jesus." Yes, faith in Christ is a personal decision that no one else can make for us. But when we decide to trust him, we're becoming part of a family. We're no longer orphans standing out in the cold by ourselves, alienated from God and each other; we're joining a lot of other brothers and sisters who are inside warming themselves in the presence of God and his love. Because of this, our faith *can't* stay in our bedrooms or prayer closets; if it's real, it oozes out—into our lives, into the world.

Living in God's presence is something we do together. Being connected to the family of God isn't just an added benefit; we actually *need* each other to keep living in him! We've seen hints of this already. King David needed the prophet Nathan to pull him out of hiding behind his sin. Andrew needed his family and an accountability partner to help him get rid of his double life. And people who suffer lean on other believers to get through hard trials. (Sometimes, fellow Christians—which means, literally, "little Christs"—are the *only* sense of God's presence we feel when we're walking in a valley of life.)

Relationships are critical. They're the most visible evidences of God's presence and self-sacrificial love in the world. Here's how Larry Crabb puts it:

> When Jesus commands us to love, He is actually issuing an invitation to experience God, *to know His presence by revealing His nature.* . . .
>
> It's His specialty . . . to stir in Jesus' followers our God-given desire and power to put Jesus on display by the way we relate to others. In this life that is our greatest good, the source of our deepest joy: the God-delighting pleasures of knowing Him and making Him known.[3]

It Was Not Good

In the first pages of our Bibles, God tells us some of the most important things we'll ever know. There we learn God is our Creator. We learn about our dependence on him and the dignity he gave us by making us in his image. We also get our first lesson on community: "The LORD God said, 'It is not good for the man to be alone'" (Genesis 2:18).

Sure, the beginning of Genesis is a story about man and woman, but it's also about living with God in community. Trinitarian theology (the idea that God is three persons in one: Father, Son, and Holy Spirit) is the foundation for human anthropology (who we are: the story of humankind). These early words of the Bible tell us that ultimate reality is a personal Being. And this personal God isn't just one person but is himself a community of three coequal, coeternal persons who are fully God, yet not each other. It's a deep and profound mystery about unity and diversity that you won't find in any other world religion. God, at his core, is relationship.

Contrary to what some people believe, God didn't create us because he was lonely. He didn't make us out of a deficit but out of an overflow of deep and glorious love. And because we were made in his image, we're made for community too. God gave the man a partner (woman), and God put them both in a garden where he would come and spend time with them. And for a time, he did: Adam, Eve, and God had perfect, unbroken community.

But it didn't last. Sin came into the world, changing everything. People became alienated from God and each other. The perfect community was broken. But God's plan has always been to bring this separation to an end. Our eternal God will one day bring those who choose him into perfect community with him *and with each other* (Revelation 7:9). Until then, we're the world's best picture of what life in his presence looks like.

That They May Be One

Days before Jesus was tried, falsely convicted, and murdered, he prepared his closest friends and followers—a small group of unschooled, ordinary people—to carry out the most important mission in the world. John 13–17 gives details of what he said to them, including his "new command" to love others as he loved. It was really an old command, but it was new in that they now had a perfect, living example of what true, godly love looks like. And he repeated the command twice, in both John 13 and John 15, which is the Bible's version of bold and italics.

Finally, he prayed this, which would be the key to *how* they'd be able to fulfill his command:

> Holy Father, protect them [my disciples] by the power of your name, the name you gave me, so that they may be one as we are one. . . .
>
> My prayer is not for them alone. I pray also for those who will believe in me through their message. . . . I have given them the glory that you gave me, that they may be one as we are one—I in them and you in me—so that they may be brought to complete unity. (John 17:11, 20, 22-23)

That's a lot of pronouns, but don't miss the profound truth of Jesus' prayer: he was asking the Father to give his disciples unity with himself and with each other. And he was praying the same thing for anyone who would come to believe in him through their message. *That's us.* We're the "they" he was talking about! Jesus was letting his followers, both then and now, know that the close fellowship he enjoys with his Father is available to all of us. And it's meant to be enjoyed *together.* Amazing!

Yet, during the three years of following Jesus, his disciples had never managed to do this. As Andrew Murray said, "All Christ's teaching could not make them of one heart and one soul."[4] But that is exactly the description we read of their community *after* Jesus left earth (Acts 4:32). What changed? The Holy Spirit—God's presence in us—had come to dwell in them, guide them, and bind them together, just as Jesus had promised (John 16:13, 15; Acts 2:1-13).

The reason we love each other is because the Holy Spirit brings God's love and plants it in our hearts. Those of us experiencing or longing for deep relationship with God will naturally be drawn to other people who know him. In the world, people come together because of common interests. But what Christians have is far deeper. We're a *koinonia*, a Greek word that translates to mean a communion of people held together by the glue of Jesus Christ. This is more than a social club and more than a group of people who come together to hang out. Our fellowship is about even more than the church activities we gather to do in common. We're a stuck-together community united by his grace and love. This is a community reflecting the divine community: made up of unique individuals, each different in our functions and gifts (Romans 12:4; 1 Corinthians 12), but forever linked to the worldwide, visible, and invisible body of Christ. And when this spiritual family is loving and serving well, like Jesus did, we become a multifaceted prism refracting the beauty of the One who made us.

What about you: Is there enough evidence in your life to show your faith? Do people see you living in a loving community with people who might not naturally be in your friend groups? The unity and diversity and love in the body of Christ can be strong evidence of God's reality and goodness in a world where unity and love always seem to come with a condition or an angle for manipulation ("I'll scratch your back if you scratch mine"). People in your church might be disassociated along socioeconomic or racial lines, or some other category the world has set. But to you, they are brothers and sisters and friends. We're all one in Christ, and when we give evidence of that by loving fellow believers deeply, we show others there's a higher law than all our natural laws, a law of grace, which says we're loved and forgiven even when we don't deserve it. When people see this, they see God's *shalom*—a deep peace in our lives and in our relationships with one another—that they can't help but wonder about.

When Charles Colson went to jail on Watergate-related charges in 1974, he was a brand-new Christian, just learning what it means to be part of God's family. He'd experienced this deep *koinonia* already through gatherings of politicians who stepped across the political aisle to offer their spiritual support and prayers for their new brother in Christ. But this new identity and community in Christ was put to the test when he, a former aide and close confidante of President Nixon, found himself sharing space with convicted criminals, some for violent felonies and some who'd become believers in Christ. This is the verse that struck him, as he realized that *no* barrier or allegiance on earth overrides a Christian's duty to love fellow believers: "Both the one who makes people holy and those who are made holy are of the same family. So Jesus is not ashamed to call them brothers and sisters" (Hebrews 2:11).

When one of the most influential people in Washington, DC, reached out in love to fellow prison inmates, his witness was a demonstration of the presence of God to a watching world. And when he followed through on a promise to return to help prisoners—spending the rest of his life serving "the least of these"—the love of Christ spread like wildfire. The world couldn't help but notice.

Alone and Together

Dietrich Bonhoeffer warned, "Let him who cannot be alone beware of community. Let him who is not in community beware of being alone."[5] Walking in God's presence and working out our salvation happen on both the personal level *and* the communal level. We need time with God away from the noisy world, but we also need the encouragement, edification, rebuke, correction, and accountability of a body of believers. So many of the things we've discussed—seeing the world in a new way (God's way), battling sin so we can regain intimacy with God, experiencing and rejoicing in him despite suffering—are much easier done with fellow believers in our lives. This is the system God gave us, and to think we can ignore the many parts of the Bible that talk about it is not only astonishing to me but also foolish. It's become popular to say, "I love Jesus; I just don't love his people," or "I just don't like institutionalized religion." But there is a very real sense in which this is impossible, because refusing to love God's people is rejecting what he told us to do.

Americans are entrenched in a culture influenced by people like Ralph Waldo Emerson (author of *Self-Reliance*). Personal practice is great, but offering up our lives to a group of other people in submission and service makes us uncomfortable, to say the least. Self-sufficiency and self-determination pervade our education system and our thinking. Societies that emphasize honoring family and country first have their own problems, but Christians in those cultures often get something more right than many American believers: they understand the deep connectedness and devotion Christians have to the body of Christ as a whole.

The context of community is important for living in God's presence for so many reasons. But here are a few tangible ones.

1. Growth and encouragement. What we learn alone, we share in community. We benefit from hearing what others have learned from their times with God. What we read in the Bible this morning may be very useful to someone else this afternoon. And what a friend studied last night might be exactly what we need to hear this morning. It doesn't *always* work this way. It's more mysterious and less methodical than this. But it happens.

I know of a friend who, a couple of years ago, shared something in passing with another friend. That friend—older and more advanced in age—happened to have been through the exact same trial (a long period of infertility) two decades earlier. She knew the deep heartache it causes and the strain it places on a marriage and other relationships. She also knew how to trust God fiercely through it, surrendering to him each time the pain of barrenness returned. Over the next year, my friend and her husband met with this older couple in a spiritual mentoring relationship. Now, even though the trial isn't over, my friend has been spurred along in her faith in a way that never would've happened if she'd kept her struggle to herself.

Community with other Christians is a primary way God builds us up and encourages us (1 Thessalonians 5:11; Hebrews 3:13; 10:25), and it's a primary way, whether through formal teaching and preaching or in one-on-one relationships, that he helps us see our wrong thinking and ways we need to grow in him.

2. *Accountability.* Remember, sin thrives on secrecy and hiddenness. It's for this reason that community (even just two people meeting or sharing together by phone or email) can be so important to our relationship with God. If we try to fight sin without the accountability and encouragement of other people, it's easy to start sliding back down that slippery slope toward destruction. It's also easy to get discouraged when we fail again.

You might've noticed how tempting it is for us to pull away from fellow believers when we've started down a path that we know will lead us further from God and into sin. We may keep up appearances by attending worship services, but we'll distance ourselves from anyone who'd force a more honest examination of ourselves. According to Proverbs, the wise person heeds a rebuke and is open to correction, because they know it ultimately brings them to a more abundant life (Proverbs 10:17; 15:31). Staying connected to a community of genuine Christian believers can lead us to confront our sins *before* those sins master us.

3. Living the gospel. The everyday context in which we walk with Christ and "work out [our] salvation" (Philippians 2:12) is relationship. Some parts of the Bible can't be lived out if we don't live in community! All the many "one another" commands—love one another, serve one another, forgive one another, bear one another's burdens, encourage one another, pray for one another (and so on)—are essential ways that God calls us to embrace his presence while living in the world. It's why so many of the exercises in this book (and in the companion, "A Guide to Practicing God's Presence") relate not just to sitting and meditating alone, but to taking what he's taught you in secret and making it known, through your words and actions, to others.

Being involved in a community makes us more than we are alone. We're called to encourage, inspire, and hold each other accountable. We can't do these things for ourselves. And while it's possible to believe in Christ in isolation, without the support of fellow believers, it ultimately impoverishes us, causing us to miss a rich level of spiritual engagement and fulfillment that we were meant to have and that the New Testament talks so much about. Keith Anderson and Randy Reese talk about this in their book *Spiritual Mentoring*:

> You can learn to speak a foreign language by sitting alone in a room, reciting grammar and memorizing vocabulary cards, but you will never know the rich taste of the language on your tongue until you hear it spoken by others who love the language and speak it with a fluency rich in the experience of their own lives. The way to nurture our lives of faith most deeply is by spending time with experienced and wise mentors who can help us discover the way, [and] to read stories of the great men and women of faith who preceded us in the body of Christ.[6]

Although we come to faith in Christ individually, and we certainly grow in time spent alone with God, we can't grow to our full potential—and we can't display God's distinguishing mark, his love (as an action, not a feeling)—absent community. Life in Jesus is personal, but it's also shared and collective. It's in community that we prove the seriousness of our personal commitment to Christ (if we'll follow his commands). It's also in the midst of corporate fellowship and worship that the presence of God can be the most real and palpable. Maybe because he promised that "where two or three [or more] gather in my name, there am I with them" (Matthew 18:20).

Practice Tip: Pray for Others

Prayer is perhaps the most underutilized tool of God's people, and yet it's the most effective way that we invite his presence into our lives and the lives of others. Andrew Murray said, "It is only love that can fit us for the work of intercession [prayer for others]."[7] If you find yourself lacking in a passion to pray for others, ask God to help you love them as Jesus did, and your desire to pray for them will follow. Once we're motivated and intend to pray for others, it can still be easy to forget to follow through. Today, make a list of people you want to remember to pray for regularly. Keep the list by your Bible, maybe even using it as a bookmark. It might help if you make three categories of people: (1) family (blood relatives), (2) fellow believers, and (3) nonbelievers. For the last group, pray for salvation in addition to their temporal needs. Thank God for all three groups and then intercede on their behalf for both spiritual and temporal needs. (Hint: You may want to split up the names—a few people per day, for example—so you're not just rushing through a list of names.) Not sure how, or feel like you're in a prayer rut? Consider letting one of Paul's four "life-changing prayers"—from Ephesians 1:17-19; Ephesians 3:16-19; Philippians 1:9-11; and Colossians 1:9-12—guide your prayer, inserting the person's name into the verses as you go to God on their behalf.[8]

Soul Care

If you're active in a local church, you probably experience the community of other believers in small group and large group settings weekly. I myself am involved in teaching four weekly groups (one at my home church) and seven monthly gatherings, which have become their own communities, where we all share and practice the presence of God together. Traditionally, though, there's another kind of relationship that belongs in the life of believers: one-on-one relationships, for the purpose of soul care.

In Hebrews 13:17, soul care is clearly a charge of the elders and deacons of a church: "Obey your leaders and *submit to them, for they keep watch over your souls* as those who will give an account" (NASB, emphasis added). We all need this kind of care from a local church, but the Bible suggests we need even more than that: "Let us consider how we may spur one another on toward love and good deeds, not giving up meeting together, as some are in the habit of doing, but encouraging one another—and all the more as you see the Day approaching" (Hebrews 10:24-25).

From this passage, it's clear that believers not only need to gather together, but we also need the regular encouragement and guidance that comes only through intentional, one-on-one relationships. Throughout history, these kinds of relationships (whether more organic and informal or formal) have helped Christians grow deeper in their walk with God. In one sense, every Christian is charged with this type of ministry—to "watch over one another in love," as John Wesley put it. These kinds of spiritual care and relationships can take various forms. Here are a few of them.

1. Spiritual friendship is the most natural and spontaneous form of personal soul care. This kind of friend is more than a buddy, but someone you have a relationship with that goes beyond the surface level and involves the give and take of unstructured but spiritually infused conversation. These relationships deepen over time as you share experiences with Jesus together. This could be a friend or a close relative, such as a spouse.

There's an old Gaelic term for this kind of relationship: *anam cara*. A "soul friend" or "soulmate," an *anam cara* is someone who cares for you beyond your physical life, whose aim in friendship is to see you through to eternity. I have a friendship like this. My friend (I'll call him Raymond) and I sometimes take spiritual retreats together to a place near where I live, Ignatius House, which is designed especially for spiritual retreats. It's a beautiful setting that includes a trail down to a bench by the Chattahoochee River. On one visit recently, Raymond and I sat on that bench and decided to read through the Gospel of John together. We'd done this before, but because we always read slowly, we didn't usually make it past chapter 3. This time, though, Raymond couldn't start. He spoke the opening words of chapter 1, "In the beginning was the Word," but then he stopped, unable to continue. For about five minutes afterward, neither of us could speak. We sat wordlessly pondering this idea: that before there was time, when there was no energy, no matter, nothing at all, God *was*. And God *is*. It was impossible to wrap our minds around. This was just one of a number of ineffable and profound moments we've shared together. Of course, most of our times together are not nearly that intense. Spiritual friendships are mostly just about walking through life together and encouraging one another in faith.

2. *Spiritual guidance* happens when you're friends with someone who's further along in spiritual maturity than you are. Spiritual guides are people we feel comfortable turning to for advice and direction. They may not be formal relationships. We may not even know them face to face. These relationships could happen over the phone or via email, and they may involve daily or sporadic communication. C. S. Lewis used to carry on lengthy correspondence with people on other continents, teaching them to pray and to understand the faith and the Scriptures (Sheldon Vanauken, author of *A Severe Mercy*, was one of those people).

I consider authors like A. W. Tozer, Blaise Pascal, and St. Augustine to be some of my greatest spiritual guides. Although I never met any of them except through their writings, I feel like I know them personally. Words are strange like that—able to convey the spirit of an eternal soul, so that they keep on living, right there on the page. Much of what these authors taught me had, and continues to have, a great impact on me. As an author and teacher myself, I pray God uses me in this way in the lives of my readers and those who attend my monthly and weekly gatherings, since I know there's not the time for me to deeply invest in more than a handful of people.

3. Spiritual mentoring involves a more formal relationship, one you seek out intentionally. Mentors are also people further along in their walk with Christ. They can expose you to teachings in Scripture as well as spiritual training and practices. They're like coaches and often take joy in seeing you grow. They equip, encourage, and build up. They listen and counsel and help you to know both God and yourself, so you can discern his gifts and calling in your life.

Many of my spiritual mentors, sadly, have passed on. As I enter the prime of my life, I find myself mentoring *others* more, but this helps me grow spiritually too. Here's something I've learned from these relationships: before agreeing to invest time in a new mentee, I try to discern if the person is serious about following and growing in Jesus. Jesus' question, "What do you seek?" is one of the first things I find out about the person. It's hard to help people who don't know what they want, or who can't be persuaded that seeking God is the true key to happiness and meaning in life (even if they're currently seeking it elsewhere). When my mentees follow through on advice or suggestions, I know mentoring them is a worthwhile time investment.

4. Spiritual direction is an ancient art of soul care that has been largely forgotten by today's Christians, although it seems to be making a comeback. These are usually the most formal and one-directional of the four levels of soul-care ministries. Spiritual direction focuses on cultivating prayer, discernment, and practical implementations of spiritual truth. In the early centuries of the church, spiritual direction was associated with desert monks, and it continued with people like Brother Lawrence, whose wisdom and practices were collected in *The Practice of the Presence of God* specifically to aid *other* spiritual directors.

To be effective, spiritual directors should have a combination of knowledge, discernment, and character, including humility and sensitivity to the difference between walking by the Spirit and walking by the flesh. These people must be sought out, and if we're fortunate enough to find one, we should be ready to open up to them honestly about what we think, feel, and desire. A good spiritual director

- asks appropriate questions,
- listens skillfully,
- reveals barriers to growth,
- assists in confession and repentance,
- shows how to listen to God and implement spiritual disciplines,
- rebukes and encourages as necessary, and
- offers presence and compassion.

Spiritual direction is deeply personal and can feel invasive, but it's also one of the most effective ways to make real spiritual progress. All of the exercises and principles of this book are *much* easier to inwardly digest and implement if we have someone alongside us, lovingly and skillfully assisting us, praying for us, and helping us see our own blind spots.

Spiritual directors (and mentors) are a lot like personal athletic trainers. Just as professional athletes hire personal coaches to work with them one-on-one, spiritual directors are for Christians who are *serious* about their growth and are willing to invest the time to meet and to put into practice the direction they receive.

You should be cautious when seeking a spiritual director. This isn't someone just keeping tabs on your tendencies to sin. Spiritual directors spur you on toward love and good works in an intentional way. They're willing to be used as God's instrument of grace, and they truly care about you. When we're too close to ourselves to see things as they really are—through the lens of God—a mentor or director can help correct our vision. Like a good coach, a spiritual director or mentor helps you identify *both* your weaknesses and strengths, and then encourages you to train to overcome your weaknesses while looking for ways to use your God-given gifts.

Spiritual direction or mentoring works best as a two-way street. I typically meet my mentees once a month or several times a year, but more or less often depending on their availability and location. Because I can't read their minds, it's helpful if they come to me with a list of *their* questions. Then I can offer what I've learned that might help them. Sometimes I answer their questions with my own questions, so I can better understand the root issues or find out which questions are worth asking them.

It's important to keep in mind that a good spiritual director, mentor, guide, or friend will *always* point you to Christ and his Word as the ultimate source of wisdom and guidance. When giving advice, direction, encouragement, and support, they do so *not* with a controlling attitude, as though they have all the answers, but in humble submission to God, the ultimate caretaker of our souls.

Practice Tip: Invite Mentorship

Think of one person you know and consider to be a spiritual guide or mentor. If you don't have anyone like that in your life, seek one out, if you're willing and open to it. Invite that person to be your mentor, and if he or she is willing, set a regular appointment time (it could be weekly, monthly, or even quarterly or annually) when you can review your spiritual progress and struggles, and pray together. If you're further along in your own spiritual journey, consider whether there is someone you could mentor. If so, reach out to that person and, if they invite it, set up a regular time to meet.

Real Relationships

An investment in spiritual relationships, whether one-on-one or in a larger community, needs to come from an overflow of our relationship with God. When Christ becomes the source and provision of all of our fundamental needs, then we'll approach people out of the overflow of his life in us rather than out of selfish motives or hidden agendas. God gives us this capacity for true, divine love, which is very different from the world's approach to relationships. Instead of always posturing and comparing, coveting and envying, and wondering what favor someone might hope for in return, we aim to love freely and live as Jesus did, expecting nothing in return.

This kind of community life doesn't happen overnight, and it doesn't happen over a text message. It takes time, and, in our era of digital excess, inertia fights against these kinds of genuine, Christlike relationships. The French philosopher René Descartes said, *Cogito ergo sum* (I think, therefore I am). Today, we're a society being shaped by a practice of sharing *before* thinking. The identity of far too many people is "I share, therefore I am." But deep spiritual relationships aren't formed electronically or virtually. We need real, undistracted, face-to-face time. Electronic communication can serve as a *tool* in these relationships, but it can't substitute for the time we need *in person* to learn and practice things like love and respect, courtesy and civility. If, instead, we spend the bulk of our time fixated and constantly distracted by our screens, we lose something of our humanity, becoming more like conditioned rats hitting certain buttons over and over, for a short moment of positive reinforcement or pleasure. (That shot of pleasure is actually a chemical called dopamine, and our technology can send us into a "dopamine loop" that makes us physically addicted to checking our email or text messages, until we stop the loop by shutting off the ding, or whatever sound we've set, that cues their arrival.)[9]

The field of captology (I probably don't need to point out the root word for you) is devoted to developing technologies that will "motivate and influence" (persuade and addict) users. These technologies depend, partly, on people's FOMO (fear of missing out). They're hard enough for adults to exert self-control over, but children's minds are even more malleable and impressionable. Their brains reprogram quickly, creating new neural pathways that they'll take with them into adulthood. I don't think it's an overstatement to say that their very souls are at stake!

In this crazy, "brave new world," we regularly undervalue one of the most fundamental aspects of our divine image: we are relational beings.[10] We're designed to draw our greatest joy and satisfaction from relationships—first from an ongoing, daily relationship with the personal and living God, and second from relationships with others. All the false forms of connecting are to our spiritual health what vinegar is to our cars' gas tanks. Cars aren't meant to operate on vinegar, not for long anyway, and we weren't made to be enslaved to screens. At some point, like vinegar-fueled cars, we're bound to break down. Already, a few people are catching on to this; for example, David Sax, whose 2016 book *The Revenge of Analog* is tellingly subtitled "Real Things and Why They Matter."[11]

How will the world "know we're Christians by our love" if what we really love isn't Christ at all?[12] We may have to give up some false "relationships" to maintain real relationships in our lives (and in the lives of those we mentor). Within the body of Christ, we have a direct charge to love and serve one another, valuing and honoring others above ourselves (Romans 12:10; Philippians 2:3). Following this charge might require some rewiring in our brains, but the result is worth it. Remaining in community isn't an option for us; Christ has called us to it. We're a holy people, "God's special possession," called to "declare the praises of him who called [us] out of darkness into his wonderful light" (1 Peter 2:9). We do this corporately, as well as individually, to those he's placed in our lives, one person, one opportunity, at a time:

> We cannot keep the love of God to ourselves. It spills over. . . .
>
> But in our love of people are we to be excitedly hurried, sweeping all men and tasks into our loving concern? No, that is God's function. But He, working within us, portions out His vast concern into bundles, and lays on each of us our portion.[13]

Listen to God in His Word

Read Romans 15:1-7 a couple of times. Then reflect on these two questions: (1) Based on the Romans passage *and* what you read in this chapter, what does unity in the body of Christ—being of "one mind and one voice" (v. 6)—have to do with practicing God's presence? (2) What's one thing you can do to *be* Christ to others by treating them in the way Romans 15 talks about? (If you're not sure, home in on verses 2 and 7, and think about either a believer you know who's struggling or a person you've always found difficult to accept or get along with.)

Practice His Presence
Every Encounter

Keeping an eternal perspective means seeing every person you meet through the lens of God's grace, realizing we never meet someone at random or by accident. God can magnify a small deed or word to large effect in another's life. Starting today, seek to respond to God's initiatives in your everyday encounters. For each person you meet,

- Assume God is working in that person, somehow.

- Ask yourself, *Is there some way I can share the love or presence of Christ with this person?*

If this feels too overwhelming, try this exercise with a certain category of people, for example family members, colleagues at work, those who serve you (e.g., waiters, cashiers, salespeople, mail carriers), or anyone you meet for the first time.

Reimagining Life

All their life in this world and all their adventures in Narnia
had only been the cover and the title page: now at last
they were beginning Chapter One of the Great Story,
which no one on earth has read: which goes on for ever:
in which every chapter is better than the one before.

C. S. LEWIS, *THE LAST BATTLE*

Christians live within the context of a great story,
a story much bigger than ourselves, with a plot that we know
begins and ends well, even better than well, in *eternal perfection*!
But many of us don't yet feel or look like people living that kind
of amazing story. The words *eternal perfection* don't sound exciting to us, but rather dull. This is a deficit in *our* imagination,
not in eternity itself. Scripture is clear that none of us can fully
fathom the place God is preparing for us, how great it really is.
And most of us don't try very hard to imagine it either.

But if we can't imagine even a little of what eternal life in God's
presence will be like, then how will we be motivated to live *today*
in his presence? Why would we persevere in suffering and in

spiritual training if the end result doesn't interest us all that much? To deny earthly pleasures now, we need to believe that the eternal pleasures at God's right hand are more satisfying than anything else. For this, we need our imaginations.

C. S. Lewis wrote, "For me, reason is the natural organ of truth, but imagination is the organ of meaning."[1] Imagination played an important role in Lewis's conversion. His words about his view before he came to Christ are telling: "Nearly all that I loved I believed to be imaginary; nearly all that I believed to be real I thought grim and meaningless."[2]

The question arises again: if we believe heaven to be real but monotonous, and if we love things in our lives now but know they won't last, how will we be motivated to pursue God in our daily living? I think many of us fail to see heaven as a place where we'll be always growing, both cognitively and relationally, and in our capacities for beauty, goodness, and truth. We don't think about heaven as a place where we'll enjoy endless creative activity, according to our unique personalities, without frustration, and to the glory of God. Eternity won't be disconnected from what happens on earth (as C. S. Lewis observed in *The Last Battle*), but far better and beyond it.

How do we catch this vision? We need more than training for our minds. We need to train our imaginations. When we do, it'll fuel a hunger not only for godliness in heaven, but for godliness here on earth. And a hunger for godliness is always filled, Jesus said (Matthew 5:6). We'll be able to see ourselves in a story in which every chapter is better than the one before, because more of God's presence is in each one.

Being Versus Becoming

C. S. Lewis walked in the same circles as another author famous for his emphasis on the imagination: J. R. R. Tolkien. In the third of *The Lord of the Rings* movie trilogy (based on Tolkien's books and directed by Peter Jackson), *The Return of the King*, there's a particularly powerful scene. Earlier in the story we meet Aragorn when he's known by another name, Strider, a ranger from the north, a nobody. His true identity is veiled. The truth is that he is the rightful king of the great realm of Gondor. In this moving scene, the mighty ruler Elrond gives Aragorn a commission and a warning. Aragorn will face Sauron (the Dark Lord of Mordor) in battle. Elrond tells Aragorn that he'll be outnumbered and will need to rally more troops. But the only other men available to fight are the kind of people who answer to no one, Aragorn says. They will answer to the king, Elrond tells him. Elrond pulls out a sword called Andúril, Flame of the West, reforged from the remains of an old sword from Aragorn's family line. Elrond hands Aragorn the sword, and says: "Put aside the ranger. Become who you were born to be." Aragorn was born to be king, but he was going to have to fight for it. He now had in his hand everything he needed to do so. It was up to Aragorn to become who he was born to be, to live for the greater purpose and with a greater certainty of his calling.[3]

When you discover who *you're* created to be, you have to put aside your false self, your false identity. Casting aside those lies and false stories made up about you, you can, by the grace of God, become the son or daughter of the living God that you were born to be. You're meant to rule and reign with Christ. You're an heir of your heavenly Father, a co-heir with Christ. You've been adopted into and now belong to the household of God! No longer under condemnation because of sin (Romans 8:1), you're a beloved child of God because of Jesus. You are *his*! These facts need to shape your view of yourself and inform your hope of the future, so they can lead you to become who you were meant to be.

Paul talked a lot about who we are in Christ—our new nature and identity—and who we're becoming. We were dead. Now, we have to count ourselves alive to God in Christ Jesus (Romans 6:11). We're no longer identified with our sin nature; that's not the deepest us anymore. God has given us a heart transplant. We're "new creations," Paul said: "The old has gone, the new is here!" (2 Corinthians 5:17). We start counting ourselves dead to sin and alive to God by making adjustments, realigning our minds with God's thinking about who we really are, and reimagining our lives in light of what God's Word says is now true about us.

At the same time, we'll still struggle, because our outer selves aren't yet in complete conformity with our new inner selves. We may know our *being* has changed, but our *doing* seems to tell a different story. That's because we're still *becoming*. In fact, when we first begin drawing near to God and training in godliness, it sometimes only increases our awareness of this discrepancy between the person we're called to be and the way we see ourselves behaving. Everyone wrestles with this at some point, as God reveals the true ugliness of our sin, including things like pride and selfishness, which we never noticed much, if at all, before.

In Romans 7, Paul explained the predicament well, and his words resonate with the experience of many (if not all) of us: "I find this law at work: Although I want to do good, evil is right there with me. For in my inner being I delight in God's law; but I see another law at work in me, waging war against the law of my mind and making me a prisoner of the law of sin at work within me" (Romans 7:21-23).

Romans 8 tells us how to solve the problem. The solution is that we learn to live by the power of God's Spirit instead of by our own strength. Even the apostle Paul couldn't live as he was supposed to live; why should you think you can? When you throw up your hands and say, "I can't do this. I can't live the way God wants me to live," you're in a better position than you might think, because this great realization is the start of learning to depend on the power of God's Holy Spirit instead of trusting yourself.

We don't save ourselves. We say we believe this, but until we reach the point where we throw up our hands and scream, "God, I can't do it!" we are still trying (instead of training). God works in us and through us. He's implanted the Holy Spirit inside us to provide all the power we need to live as we are called to live. But until we learn to rely on that power instead of our own, we'll find walking with God difficult and wearying, instead of lightweight and freeing.

When we become new *beings* in Christ, we are also *becomers* in him. Gradually, through the Spirit's work in us, we're *becoming* who we already are. Like Aragorn, we're in the process of throwing off our false selves and awakening to the person we were always meant to be. This process happens from the inside out. We can't work our new identity into ourselves; that would mean we're working *for* our salvation (which Jesus already paid for). We can only work *out* the identity and the salvation that God has already worked in us (Philippians 2:12-13). As I've said from the beginning of this book, this dynamic process never ends as long as we're on this earth. We're never finished with learning how to walk with God. We're never done learning who he is and who we are in him. It's always "further up and further in," in a growth process that continues into eternity.[4]

Attitude Check

As our mindset and imagination shift, and our identity comes into sharper focus, there's one attitude we need more than any other: humility. Our humble Savior told us about having this same attitude: "So you also, when you have done everything you were told to do, should say, 'We are unworthy servants; we have only done our duty'" (Luke 17:10).

We can't walk in God's presence and live in light of eternity for any other reason besides God himself. We walk in his presence because it's who we're called to be. In many cases, we'll be rewarded in small, earthly ways for our faithfulness, but he never promises these kinds of rewards. The *great* rewards come in intangible forms, and we won't know the *greatest* rewards while on this earth.

One of the most challenging spiritual disciplines is secrecy; that is, doing something good and intentionally *not* telling others about it. This discipline is difficult in a time when everyone posts or tweets about almost everything they do. But secrecy isn't impossible, and it helps us check our motives. Who is our audience? Who are we living for? God must be our sole audience. Everything we have is a gift from him and his grace to us. If we understand this, it won't matter when our good works aren't seen by anyone else, and we won't be as tempted to boast about what we have.

Most of the impact we have on this world will be hidden from us. It's better that way, because if we got immediate, external feedback for every good thing we did, we would too easily live for people's praise. Instead, we walk with him only for the sake of our relationship with him and not for anything else. Most truly spiritual people are also humble. We only see the depth of their spirituality in how they authentically love other people.

Our Eternal Destiny

Our faith is only as good as the object in which it's placed. People of all different levels of faith will enter heaven. The determining factor isn't the level or depth of faith but the object of it. Our faith is either in Christ, or it's not.

Say two people hop on a plane. One is an experienced traveler, and the other has never flown. The woman who flies every month hardly notices when the plane takes off. She has complete confidence in the plane and the pilot. But our first-time traveler is terrified. He asks about the pilot's credentials and then spends the rest of the flight with white knuckles, wondering if he's about to go careening into the ocean. But at the end of the trip, both passengers—one terrified and the other at peace—arrive safely. Whether we have a little faith or a lot isn't nearly as important as the object of our faith. As long as we're trusting in the right Person, we'll still get to the same destination. It's still good to grow in our faith, but when we do, the greatness is really about *him*, not us. Even faith, the Bible says, is a gift from him (Ephesians 2:8)!

People who don't choose to seek Christ on earth are headed to an eternity without him. If we do nothing, the Bible says there's a "second death" (Revelation 2:11; 21:8). They were dead spiritually on earth and their flesh will die too. The second death is eternal. Yet, in spite of this terrible desolation in the human spirit, God has given us a way out of that default destination. If we allow him, he places us in a new family line, the line of Jesus. As a result, we're rerouted to a new and glorious destination, a Christ-filled eternity.

Our destiny determines where we fit within God's larger story. Our physical life is only a temporary setting for our individual part in this greater story. When we think of eternal life, we have to imagine that it's not something up there, or far off, for later; it's an enduring quality of life that begins as soon as we first trust Christ. This new life lasts forever, and Jesus defined it as "knowing him" (John 17:3). Walking with God in the mundane details of our earthly lives *is our first act in eternal life with him*. How many of us see our lives that way? It takes some imagination, but we can, and when we do, even our everyday tasks and encounters become significant.

In some mysterious way, Jesus' death becomes our death, his life becomes our life, his resurrection our resurrection, and his ascension our ascension. While we're waiting for Christ to come again to make *all things* new, this new life is already a reality: "God raised us up with Christ and seated us with him in the heavenly realms in Christ Jesus, in order that in the coming ages he might show the incomparable riches of his grace, expressed in his kindness to us in Christ Jesus" (Ephesians 2:6-7).

Even if we don't wake up in the morning *feeling* like we're seated in the heavenly realms, the Scripture says we are! This kind of truth has to begin to shape our imagination of what life *is* and *will be*. If we search the Bible a little more like we're digging for hidden treasure (Proverbs 2:4), we'll start to dwell a lot more on how amazing our future is, though our imaginations will never be big enough to contain its wonder (1 Corinthians 2:9). The result of focusing our thinking and imaginations on these truths is powerful. It's the secret to how ordinary life for regular people—whether you're Brother Lawrence living in a French monastery in the 1600s or a young homemaker fighting cancer in Colorado (like Kara Tippetts)—gets transformed into extraordinary life. *This* is the kind of abundant life Jesus died to give us. *This* is the supernatural-infused life I hope you're learning to live!

Reimagining the Good Life

If you have a hard time imagining all of this for yourself, you're not alone. Most people, even many followers of Christ, I think, have anemic imaginations. Our world is full of imagination killers—television and the Internet being chief culprits in today's world. Most of us let the news media tell us what's important, and our days get filled with soundbites they've chosen for us, without us even thinking about the fact that maybe some of the most important things that happen each day never make it into the news, much less the front-page headlines.

Many of us need to work on developing (or at least focusing) our imagination. Besides the Bible, other books (good ones, which sadly means mostly older ones), films, nature, and relationships (real ones!) are some of the ways we can do this. However we do it, God's Word is not only our primary inspiration but also our measuring stick, and his Spirit helps us discern good and evil, so we can "take the gold and eschew the gravel," so to speak. When we challenge our minds and hearts in this way, our aspirations and longings will change and expand. The deepest desires of our hearts will be elevated, and we'll be less likely to settle for the cheap substitutes of the temporal world. We'll realize there are deep desires in us that can't be fulfilled on earth, and these point us to the next one, where God will fulfill us *completely*.

We become conformed to whatever we aspire to and long for, so the person we become will have everything to do with the destiny we're able to imagine (with God's help). And let me submit to you that most of us living in twenty-first-century America need to reimagine what the good life, the fruitful and flourishing life, really looks like for those who belong to God's kingdom.

Preparing for Eternity

Suppose you just made plans to visit another country, not merely for a weeklong tour but for a year or two. You need more than a few phrases and a pocket dictionary. You need to learn the language with fluency, and you need to be familiar with that country's culture and customs.

We too are headed for another place—a better country, a heavenly one. What do we need to do to prepare? We need to envision what life might be like when we're with God forever. When we do, it helps us train more wisely (like we've been learning to do in this book), so that when we go through that second birth canal called death, we'll hear him say to us, "Well done, good and faithful servant!" (Matthew 25:21).

Thomas Kelly warned that we shouldn't put off this preparation until some future time when circumstances seem more dire. Here are his words, which, interestingly, he wrote before dying suddenly of a heart attack:

Don't be deceived. *You* must face Destiny. Preparation is only possible now. Don't be fooled by your sunny skies. When the rains descend and the floods come and the winds blow and beat upon *your* house, your private dwelling, your own family, your own fair hopes, your own strong muscles, your own body, your own soul itself, then it is well-nigh too late to build a house. You can only go inside what house you have and pray that it is founded upon the Rock. Be not deceived by distance in time or space, or the false security of a bank account and an automobile and good health and willing hands to work. . . . Be not fooled by the pleasantness of the Main Line life . . . and the quiet coolness of your well-furnished homes. For the plagues of Egypt are upon the world, entering hovel and palace, and there is no escape for you or for me.[5]

When we stand before God at judgment, the hourglass will have emptied. No time will be left. Now is the time to prepare and draw near to him; *today* is the day of salvation (2 Corinthians 6:2).

Practice Tip: Living in Light of "Well Done"

When we're before the judgment seat of Christ, the best words we can hope to hear are, "Well done, good and faithful servant" (Matthew 25:21), while the most terrifying words will be, "I never knew you. Away from me" (Matthew 7:23). Are you living each day in light of the former words: "Well done"? Seek to do so each day. Think of a creative way to remind yourself to live in this way (or maybe it's just a note or picture on the fridge), so that you live each day with the sole purpose of pleasing and honoring him (not other people or even yourself).

His Story, Our Story

In 2005, I made a DVD called *The Decline of Nations: The Roman Empire and the United States*. In it, I examined ten characteristics of Rome before its demise (entertainment and media, government debt, etc.) and compared them with the United States. I shudder to think about how much further America has declined since I made the video. I said at the end of that presentation that I believed we were past the tipping point. I can say with confidence now that we *are*. But I'm not wringing my hands in fear or despair. Christians everywhere talk about the terrible condition and direction of the United States—and the whole world, for that matter. It's not that I don't agree. But I also think we listen to the media's narrative far too much and allow it to shape our view and attitudes about the world. We listen to what they craft to intentionally alarm and shock us. In the process, we forget we're part of a greater story, which has an indescribably good ending and continues forever.

To live well in the current times, we have to embed our little stories in God's. Doing this helps us know that even the greatest difficulties, pains, and mess-ups on our part can't thwart the ending that he's already written. Through training and trust, we can adopt this transcendent narrative and live it out in our present world, in this present darkness. We do this as agents sent from another world to this world. We're agents of God's *shalom*—the Hebrew word for peace that encompasses the ideas of harmony and rhythm in our relationships with God and his people. Far more than a superficial peace, *shalom* is an inner rest and wholeness brought to bear on this passing world. This *shalom* is why we can look at the world today, compare it to the patterns of nations in Scripture and to what God says happens to a people who grow prosperous and comfortable but forget him, and *still* not throw up our hands. We do what we can to call others back to him, but we do so knowing our hope is transferred; and the troubles of this world, from an eternal perspective, can't hurt us or take away our inner peace.

If we look across national borders, we'll see much good *is* taking place. God *is* at work, doing things the media will never report. In the past few decades, the Spirit of God has been moving remarkably through people in Asia, Africa, and South America. For all the turmoil in the headlines about the Middle East, did you know that Christianity is growing the fastest in terms of per capita growth in the country of Iran? China too has seen tremendous growth of the church in spite of tightening government oversight and persecution. In fact, Chinese believers are now sending missionaries to America, and many of them have a wonderful vision to take the gospel back to Jerusalem along the Silk Road.

God isn't absent. He's present everywhere, if we'll only open our eyes to it. There's tremendous excitement and fervor in the worldwide body of Christ. In many cases the church is most vibrant where it's more difficult to be a Christian. Of course, history teaches us that this pattern is not uncommon; the gospel often spreads amid severe persecution. Christians know our lives are hidden with Christ (Colossians 3:3) and that there's nothing to fear (Matthew 10:28) because we know God *will* prevail in the end. This frees us up to stay focused on a kingdom that is to come, even if our earthly one is in decline or full of injustice.

Living Out of the Depths

"A man is responsible for his face after he's forty years old" is a proverb credited to Abraham Lincoln. America's sixteenth president wasn't talking about being a good-looking guy. He was talking about the cumulative effect of a life lived either well or poorly. The last photograph of Lincoln before he was assassinated is well known. The picture shows a man of sorrows, of wisdom and integrity, a man whose face immediately tells you he's been through some very real pain. This wasn't a man who lived out of the shallows. He exhibited depth of character.

We too should aim to live out of the depths rather than the shallows. To do this, we have to sink our roots deep into the soil of God's Word and love. In this way, our root system can grow deeply and profoundly, though the growth will be largely invisible to others.

Training is an important aspect of this deeper life. As I was completing the manuscript for this book, I picked up Rod Dreher's latest, *The Benedict Option*. His insights convince me I'm not alone in believing that we, as Christians, need to develop a more coherent strategy in how we approach our lives, our work, and our time so we're less likely to be swept away in the strong current of today's post-Christian culture (and not only in America, as Rod's book focuses on, but worldwide). This doesn't mean we seclude ourselves and hunker down, but we're naive to think we can adopt many of the same life practices as the nonbelieving world and still, somehow, maintain our identity as God's set-apart people. Rod is right to point us to the ancient church, specifically the Benedictine monks, who found "true liberty by submitting to a rule of life, which is to say by ordering themselves to God in a structured way." When we do this, he explains, we develop "the cognitive control that leads to a more contemplative Christian life"—the "key to living as free men and women in post-Christian America," and not as captives to the culture.[6]

The kind of living Rod is talking about is not unlike the kind I've been proposing in this book. It's a life that contrasts starkly with today's image-obsessed society, where impressions are more important than character, and people move through their lives more like machines (controlled by our devices) than free humans.[7] The trouble with social media is that it can't show our character— who we are when we aren't taking our own picture. If we dedicate too much time to an online profile, we risk becoming all show and little substance. And people without substance, without deep inner roots, will be toppled when the wind comes. We'll reach the end of our lives with nothing eternal to show for them. The most important part of the building is the foundation, the part few ever see. The part of us that will keep us standing when we're shaken is our foundation too: who we are in Christ, according to God's Word.

When we live out of the depths of a life immersed in God's presence, we can weather all kinds of storms. We'll be like the giant live oaks of New Orleans, with root systems so rich and vast that they withstood the devastation of Hurricane Katrina. Psalm 1 talks about trees like these, and the people who are like them:

That person is like a tree planted by streams of water,
    which yields its fruit in season
and whose leaf does not wither—
    whatever they do prospers. (Psalm 1:3)

Catching His Vision

Our foundation—our identity in Christ—is about much more than our careers, our families, our homes, and any other circumstances in our lives. Those things are only the context of how we live out the calling he's given us. Acts 17 says God "made from one man every nation of mankind to live on all the face of the earth, *having determined their appointed times and the boundaries of their habitation*" (Acts 17:26 NASB, emphasis added). You belong to heaven, but you're here on earth for a reason. There's something God has for you to do, and no other person has the combination of talents, experience, and context that you have. No one else will do exactly what you're called to do; no one else can. That should give you a strong sense of responsibility and stewardship.

All of us want our lives to matter in some ultimate way. The truth is that they do, even if we don't see the whole picture yet. We all want to leave a legacy, and we all will. But we'll only know that calling and be able to live it out if we *know God* and we're walking with him. Those of us who want to find our calling, leave a legacy of Christ-likeness, and live in an eternal story will prioritize knowing God above everything else. *That* will be the most important thing we build our daily agendas around, instead of getting sidetracked by secondary goals (even very good secondary goals).

So many people give testimonies in church about how they came to Christ. But I rarely hear one about how a man found his calling or how the quiet woman you never notice at church seeks God every single day. Twenty, thirty, and forty years later, people are still talking about how they came to faith as if there's nothing that happened since. God has *so much more* than that for us! Even for those of us who are older, there is a final movement God wants to play out in our lives. We are still *new creations* in Christ, looking forward to the great consummation day when he returns and everything is fulfilled in him.

To live and finish well, we *must* view and live our lives differently than most of us have been doing. We've got to realize we're called to a better good, a better love, and a better hope than this world can offer. Instead of living with divided hearts that are constantly pulled in two directions—the world and God—we need to integrate God into every area of our lives (he's there anyway!), training ourselves to live in both this world and God's kingdom simultaneously. Jesus modeled this perfectly, and we can follow his example in moment-by-moment obedience, offering ourselves up to him in small things. These little things add up and deepen our relationship with him.

There's a life waiting for you, a someone you're meant to be. You'll find that life and identity when you seek and find God. You can't find it anywhere else. And it really is possible, if you'll just begin right now, right where you are, believing with Thomas Kelly:

God *can* be found. There *is* a last rock for your souls, a resting place of absolute peace and joy and power and radiance and security. There is a Divine Center into which your life can slip, a new and absolute orientation in God, a Center where you live with Him and out of which you see all of life, through new and radiant vision, tinged with new sorrows and pangs, new joys unspeakable and full of glory.[8]

Listen to God in His Word

Read 2 Corinthians 4:17: "Momentary, light affliction is producing for us an eternal weight of glory far beyond all comparison" (NASB). What do you think it means that God's glory is weighty or heavy? Do you live in light of this destiny?

Practice His Presence
The Good Life/VIM Model

Author Dallas Willard devised the VIM model (Vision, Intention, and Means), which can help us imagine the good life as God intended it (see tables 12.1 and 12.2).[9] It looks technical, but it can spur you to the spiritual. Make some notes in a journal or notebook about your thoughts for each of these areas. Set a calendar reminder to revisit your vision a year from now.

Table 12.1. Dallas Willard's VIM model

Vision	Intention	Means
What is your vision for the fruitful, flourishing life? *What do you want more than anything else? What do you seek?* With words or images, paint a picture of that life. Make sure you're embedding your story into God's larger narrative and plan for his creation.	*What is the price tag* for the vision you articulated (i.e., what will you have to give up, and what new practices will you need to take up to see it to fruition)?	*What practices will empower you to achieve your intention?* Training involves habituation through practice. What specific disciplines will move you toward the fulfillment of your vision?

Table 12.2. VIM sample using a trivial example

Vision	Intention	Means
I want to visit Italy next summer.	I should learn some Italian so I can communicate and get around while I'm there. I will need to spend time and money to do this.	• 2-3 hours per week for study and practice • Rosetta Stone subscription: $180

Online Training Guide

For additional practices, exercises, and resources, see the companion "A Guide to Practicing God's Presence" available online at ivpress.com/life-in-the-presence-of-god and kenboa.org.

Acknowledgments

I want to express my profound gratitude to Jenny Abel for her excellent work in shaping my presentations on life in the presence of God into the chapters of this book. Jenny also assisted with the development of "A Guide to Practicing God's Presence," a training guide that will enhance this experience.

Jill Foley Turner was also of great assistance in her editorial work on the manuscript, and I am thankful for her insights and enhancements.

Notes

Introduction

[1] Kenneth Boa, *Rewriting Your Broken Story* (Downers Grove, IL: InterVarsity Press, 2016).

[2] Brother Lawrence, *The Practice of the Presence of God with Spiritual Maxims* (Grand Rapids: Spire, 2007), 32.

[3] Ibid., 36.

[4] Ibid., 11.

[5] Hannah Whitall Smith, *The Christian's Secret of a Happy Life* (Boston: Willard Tract Repository, 1885), 260. The rest of the quote reads as follows: "while internal anguish cannot find happiness in the most favorable surroundings."

[6] Watchman Nee, in the preface to *What Shall This Man Do?* (Fort Washington, PA: CLC Publications, 2012), n.p.

Chapter 1: The Secret

[1] C. S. Lewis, *Surprised by Joy* (New York: Harcourt Brace, 1955), 15.

[2] Tyler O'Neil, "New Spiritual Biography of C.S. Lewis Focuses on How Atheist Loner Changed to Joyful Christian," *Christian Post*, August 13, 2013, www.christianpost.com/news/new-spiritual-biography-of-c-s-lewis-focuses-on-how-atheist-loner-changed-to-joyful-christian-103357/#9HLUygT5Loz1rS6x.99.

[3] C. S. Lewis, *The Weight of Glory* (New York: Touchstone, 1996), 26.

[4] C. S. Lewis, *The Joyful Christian* (New York: Touchstone, 1996), 138.

[5] George Herbert, "Vanity (2)," in *George Herbert: The Complete English Poems* (London: Penguin, 2004), 103.

[6] Augustine, *The Confessions of St. Augustine of Hippo*, LeaderU.com, accessed April 11, 2017, www.leaderu.com/cyber/books/augconfessions/bk1.html.

[7] C. S. Lewis, "Christian Apologetics," in *God in the Dock: Essays on Theology and Ethics* (Grand Rapids: Eerdmans, 2000), 101.

[8]Henry Scougal, "Part II: On the Excellency of Religion and Divine Love," in *Life of God in the Soul of Man*, www.ccel.org/ccel/scougal/life.iii.html.

[9]Peter G. Gowing, "The Legacy of Frank Charles Laubach," *International Bulletin of Mission Research*, April 1983, 59, http://journals.sagepub.com /doi/abs/10.1177/239693938300700203.

[10]Frank Laubach, *The Game with Minutes*, included as a supplement in Frank Laubach, *Letters by a Modern Mystic* (Colorado Springs: Purposeful Design, 2007), 92.

[11]Ibid., 20-21.

Chapter 2: The Images

[1]Watchman Nee, *The Normal Christian Life* (Carol Stream, IL: Tyndale House, 1977), 2.

[2]James K. A. Smith, *You Are What You Love: The Spiritual Power of Habit* (Grand Rapids: Brazos, 2016).

[3]Carl Boberg, "How Great Thou Art," 1885.

Chapter 3: The Exemplar

[1]The Greek verb used for "loud voice" implies that Jesus' call was a command with great authority.

[2]Thomas R. Kelly, *A Testament of Devotion* (New York: HarperCollins, 1992), 8.

[3]A. W. Tozer, *The Pursuit of God* (Camp Hill, PA: Christian Publications, 1982), 50-51.

[4]This paraphrased retelling of the calling of Peter is primarily based on Luke 5.

[5]For guidance on and samples of flash prayers, see the prayer exercises in the companion "A Guide to Practicing God's Presence."

[6]Larry Crabb, *A Different Kind of Happiness: Discovering the Joy That Comes from Sacrificial Love* (Grand Rapids: Baker, 2016), 41.

Chapter 4: The Walk

[1]In the Bible, *death* means separation from God, not total annihilation.

Chapter 5: Training

[1]Alec Rowlands, *The Presence* (Carol Stream, IL: Tyndale House, 2014), 99-100.

[2]Dallas Willard, quoted in John Ortberg, *Soul Keeping* (Grand Rapids: Zondervan, 2014), 23.

[3]Thomas R. Kelly, *A Testament of Devotion* (New York: Harper, 1992), 4-5. Note that in the first quote Kelly's phrasing borrows from Meister Eckhart.

[4]Chapter three of John Ortberg's book *The Life You've Always Wanted* (Grand Rapids: Zondervan, 2015) is especially pertinent, and I encourage you to check it out.

[5]Rod Dreher, *How Dante Can Save Your Life* (New York: Regan Arts, 2015), 100.

[6]Frank Laubach, *Letters by a Modern Mystic* (Colorado Springs: Purposeful Design, 2007), 15.

[7]Brother Lawrence, *The Practice of the Presence of God with Spiritual Maxims* (Grand Rapids: Spire, 2007), 31.

[8]Ibid., 18, 22.

[9]Ibid., 16, 45.

[10]Ibid., 26.

[11]Laubach, *Letters by a Modern Mystic*, 32.

[12]Ibid., 8.

[13]Ibid., 19.

[14]Ibid.

[15]Ibid., 36.

[16]Ibid., 14.

[17]Ibid., 90.

[18]Kelly, *Testament of Devotion*, 33.

[19]Ibid., 12.

[20]Richard J. Foster, introduction to ibid., ix-x.

[21]Hannah Whitall Smith, *The Christian's Secret of a Happy Life* (Grand Rapids: Revell, 1952), 30, 42. "Glad surrender" is used by Kelly in *A Testament of Devotion* and has also been used by other authors, such as Elisabeth Elliot in her book *Discipline: The Glad Surrender* (Grand Rapids: Revell, 2006).

[22]Smith, *Christian's Secret of a Happy Life*, 35.

[23]For more on habit formation, I recommend Charles Duhigg, *The Power of Habit: Why We Do What We Do in Life and Business* (New York: Random House, 2012).

[24]Martin Laird, *Into the Silent Land: A Guide to the Christian Practice of Contemplation* (New York: Oxford University Press, 2006), 19-20.

[25]Ibid., 2.

Chapter 6: Rewiring Your Mind

[1]"Backwards Brain Bike," Smarter Every Day, accessed September 27, 2016, www.smartereveryday.com/store/backwards-bike.

[2]See Norman Doidge, *The Brain That Changes Itself* (New York: Penguin Books, 2007).

[3]A summary observation from Carol S. Dweck, *Mindset: The New Psychology of Success* (New York: Random House, 2006).

[4]Doidge, *Brain That Changes Itself*, 47.

[5]"Memory Capacity of Brain Is 10 Times More Than Previously Thought," *Salk*, January 20, 2016, www.salk.edu/news-release/memory-capacity-of-brain-is-10-times-more-than-previously-thought.

[6]Stephen Wiltshire's sketch of Rome was accurate down to the precise number of columns on the Colosseum. You can view his Rome and other cityscapes (London, New York, Tokyo, and others) at www.stephenwiltshire.co.uk.

[7]Sigridur Kristinsdottir, "Savant Learns How to Speak Icelandic in a Week," YouTube, March 20, 2017, www.youtube.com/watch?v=_GXjPEkDfek.

[8]William James, *Principles of Psychology* (Mineola, NY: Dover, 1950), 1:127.

[9]Doidge, *Brain That Changes Itself*, xx.

[10]James, *Principles of Psychology*, 1:127.

[11]Robert D. Richardson, ed., *The Heart of William James* (Cambridge, MA: Harvard University Press, 2010), 113.

[12]Sandra Blakeslee, "Nicotine: Harder to Kick . . . Than Heroin," *New York Times*, March 29, 1987, www.nytimes.com/1987/03/29/magazine/nicotine -harder-to-kickthan-heroin.html?pagewanted=all.

[13]Neuroscientist William M. Struthers has written an entire book on this topic: *Wired for Intimacy: How Pornography Hijacks the Male Brain* (Downers Grove, IL: InterVarsity Press, 2010). I recommend it to those struggling in this area or who know someone who is.

[14]Nicholas Carr, *The Shallows: What The Internet Is Doing to Our Brains* (New York: W. W. Norton, 2011), 126-29, 140, 193.

[15]Ibid., 140, 220.

[16]Ibid., 193.

[17]Ibid., 122-23. See also the Nicholas Carr interview "'The Shallows': This Is Your Brain Online," *All Things Considered*, National Public Radio, June 2, 2010, www.npr.org/templates/story/story.php?storyId=127370598.

[18]T. S. Eliot, *Choruses from "The Rock,"* in *Selected Poems* (San Diego: Harcourt Brace Jovanovich, n.d.), 107.

[19]Dallas Willard, *Renovation of the Heart* (Colorado Springs: NavPress, 2002), 109.

[20]The Hebrew word for Spirit, *ruach*, has a similar meaning to the Greek *pneuma*; it means "breath," "air," or "wind."

[21]As additional reading, along with Nicholas Carr's *The Shallows*, I recommend Timothy R. Jennings, *The God-Shaped Brain* (Downers Grove, IL: InterVarsity Press, 2013); Curt Thompson, *Anatomy of the Soul* (Wheaton, IL: Tyndale House, 2010); and Michael Merzenich, *Soft-Wired* (San Francisco: Parnassus, 2013).

Chapter 7: Reseeing the World

Epigraph from A. W. Tozer, *The Pursuit of God* (Camp Hill, PA: Christian Publications, 1982), 96.

[1]The recovered diaries of two crewmen, plus other knowledge gained from investigation into the incident, provide the details we know; still, we'll never know the whole truth of what happened.

[2]Thomas R. Kelly, *A Testament of Devotion* (New York: HarperCollins, 1992), 19.

[3]Ibid., 9, 10.

[4]Ibid., 89.

[5]Ibid., 91.

[6]Ibid., 118. The quote is in a biographical memoir of Kelly (written by Douglas V. Steere) at the end of the book.

[7]Ibid., 94.

[8]Martin Laird, *Into the Silent Land: A Guide to the Christian Practice of Contemplation* (New York: Oxford University Press, 2006), 17.

[9]Matthew Henry, *Concise Commentary on the Whole Bible* (Nashville: Thomas Nelson, 1997), 1098.

[10]George Herbert, "Man's Medley," in *Complete English Poems* (London: Penguin Classic, 1992), 122. I've taken the liberty to change the British English spelling of "pretence" to the American English spelling.

[11]Ibid.

[12]William Butler Yeats, "Sailing to Byzantium," 1928, www.online-literature.com/yeats/781.

[13]Dallas Willard, *The Divine Conspiracy: Rediscovering Our Hidden Life in God* (San Francisco: HarperSanFrancisco, 1998), 1, 2.

[14] *The Matrix*, directed by the Wachowski Brothers (Burbank, CA: Warner Bros., 1999), DVD.

[15] The phrase comes from a title of one of his sermons. It's been reprinted many times, but one of the latest is in a compilation of sermons, Francis Schaeffer, *No Little People* (Wheaton, IL: Crossway, 2003).

Chapter 8: Reorganizing Your Time

[1] C. S. Lewis, *Screwtape Letters* (San Francisco: HarperOne, 2015), 60.

[2] I'm covering this topic briefly, but if this is a big struggle in your life, consider reading Alan Fadling, *An Unhurried Life* (Downers Grove, IL: InterVarsity Press, 2013); or Kevin DeYoung, *Crazy Busy* (Wheaton, IL: Crossway, 2013).

[3] This section draws on my book *Conformed to His Image* (Grand Rapids: Zondervan, 2001).

[4] Rob Moll's *The Art of Dying* (Downers Grove, IL: InterVarsity Press, 2010) provides an elegant, longer exploration of *memento mori*.

[5] Jim Elliot, quoted in *The Journals of Jim Elliot*, ed. Elisabeth Elliot (Grand Rapids: Fleming H. Revell, 1999), 278.

[6] Thomas Carlyle, "Signs of the Times" (1829), in *Complete Works of Thomas Carlyle* (New York: P. F. Collier, 1901), 1:31.

[7] Frank Laubach, *Letters by a Modern Mystic* (Colorado Springs: Purposeful Design, 2007), 9.

[8] Thomas R. Kelly, *A Testament of Devotion* (New York: HarperCollins, 1992), 100.

[9] This section draws on my book *Conformed to His Image* (Grand Rapids: Zondervan, 2001).

[10] There's physical evidence that fast-paced technology, used often, increases the body's stress or fight-or-flight response.

[11] For guidance on wordless prayer, see exercise PR8 in "A Guide to Practicing God's Presence."

[12] Basil the Great, quoted in *A Select Library of Nicene and Post-Nicene Fathers of the Christian Church*, ed. Philip Schaff and Henry Wace (New York: Christian Literature, 1895), xix; emphasis added.

[13] Catherine of Genoa, quoted in *Devotional Classics: Selected Readings for Individuals and Groups*, ed. Richard J. Foster and James Bryan Smith (New York: HarperCollins, 2005), 182.

[14]Andrew Sullivan, "I Used to Be a Human Being," *New York Magazine*, September 18, 2016, http://nymag.com/selectall/2016/09/andrew-sullivan-technology-almost-killed-me.html.

[15]Richard Swenson, *Margin: Restoring Emotional, Physical, Financial, and Time Reserves in Overloaded Lives* (Colorado Springs: NavPress, 2004).

[16]Evidence abounds, but see, for example, Jean M. Twenge, "Are Mental Health Issues on the Rise?," *Psychology Today*, October 12, 2015, www.psychologytoday.com/blog/our-changing-culture/201510/are-mental-health-issues-the-rise; Jesse Singal, "For 80 Years, Young Americans Have Been Getting More Anxious and Depressed, and No One Is Quite Sure Why," *New York Magazine*, March 13, 2016, http://nymag.com/scienceofus/2016/03/for-80-years-young-americans-have-been-getting-more-anxious-and-depressed.html.

[17]Dallas Willard, quoted in John Ortberg, *Soul Keeping* (Grand Rapids: Zondervan, 2014), 20.

[18]Jim Elliot, *Journals of Jim Elliot*, 278.

Chapter 9: Rejoicing amid Suffering

Epigraph from Arthur Bennett, ed., *The Valley of Vision: A Collection of Puritan Prayers and Devotions* (Carlisle, PA: Banner of Truth Trust, 1975), xv.

[1]Joni Eareckson Tada, foreword to Kara Tippetts, *The Hardest Peace* (Colorado Springs: David C. Cook, 2014), 14.

[2]Blythe Hunt, "Homecoming," *Mundane Faithfulness* (blog), March 22, 2016, www.mundanefaithfulness.com/home/2015/3/22/homecoming.

[3]Tada, foreword, 14.

[4]Tippetts, *Hardest Peace*, 17, 18.

[5]Ibid., 18.

[6]Joni Eareckson Tada, "Joni's Story," *Joni Eareckson Tada Story*, accessed April 18, 2017, http://joniearecksontadastory.com/jonis-story-page-1.

[7]"A severe mercy," a now-common phrase, is borrowed from the title of the book *A Severe Mercy* by Sheldon Vanauken, which documents his relationship with his wife and their joint relationship with C. S. Lewis.

[8]Tada, "Joni's Story," http://joniearecksontadastory.com/joni-tadas-story-page-2.

[9]Nik Ripken, with Gregg Lewis, *The Insanity of God: A True Story of Faith Resurrected* (Nashville: B&H Books, 2013), xxx. "Nik Ripken" is a pseudonym.

[10]Ibid.

[11]Ibid., 136.

[12]Ibid., xxviii.

[13]Larry Crabb, *A Different Kind of Happiness: Discovering the Joy That Comes from Sacrificial Love* (Grand Rapids: Baker, 2016), 46.

[14]Ibid., 48.

[15]Julian of Norwich, quoted in *Devotional Classics: Selected Readings for Individuals and Groups*, ed. Richard J. Foster and James Bryan Smith (San Francisco: HarperSanFrancisco, 2005), 74.

[16]Ibid., 73.

[17]Thomas R. Kelly, *A Testament of Devotion* (New York: HarperCollins, 1992), 43.

[18]Jean-Pierre de Caussade, *Abandonment to Divine Providence* (Mineola, NY: Dover, 2008), 74.

[19]Tippetts, *Hardest Peace*, 156-57.

Chapter 10: Repenting of Sin

Epigraph adapted from Derek Kidner, *Proverbs*, Tyndale Old Testament Commentaries (Downers Grove, IL: InterVarsity Press, 2008), 39. The original quote is singular: "he deceives himself by the smallness of his surrenders."

[1]This account is based on a true story, but details have been changed for anonymity.

[2]Father Maximos of Mount Athos is quoted on the *logismoi* in Kyriacos Markides, *The Mountain of Silence* (New York: Random House, 2001), 124-30.

[3]Pornography use doesn't always lead to affairs, but if an opportunity arises, the enemy will always exploit it.

[4]Excerpted from Kenneth Boa, *Handbook to Prayer: Praying Scripture Back to God* (Atlanta, GA: Trinity House Publishers, 1993), 394.

[5]Oswald Chambers, "Where the Battle Is Lost or Won," *My Utmost for His Highest*, December 27, 2017, http://utmost.org/where-the-battle-is-won-or-lost.

[6]Kidner, *Proverbs*, 42.

[7]Thomas Chalmers, *The Expulsive Power of a New Affection* (Louisville, KY: GLH Publishing, 2015), 9.

Chapter 11: Remaining in Community

[1]Andrew Murray, *Absolute Surrender* (Chicago: Moody Publishers, 1974), 23.

[2]Charles Colson, with Ellen Santilli Vaughn, *The Body: Being Light in Darkness* (Dallas: Word, 1992), 65.

[3]Larry Crabb, *A Different Kind of Happiness: Discovering the Joy That Comes from Sacrificial Love* (Grand Rapids: Baker, 2016), 92, 95.

[4]Murray, *Absolute Surrender*, 31.

[5]Dietrich Bonhoeffer, *Life Together* (New York: HarperOne, 1954), 78.

[6]Keith R. Anderson and Randy D. Reese, *Spiritual Mentoring: A Guide for Seeking and Giving Direction* (Downers Grove, IL: InterVarsity Press, 1999), 20.

[7]Murray, *Absolute Surrender*, 35.

[8]For more prayer exercises and for printable versions of Paul's four life-changing prayers, see "A Guide to Practicing God's Presence."

[9]Susan Weinschenk, "Why We're All Addicted to Texts, Twitter, and Google," *Psychology Today*, September 11, 2012, www.psychologytoday.com /blog/brain-wise/201209/why-were-all-addicted-texts-twitter-and-google. MIT professor Sherry Turkle's book *Alone Together* (New York: Basic Books, 2012) offers a wonderful, in-depth treatment of this topic of how technology has affected our relationships. Though she does not focus on spiritual matters, Turkle's observations, rooted in scholarly research, are highly relevant to believers and the church in the twenty-first century.

[10]See Aldous Huxley, *Brave New World* (New York: HarperPerennial, 2006). Huxley's prescient book was first published in 1932.

[11]David Sax, *The Revenge of Analog: Real Things and Why They Matter* (New York: Public Affairs, 2016).

[12]Peter Scholtes, "They'll Know We Are Christians," in *They'll Know We Are Christians by Our Love*, F. E. L. Records, 1966.

[13]Thomas R. Kelly, *A Testament of Devotion* (New York: HarperCollins, 1992), 98, 99.

Chapter 12: Reimagining Life

Epigraph from C. S. Lewis, *The Last Battle* (New York: Macmillan, 1956), 173-74.

[1]C. S. Lewis, "Bluspels and Flalansferes," in *Selected Literary Essays by C. S. Lewis*, ed. Walter Hooper (New York: Cambridge University Press, 2013), 265.

[2]C. S. Lewis, *Surprised by Joy* (New York: Harcourt Brace, 1955), 164.

[3]*The Return of the King*, directed by Peter Jackson (Los Angeles: New Line Cinema, 2003), DVD.

[4]See Lewis, *Last Battle*, 176.

[5]Thomas R. Kelly, *A Testament of Devotion* (New York: HarperCollins, 1992), 41-42.

[6]Rod Dreher, *The Benedict Option* (New York: Sentinel, 2017), 227.

[7]Dreher makes this observation in his book as well.

[8]Kelly, *Testament of Devotion*, 118.

[9]The VIM model is taken from Dallas Willard, *Renovation of the Heart* (Colorado Springs: NavPress, 2002), 85-90.

About the Author

Dr. Kenneth Boa is engaged in a ministry of relational evangelism and discipleship, teaching, writing, and speaking. He holds a BS from Case Institute of Technology, a ThM from Dallas Theological Seminary, a PhD from New York University, and a DPhil from the University of Oxford.

Ken is engaged in a wide variety of ministry activities. On a local level, he teaches four studies a week and leads seven small discipleship groups on a monthly basis. He is also engaged in one-on-one discipleship, mentoring, and spiritual direction. Ken's Reflections Ministries also involves people in special outreach events and conferences. On a national and international level, Ken speaks and teaches throughout the United States and in various countries. He also creates numerous written, audio, visual, and video resources, and continues to expand the kenboa.org website as a resource center for people around the world.

www.kenboa.org
www.facebook.com/KennethBoa
www.instagram.com/ken.boa
twitter.com/kennethboa
vimeo.com/user10496586

Other Books
by Kenneth Boa

Available from IVP:
Faith Has Its Reasons
Life in the Presence of God
Passionate Living: Praises and Promises
Passionate Living: Wisdom and Truth
Rewriting Your Broken Story

Also by Ken Boa:
Augustine to Freud
Conformed to His Image
Growth in Character
A Guide to Practicing God's Presence
Handbook to Leadership
Handbook to Prayer
Handbook to Renewal
How to Study the Bible
I'm Glad You Asked
A Journal of Sacred Readings
Leadership in the Image of God
Living and Finishing Well
Talk Thru the Bible